THE ENGLISH ARE LIKE THAT

The
ENGLISH
Are Like That

By

PHILIP CARR

NEW YORK

CHARLES SCRIBNER'S SONS

1941

TO

EUGEN MILLINGTON-DRAKE

FOREWORD

THE ENGLAND which is described in these pages will not be the England of tomorrow. Changes have already been, are being and will still further be made in it to make democracy a social reality. Nevertheless, although there will be adaptation, there will be no revolution, for that is not the English way. The base will remain the same; and to know the essentials of this base is to understand what will be rebuilt upon it.

CONTENTS

I. *THE ENGLISH CHARACTER*   1

II. *JUSTICE AND PARLIAMENT IN ENGLAND*   20

III. *THE SOCIAL STRUCTURE OF ENGLAND*   57

IV. *WOMEN, CHILDREN AND HOME LIFE*   94

V. *SCHOOLS AND UNIVERSITIES*   120

VI. *THE PRESS AND ITS INFLUENCE*   155

VII. *INDUSTRY, COMMERCE AND FINANCE*   184

VIII. *LITERATURE, THE ARTS AND THE THEATRE*   222

IX. *SPORT*   257

X. *NATIONAL DEFENCE, THE BRITISH EMPIRE AND SEA POWER*   282

XI. *THE MEN AT THE HELM*   309

INDEX   343

THE ENGLISH ARE LIKE THAT

Chapter I

THE ENGLISH CHARACTER

FIRST of all, I had better explain what I mean by "English." In other countries, people are sometimes inclined to refer to the inhabitants of the British Isles, in general, as "the English." This is, in fact, both inaccurate and misleading. It is inaccurate because the British Isles are inhabited by four peoples, who are not only distinct but consciously distinct from one another. If you ask a Scotsman whether he is English, he will proudly answer that he is not. A Welshman will do the same, and, as for an Irishman, he will probably repudiate with indignation any identity with the English, and may even remind you that his country—or at least the southern part of it, which forms the State of Eire—is actually neutral in the present war, and has its own independent government and Parliament, although it is a member of the British Commonwealth of Nations. Moreover, although Scotland now forms part of the United Kingdom and sends representatives to the British Parliament, we still talk of the Border, meaning the frontier between the two countries; and Scotland has a special minister, the Secretary of State for Scotland, a separate legal system and a separate Established Church, which is Protestant, but not in the same organization as the Established Church of England.

To put the four peoples together into one category is misleading, because these political distinctions are accompanied by marked differences of temperament, of mentality and even, to a great extent, of speech. A Celtic dialect, called Erse, is spoken by most of the peasants of the State of Eire, and some of them in the west understand nothing else. As the national language, it has been made the first official language of Ireland, although most people habitually speak English, which is the second official language. In the highlands of the north of Scotland is spoken another Celtic dialect, and another again in Wales.

The Irish have a poetical melancholy and a fairylike fancy, which are quite different from the poetry and the fairyland of the English, and a delicate and rapid understanding, a realistic and quite unsentimental way of thinking, a light and whimsical wit and a combative and bitterly uncompromising rebelliousness, which are not English at all.

The Welsh have a shrewd and rather tortuous intelligence, a passion for choral music and a florid and picturesque eloquence, which are all their own; and the Scots—you must never say Scotch—have a thrifty habit, which has become proverbial in contrast with the wastefulness of the English; a conscientiousness, which is so persistent that they are its slaves; a tradition of learning, which has developed their higher education into something really democratic; a manual and mental skill, which has made them the working marine engineers of the world; a logical manner of constructive thinking, which is much nearer to France than to England; and long political and personal memories, which are quite foreign to the English tendency to forgive and forget.

It is a surprising thing that with all these independent and sometimes defiantly independent characteristics, distinguished Scotsmen, Welshmen and Irishmen have played such important parts in building up a political, social and intellectual world which nevertheless remains fundamentally English. Mr. Bernard Shaw, himself an Irishman, has pointed out that the cool and clear-thinking Wellington was Irish, while the imaginative and sentimental Nelson was English. Mr. Lloyd-George is a Welshman, and, with Lord Balfour, Sir Henry Campbell-Bannerman and Mr. Ramsay MacDonald, who were Scotsmen, he makes up the four non-English Prime Ministers, who, in the last forty years, have been at the head of the British Government for a longer time than the five Englishmen who held office during the same period.

Nevertheless, England remains England, and the guiding spirit of Great Britain, in politics and in everything else, remains English at bottom. Consequently, although it is mistaken to assume that all the British are English, a study of the character of the Englishman will reveal the essential motives which animate the British nation as a whole.

I say the Englishman, and not the English gentleman; for although the latter holds a very important place in the English social system, which must in due course be examined, he is a special product, and it is first necessary to understand the character of the people of which his class is, after all, only a part.

I want to tell you how the average Englishman thinks, how he feels, how he behaves, how he acts and what are the ideals for which he lives.

In the first place, it can almost be said that he does not think at all. At least, he does not consciously build up anything in his thoughts. He dreams. He puffs at a large pipe and ruminates. It is not by the aid of reason or logic that he reaches his conclusion, nor does he constantly submit the embryo of it to critical analysis, as a Frenchman does, in order to reach something well rounded and proportioned. He relies, above all, upon his instinct, and then upon a series of mental experiments, which seem at first to be undertaken entirely haphazard, but are shown afterwards to proceed from a real intuition, even though they may be too vaguely empiric to constitute a method. He has none of the sense of balance and studious avoidance of exaggeration which restrain the Frenchman in his mental processes. When he has reached his conclusion by the devious ways which I have indicated, the one touchstone which he applies to it is to ask whether it works, whether it gives results. If it does, if, that is to say, it seems to be practical, he is quite indifferent as to whether or not it is based on premises which are completely contradictory.

I do not mean to suggest that the Englishman's mind is chaotic. He has a great sense of practical orderliness; but he has an inborn distrust of anything that is based merely on an intellectual justification. Indeed, he even distrusts intelligence in itself, as being something rather dangerous. He is inclined to think that a man who is intelligent, and still more a man who is brilliant, will be wanting in solid judgment when it comes to forming an opinion—judgment being the slow and almost instinctive estimation of men and things and circumstances, which is the Englishman's sheet anchor through life.

For the same reasons, a man who talks much, and especially a man who talks about himself, is to be viewed with suspicion. It was a Frenchman who coined the maxim "catch hold of eloquence and wring its neck," but it is the English who are the most ready to put it into practice. I do not mean to say that a man with a ready flow of language does not take in simple people in England, as elsewhere. It could hardly be otherwise in the native land of Autolycus. Sometimes he even takes in those who think themselves far from simple; but in a general way he is best advised to talk only when there is an opportunity for a speech to be made, and not in conversation. There the man who keeps his mouth shut most of the time is considered to be the sounder fellow. You remember André Maurois *Silences du Colonel Bramble*. It is the same instinct which makes an Englishman distrust versatility. It is too "clever." Besides, the mere fact of being able to do a number of things seems to him to indicate a probable incapacity for doing any one of them well.

All this may make you think that the average Englishman is gloomy. You would be mistaken. He is not gloomy; but I am afraid he is sometimes dull.

In matters of both the intellect and the imagination, and in other things as well, the Englishman never quite grows up. He is always a bit of a schoolboy, and even a bit of a child. He reads a lot—more than people of some other countries, who talk more and are more intelligent—but what he reads consists almost always of stories, and they must be stories in which something happens. The improbability matters little. It is the inventiveness which counts. The Englishman is in fact always reading fairy stories. He may sometimes call them detective stories, but it is the romantic adventure which attracts him. It is also towards the fairylike, the romantic and the rather nebulous that he turns when he wants something more serious in literature.

In fact, the Englishman does not care for conscious and precise art. That is to say, he takes little pleasure in admiring the skill and perfection of the artist. Indeed, there are few societies more philistine, in an artistic sense, than the English middle class, in spite of a certain pretense and snobbishness about artistic matters, which has obtained in London during the last twenty years.

However, if the Englishman has very little artistic sense, he has a very profound poetic sense. The two are by no means the same thing. Perhaps the most lasting monument which England will hand down to future ages will be, neither her political system nor her imperial greatness, but the magnificent body of lyric poetry which she has produced, almost without interruption, for four centuries. Being possessed, as he is, of this poetic sense, the Englishman, without having any artistic taste, has nevertheless a sure instinct and a real love for the beauties of nature. On the most cunningly chosen site in each of the most magnificent landscapes of the world, there is generally an Englishman who has built himself a house. The same love for the beauties of nature inspires the passion for flower gardens, which breaks out, not only in these favored places, but in the most unlikely and thankless spots—indeed, wherever the Englishman sets his foot.

Perhaps the most important part of the imaginative side of the Englishman's character is his sense of humor. What he means by that it is very difficult to explain to any one who is not English. The difficulty is not merely that what one people considers to be funny will very often not raise a smile in another. The feeling for the merely comic has always been very much a matter of place and also of time. For instance, much of what must have considerably amused Shakespeare's contemporaries in the adventures of Falstaff no longer amuses us at all. Nevertheless, the character of Falstaff remains titanically humorous.

Humor, therefore, is something more than the comic. Moreover, it has nothing to do with it. It is a matter of the character, and not of the mind. I think it has its origin in the fact that when an Englishman feels that he is ridiculous, either physically, socially or morally, he does not enjoy the discovery any more than other people, but he has the courage to admit that he is ridiculous, and to admit it, not only to other people, but to himself. This gives him a certain sympathy for those who are ridiculous or are placed in ridiculous situations. He discovers something in their characters which is rather whimsically sympathetic though it is comic, and rather picturesque, though it is absurd.

Moreover, humor is closely allied to another of the inherent characteristics of the Englishman, his inveterate habit of understatement, which must not be confused with irony, for it is something very different. In moments of crisis it gives him that quiet courage without a smile but with the mere suggestion of one at the corners of the mouth, which Mr. Winston Churchill has so admirably described as being both "grim and gay." It comes out in the grocer who is not content to announce that his shop, of which the front has been bombed, will carry on "business as usual," but puts up "more open than usual." It is expressed by the bride, who sets out for the church from a wrecked house in her wedding dress, as much as by the golf club, which posts a notice to the effect that a player who drives his ball beyond the red flag marking the area of an unexploded enemy shell in the ground may take another stroke with a new ball without penalty. In ordinary times, understatement is not only a form of the Englishman's humor which is sometimes irritating to those who are not accustomed to it, but is often, for himself, a safety valve which enables him to keep his temper.

Having given you a few indications of the working of the Englishman's mind and his imagination, I will try to explain something about his feelings.

He feels deeply, but all his instincts tend to prevent him from giving expression to his feelings, and these instincts are reinforced by the training to which he is subjected by his elders—the famous English self-control.

The instincts themselves are not one, but several. First, a certain modesty, a sense that there is something indecent in displaying emotions which are private and personal, and even admitting that you are moved at all. Then a certain fear, a fear that emotions, if they are given rein, will take command, and that a man will no longer be captain of his soul, to borrow the expression from the last line of Henley's magnificent poem. As an old Yorkshire clergyman once said to me, "In our country, we distrust the passions." Then there is the childlike quality in the English spirit, to which I have already referred, the refusal quite to grow up, and consequently the determination to go on pretending that everything is still a game. It is perhaps this instinct which makes an Englishman always disposed to be superficially flippant in moments of danger, suspense or crisis.

However, the dominant instinct of all in the matter is shyness.

If only people of other countries could understand that Englishmen are, almost all of them, painfully and incurably shy, how many misunderstandings would be avoided, how many accusations of churlishness and insolence and haughtiness, which are brought against Englishmen, would be withdrawn. Those who have the gift of ease and self-possession cannot imagine the torture of those who are shy, and they cannot even believe that such an absurd thing as shyness can exist. Still less will they believe that an Englishman, who presents a look of such assurance, can be consumed by shyness, but he can.

The Englishman has no social ease. He has no ready politeness in word or in deed. He cannot pay compliments. He has no conversation. All of this is due to his shyness. He is sometimes curt, and even seems aggressive—a protective shield for his shyness. He is uncomfortable if he is in the company of more than two people, and especially if those people are ladies—his shyness again. He sometimes imagines that others are inoculated with the same virus as himself, and I have known him apologize for inviting a lady to a luncheon party at which only men are to be present, as he is afraid she will be uncomfortable, when really she is delighted.

The attitude of the Englishman when he is in love is largely conditioned by shyness. It is this which makes him inarticulate at a moment when most other men would be eloquent. It is also partly shyness which so often prevents him from consulting his wife and becoming her companion in the way in which husbands and wives are companions and even business partners in Latin countries, and leads him to withdraw into himself for the examination of the problems of his work, and to seek the society of men for his relaxation;

but another element helps to produce this result. The respect or even reverence for womanhood which the Englishman hardly loses is perhaps a development of the childlike quality of his sentimental composition. It is certainly a barrier in the way of his relations with the other sex easily reaching the stage of familiarity.

Many things about a man's nature may be learned from what other people think of him, and the behavior of Englishmen in general is reflected in the impression which they make on the peoples of other countries.

This impression is not always favorable. It should be remembered, however, that it rarely happens that the impression made in any country by those who belong to another is favorable. They are never forgiven for being different, and they frequently react by being rather aggressively national. Besides, they are usually misunderstood. Particularly is this the case with regard to the Englishman. For one thing, his shyness, as I have said, makes him appear to be disagreeable, when he does not mean to be. For another, his readiness to expatriate himself only on the condition of taking England with him to every country in the world—English habits, English food, English clubs, English games, English furniture, English clothes and so on—makes him seem to be perpetually on the defensive, when he probably thinks he is merely being natural. For a third, his lack of imagination, his usually complete inability to guess what the other man is thinking and feeling, permits him to say and do things which give offense, when he probably does not suspect for a moment that he is being tactless. I have, for instance, known Englishmen wear plus-fours and flannel shirts in the Champs-Elysées, when they would rather die than do so in Piccadilly, and be quite surprised when they were told that the French did not like such things.

Finally his lack of curiosity about others, his complete indifference to what others—even when they are his own people—think of him, his long-established social convention that every one should keep to his place and neither interfere with any one else nor be interfered with, and his absolute refusal to lay himself out to be ingratiating will often make him appear to be unfriendly, when all he wants is to be left alone.

This last desire is understood by hardly any one who is not English. Nearly every one in other countries is easily companionable, is glad to make new friends, to knock up casual acquaintances or at least to enter into conversation with strangers. Most Englishmen are not.

There is no doubt something of snobbishness in this reserve—a fear lest the new acquaintance should be of a class with which one would prefer not to associate. Even between Englishmen, the danger of being involved in anything so deplorable leads to the most searching precautions being taken. I have known an Englishman on board ship give a test "good morning" to another on the first day out, and decide to avoid his company for the rest of the voyage in consequence of the tone in which his fellow countryman said "good morning" in reply.

Apart from snobbishness, however, there is also a great deal of shyness. The Englishman's first instinct is to retreat into his shell, not because he wants to be rude, but because he knows that if he responds to the advance, he will have to be conversational, and that is such an effort to him that he prefers to retire. His disinclination to talk may even not be due to shyness, but merely to the fact that he can think of nothing to say. The Englishman's silences have much to answer for.

The unfavorable impression is therefore often the result of misunderstanding, and the misunderstanding can be explained away. The English are not really so ungracious, so stiff, so unfriendly, so frigidly remote, so unresponsive, so selfish, so inconsiderate, so consciously and contemptuously superior as their manner may make them seem to be. They are proud, proud of being English and perhaps sometimes rather sensitive about the importance and even the duty of maintaining the dignity of being English. But when once the ice is broken, they can be as good friends as any—perhaps better. Their very reticence and reserve sometimes find admirers; and I remember Léon Daudet once saying to me that he liked meeting Englishmen, as "they never ask you questions about yourself."

It may be added that much of the impersonal manner which seems so cold in the Englishman when he is out of his own country is by no means reserved for foreign travel. He is like that at home, and towards every one. It is the outer crust, in which his whole life is wrapped. A hotel keeper in England, for instance, will never give you the same friendly welcome as will be shown you almost everywhere else. He never, at least at first, betrays any desire to make you think you are his guest. You are just a customer, and might even have been a number instead of a name, like your room. The waiter at a restaurant will take no interest in your meal. He will just be frigidly formal. A shop assistant will studiously avoid adopting anything like a personal attitude towards you.

You must not imagine that all his neutrality expresses only the individual feelings—or lack of feeling—of the hotel keeper, the waiter or the shop girl. It arises just as much from the fear, or even the conviction, that anything else would be regarded by you as an impertinence. "You keep your place, and I will keep mine."

Nor must it be thought that the air of indifference, which is that of the Englishman in social relations, is adopted merely for use abroad and towards people who are not English. It permeates the whole of middle and upper-class English life. It is perhaps considered to be good form, and there is therefore something of snobbishness in its ubiquity. At any rate it is there; but, once again, it is only the outer crust.

The Englishman in action is like the Englishman in thought. Just as he does not arrive at an opinion by reasoning, but by browsing indiscriminately all over the intellectual field, so it is not by reflection or any consecutive mental process that he makes a decision. Indeed, the more he reflects, the more he hesitates and the less ready he is to decide.

It may even be said that the Englishman never really makes a decision. He broods; and when he has been brooding for a certain time, he suddenly realizes, not so much that he has decided something, but that something has been decided. How does he realize this? It is when he discovers that he has begun to take action. It may be that an event has suddenly happened which has forced him to take action immediately. In any case, once he has made the discovery, he hesitates no longer. The action which he has taken rapidly and instinctively has committed him. He follows it out to the end, without asking where it is going to lead him, without a plan, but without turning to the right or the left and without letting go. Later on, he finds reasons to explain his action, but it is not as the result of reasoning that he enters upon it at the beginning. You may say that all this—we call it muddling through—shows a certain lack of imagination, but it is the English way.

At the same time, it is perhaps an exaggeration to say that it is entirely by instinct that the Englishman takes the first step in action, the step which commits him to a decision. It is perhaps an exaggeration to say that reasoning does not enter into the matter at all. The full truth is that he is incapable of making a decision on a question about which he has reflected for a long time, and he cannot make a decision by reflecting slowly. He will always postpone the decision to which he has given a great deal of thought; but if a decision becomes urgent and inevitable, because action is necessary, the Englishman is then capable of reasoning with an unsuspected and lightning rapidity, and it is not therefore quite true that the decision which he then makes is entirely instinctive. A brilliant Spaniard, Salvador de Madariaga, compressing the whole thing into an epigram, has said that the Englishman thinks with his instincts and acts with his mind.

All this is admirably illustrated by Shakespeare's *Hamlet*. *Hamlet* is sometimes spoken of as the tragedy of a man incapable of action, but nothing could be more profoundly untrue. Hamlet kills his man three times in the course of the play—he kills Polonius, he kills Laertes and he kills the King. We also learn that he has shown conspicuous bravery in battle. A man who can do all this is certainly not incapable of action. The truth is that Hamlet can act very decisively in a case which presents itself suddenly, and upon an issue on which reasoning can be conducted rapidly; but he cannot bring himself to act upon an issue about which he has reflected for a long time. He cannot kill the King in revenge for the murder of his father; but he can kill Laertes when he suddenly finds that he has poisoned the fencing foil, and he can even kill the King himself, when he suddenly learns that he has poisoned the wine. He may even be said to have killed the King twice, on a sudden issue of this sort; for when he killed Polonius for listening behind the tapestry, he thought it was the King.

The fact is that the English have to be sharply waked up before they will act decisively. Mr. Bernard Shaw has said that Hitler made the great mistake, from his point of view, of frightening the English; for it was only when they were frightened that they began to do anything serious. Some one else said that the peoples of the British Commonwealth ought to put up a statue to Hitler; for he had pulled them together as nothing else could have done.

The methods of the English in ordinary times are slow. All their tradition induces slow action—their tendency to form committees, in which everything is discussed with a reasonable give and take on both sides, and is finally settled by a compromise, which may not be very decisive, but which antagonizes nobody.

The tolerance of the English is in itself an element of slowness. They easily forgive and forget, and they find it difficult to suspect and still more difficult to hate. Their guilelessness up to a certain point—one might even say their gullibility—has before now led both nations and individuals to assume that they would be easy prey. An Englishman is not readily suspicious, and, for a moment, he can be cajoled; but if he suddenly begins to suspect, he bides his time, and the swindler finds to his surprise that the man whom he took to be such a simple fellow has turned the tables on him.

There is one more characteristic of the English, which is hardly ever understood out of England. Both individually and as a nation, they are generous and charitable, alike in money and active help. Moreover, they have shown, again and again, that they have been inspired by altruism to a high degree. And yet they have an instinct of self-interest, an instinct for turning circumstances to their own material advantage, which never deserts them.

What is the explanation? Are they hypocrites?

The answer is that all men—or nearly all men—are hypocrites in the sense that their own interest comes first and they pretend that it does not, even if they are not hypocrites in the sense of pretending that they are highly moral when they are not. Nor would it be possible to deny that hypocrisy—especially in the second sense—exists in the country where the immortal figure of Mr. Pecksniff was created. Each people has its own type of hypocrisy. What appears to offend other nations in our own particular type is that the Englishman is not satisfied with taking in others, but is determined to take himself in, as well. But if he does take himself in, can he be said any longer to be a hypocrite?

As far as public action is concerned, the truth, I think, is this.

The average Englishman cannot rise to any great effort or sacrifice unless he can persuade himself that he is serving some moral purpose, or else in the extreme case when he is at last convinced that he is in real danger. He is naturally generous towards those who are suffering from unexpected misfortune, or indeed to any "under dog"—to use an expression which is as common in England as another one about helping lame dogs over stiles. Both of them reveal something about the Englishman's love for animals, as well as his pity for any one who has had a piece of bad luck. This pity finds expression, not only in individual cases which come under his notice, but in wider cases which concern people whom he has never seen. Thus he is very charitable at home, and he is easily touched by the plight of those suffering from disaster abroad—as witness the invariable and immediate response in London to appeals for funds to help the victims of such disasters. He is also generous to the vanquished—foolishly generous sometimes, but not always, as was proved by the success, to the amazement of the world, of the policy of almost immediately granting self-government to the Boers after the South African War.

But the Englishman also has a keen eye to business. Napoleon contemptuously called us a nation of shopkeepers, and what he then intended as an insult remains true today, when it is so little of an insult that the people of every nation would like to be shopkeepers also. No Englishman can readily bring himself to let an opportunity for doing business pass him by; and he will seize those opportunities, even when they occur in the course of an adventure which he has·undertaken from generous motives. It is natural enough that he should be accused of seeking the adventure in order to make the business opportunities, and the long line of heroic missionaries who have set out from England to carry Christianity into savage lands have often been called hypocrites; but they were not.

It is true that in England there have always been certain cynics ready to take advantage of the generous impulses of the majority, particularly of the young majority, and to exploit them; but similar cynics exist in every country, and the man who does good deeds because he is an enthusiast usually finds that some one else has made a profit out of them, just as the man who does good work, either because he is an artist or a conscientious craftsman, usually finds that he has been underpaid for it. It is no doubt true also that governments do not allow themselves to be carried away by generous impulses, but always hold coolly and calmly in view the ultimate interests of the nation. They would be failing in their duty if they did not do so; but that does not make them, and still less their people, into hypocrites.

There is one characteristic of the English which certain other nations—including the Scots in the same island—disapprove and indeed despise. This is their carelessness and prodigality in money matters, and indeed in all material things. The Englishman, at least of the working classes, does not save, as the Scotsman does. He does not observe either of the two parts of his own proverb, "Look after the pence and the pounds will look after themselves"; for he neglects the pence, and at the same time he does look after the pounds in the sense that he has a keen eye for making money. This lack of thrift may come in part from a certain natural generosity; but I think it comes still more from the Englishman's almost unerring instinct for seizing upon essentials, and not bothering much about details. He works hard at these essentials, but he cannot exactly be called industrious. He has been described as plodding; but he plods for only a limited number of hours a day, and only at the things which he considers really to matter. For the rest, he insists upon having his leisure.

One of the qualities of the Englishman which is a great part of his strength is that he is always ready to learn by his

mistakes, when once he is convinced of them; and he sometimes learns much more rapidly than might be expected from
one who is naturally so slow. In one sense it is all the easier
for him to change, in that he has never had any preconceived
plan or principles, which it would be a wrench to abandon.
At the same time, his respect for tradition often makes him
hold on to methods which are superannuated, and it is not
any amount of argument or even of theoretical proof, which
will persuade him to abandon them. I have said that he
learns by his mistakes, when once he is convinced of them;
but it is only the brutal evidence of hard facts which will convince him, and, until these hard facts hit him in the face, his
doggedness will make him hold on. It has been said that the
English lose all the battles and win all the wars; and it is
only after he has lost a certain number of battles that the
Englishman changes his tactics. Until then, his lack of imagination prevents him from understanding what his adversary
is doing and thinking, and prevents him from seeing that he
really has made a mistake; but when he does see it, he
changes wholeheartedly.

Moreover, before he has adopted any method at all, his
habitual opportunism leaves him open to make his choice
entirely according to circumstances, and his pragmatic temper
of mind enables him to select his method on the experimental
and purely practical basis of trial and error, and without
being hampered by theory.

The Englishman has, in fact, little use for mental principles, but there are certain moral principles which he has
constantly before him.

The first is that he must keep his head and also his temper whatever happens. He must never allow himself to be
"rattled." In moments of crisis, he must remember those
words, "Steady, boys, steady," from one of the great songs
of the British Navy, words which have been shouted by how
many British officers to their men in how many battles! He

must be completely master of himself and never exhibit his feelings be they of fear or affection; and he must have confidence in himself.

He must have patience—patience with others, patience in the face of misrepresentation, patience to wait for the turn of the tide, patience to begin again after failure, patience to endure to the end.

For this he must have courage, courage to hold on. "Any one can row as long as he still has his wind," they say to young undergraduates at Oxford. "The real oar is a man who goes on rowing when he is dead."

There is a very old English proverb, "Brag is a good dog, but Hold-Fast is a better," which expresses this English ideal of tenacity and also expresses the equally English ideal of modesty. "Le moi est haïssable" is a French saying, but it represents an attitude which is typically English. A man must not always be thinking of himself and, still less, talking of himself.

He must have enough fortitude to resist failure, but he must also have enough poise to resist success, and the poise is a rarer quality than the fortitude. There is the sort of horse who, as the saying goes in hunting circles, "can't stand corn"—to whom you cannot give rich feeding because it excites him too much. The Englishman has a healthy sense of the danger of letting success go to his head. He is indeed aware of the danger of letting anything go to his head, of being carried away by anything, be it passion or enthusiasm or even intellectual facility or brilliance. That is why he distrusts clever and versatile people and prefers those who have solid and instinctive judgment. It may even be said of him that although he has little sense of moderation and proportion where the intellect is concerned, he has the keenest sense of them when it is a question of action.

His sense of duty extends to the scrupulous observance of regulations, and also of social conventions. He has a horror of doing what in any circle in which he moves will be considered the wrong thing—wearing the wrong clothes or going to the wrong places.

He feels the obligation to be just to all men, deferential to all women, and kind to all children, and hardly less of an obligation to be kind to animals, with whom he has a constant and instinctive sympathy; for he is nearer to simple nature than most men.

This sympathy will not prevent him from killing the animals which he hunts, but it will prevent him from allowing them to be tortured.

He must be so honest that no one will think of offering him a bribe and so trustworthy that it will occur to no one to doubt his word.

Finally, the Englishman has a conviction that every circumstance in life must be met with what he calls a sporting spirit.

What is a sporting spirit? It means playing your hand fairly and taking your chance without trying to mark the cards. It means giving your opponent an equal chance, so that the conflict shall be an even one. It means granting to the conquered the possibility of not being entirely crushed, if not an opportunity of escaping. It means losing with good humor, if you must lose. It means that a thing may be worth doing merely for the sake of the adventure—that is, for the sake of the very danger and the discomfort.

The sporting spirit even means that one must never forget that the whole of life is only a game, which must be played keenly, according to the rules, but without taking the whole thing too seriously, and that its greatest moments should be lived not only with a sense of the game, but with a sense of the sports of the field.

Chapter II

JUSTICE AND PARLIAMENT

IN ENGLAND

MY TITLE for this chapter is "Justice and Parliament in England," and I have chosen the title with intention. I am going to say something about the way in which England is governed; but, in doing so, I want to emphasize from the beginning that the English parliamentary system, which has been so much admired by the whole world, and has been so often imitated—not always intelligently or with understanding—is the expression, not only of the English passion for liberty, but of the English passion for justice.

This fact is not always appreciated. The part which the principle of liberty plays in English parliamentary institutions—government of the people, by the people, for the people—has always been recognized. The share of the principle of justice has less generally been admitted; but it is equally essential to the English conception.

What is not so essential is the principle of equality. If the Englishman can secure liberty and justice, he is not particularly inclined to demand a theoretical, or even a practical, equality. A certain measure of equality—that is to say, equality before the law, is necessary in order to obtain justice and liberty. Upon this degree of equality the Englishman

has always insisted, and he obtained it at a relatively early
stage in his history; but about social equality he has never
bothered very much. Both socially and to a large extent
politically, the framework of England is essentially aristocratic—that is, inconsistent with complete equality; and it has
been well said that England is a democracy because she is
an aristocracy, which means that in face of the advancing tide
of democracy, the aristocratic class, while it has been forced
to surrender some, but by no means all, of its powers, has
abandoned none of its responsibilities, and, instead of either
being absorbed or sulking in its tent, has cooperated with the
democratic forces and has to some extent absorbed them.

It is indeed largely because certain other peoples are, on
the contrary, possessed by the passion for equality, that some
of their imitations of the English parliamentary system have
been thrown out of balance.

You will have noticed that I have been talking of the
English parliamentary system. I have not used the word
British. I have two reasons for this. The first is that, although
the four peoples which compose the population of the British
Isles—the English, the Scottish, the Irish and the Welsh—
are all living, and have long lived, under the parliamentary
system, and although there are Scotsmen, Welshmen and
Irishmen, as well as Englishmen, today sitting in the British
Parliament at Westminster, the parliamentary system is, in
its origins and in most of its developments, specifically English. The second is that the parliamentary system, even as far
as British peoples alone are concerned, extends far beyond
the British Isles, and has long flourished in the States which
form the component parts of what is now officially known as
the British Commonwealth of Nations, but which is still
loosely spoken of as the British Empire.

I have said that the English Constitution expresses the
national passion for justice as well as for liberty. The Englishman has an ingrained respect for law. This is not quite

the same as saying that he has a respect for the law. He does not respect it simply because it is *the* law, because it is the emanation of high authority, which is the Hebrew conception. Nor does he respect it because it represents irresistible force, which is the German conception. He respects it partly because he is an orderly fellow, and realizes that if confusion is to be avoided in life, every one must agree to follow some kind of system. His instinct is not, like that of the Frenchman, to rebel against a regulation merely because it is a regulation, nor, like the German, to accept it for exactly the same reason. He is inclined to observe it for the sake of orderliness, and if it is intimated to him without arrogance, but only on condition that there is nothing in it which offends against his own instinctive conception of what is fair and equitable. He respects the law not merely because it is the law, but also because he considers the law to be just and reasonable, and only when he so considers it. In his subconscious mind, the real and ultimate tribunal is the general public conscience.

In England, laws and the interpretation of laws are constantly being referred to this decisive test, and there are numerous statutes, which have never been repealed, and are therefore nominally and legally still in force, but which are in fact inoperative and have fallen into desuetude, simply because they are no longer in conformity with public opinion. Still more effectively is this principle applied when the law in question is not a statute, whose terms can be found in black and white, but forms part of what in England is known as the Common Law—that is to say the custom of right and legality, which has never been written down at all, but is passed on from generation to generation and is interpreted by the trained minds of the Judges, partly by reference to tradition and precedent, but also partly under the influence of whatever evolution may have taken place in public feeling.

The Englishman therefore has a deep sense of justice, as

interpreted by the dictates of humanity and common sense. He also has a great regard for the forms of judicial procedure. This is based largely on the feeling for orderliness and decency, to which I have referred, and on the ingrained conviction that nothing sensible is ever done if people allow themselves to get excited. In an English Court of Law, you will invariably see the proceedings conducted in an atmosphere of great decorum and calm. Even when the conflict between opposing advocates is acute, you will never find the violence of protest or the outspoken appeals to passion and sentiment which are the commonplaces of forensic eloquence in some other countries. Never, above all, will you hear several people speaking at once.

This general respect for legal forms has, however, another origin as well. For hundreds of years, the ordinary Englishman has been familiar with the practice of justice, because he has been liable, at any moment, to have to take a hand in it. It is still the law of England that the police have the right to call upon any private citizen to lend assistance in apprehending an evil doer or in maintaining order, and it is a crime to refuse. Moreover, any citizen may be summoned to contribute to the administration of justice by serving upon a jury, and is obliged to leave his personal business in order to do so. Most important of all, a man of the middle or upper classes, all over the country, has long been accustomed to think in terms of legal procedure, because he might be called upon to form part of the bench of unprofessional and unpaid magistrates, who preside over the Courts of First Instance in all criminal matters, and exercise final jurisdiction in minor crimes.

The importance of these Justices of the Peace, as they are called, in the development of the political and legal consciousness of England lies not only in the fact that, although they have a trained lawyer as clerk to advise them on legal matters, they have to base their decisions principally on their own fairness and common sense, but also in the fact that, for centuries, noblemen have served as justices in exactly the same way as commoners, while in our own time members of the working classes have been nominated as well.

The Justices of the Peace have thus contributed to this remarkable state of things, that while in England the social organization has long been, and still is to a great extent, definitely aristocratic, the legal and political organization of the country has avoided the creation, either of a separate class of nobles, removed by privilege from common interests or common obligations with the rest of the people, or of a separate magisterial or administrative class, removed by being subject to a special kind of law.

There are no doubt other influences which have had their share in this double result. With regard to the nobles, there is the rule of primogeniture, under which younger sons bear no titles, but are just commoners like other people, and eldest sons inherit the great bulk of the property. There is also the happy historical fact that in the earliest House of Commons, the "knights of the shire," who were the socially aristocratic if not exactly noble representatives of the country districts, were summoned on an equality with the burgesses, who represented the commercial interest of the towns. It is here that one can find the origin of the fact, which I have already indicated, that the English democracy is essentially aristocratic. For centuries, and almost up to our own time, the House of Commons was mainly composed of members of the country gentry, for whom it was a sort of London club.

With regard to the absence of a special class of magistrates, there is this dominating condition of legal advancement in England that it is through being a member of the Bar, and in this way only, that a man either can become a Judge or can conduct an official prosecution. The Judges, the more important, as well as the less important, are appointed for life from among the ranks of distinguished barristers, and there is no promotion among them. On the other hand, there are no official advocates, unless the two lawyers who are political members of the Government, the Attorney General and the Solicitor General, can be so described, and there is certainly no separate class of salaried official advocates. Any barrister may be entrusted by the State, at a fee, with the duty of conducting the prosecution, or representing the Crown, as it is called, in a particular case, just as he may be entrusted, by a private person, at a fee, with the duty of conducting the defense. A private person may even institute a criminal prosecution, although this is not often done.

All of these things have been conducive to moulding the political mind of the Englishman in the legal way of thinking and the legal habit of ordered and precise procedure. It is this which has caused the forms of carrying on business in Parliament to be so elaborate and so scrupulously observed, and it is this which has maintained in the whole of English public life the tradition that the proper way of reaching a decision on any matter is through the sequence of presenting a case and examining the evidence by question and answer.

Other circumstances have also contributed to this result. One is that from an early stage in English history, the administration of justice was centered in Westminster. When cases too important to be dealt with by the local Justices of the Peace had to be tried in the country, they were kept until Judges from Westminster arrived on circuit to hold assizes, and even the work of the local Justices of the Peace, as well as that of other local officers of a judicial character, was controlled from Westminster. This gave to the interpretation of the law a certain unity, which would not have been maintained if there had existed independent provincial centers of justice, as in most other countries.

Another and very important effect of this centralization of the judiciary at Westminster was that the Judges, and particularly the barristers, were in constant touch with Parliament, which was at Westminster too. Indeed, the High Court of Justice and the House of Commons were, until within living memory, housed in adjacent buildings, or in what were almost two wings of the same building; for the House of Commons was next door to Westminster Hall, where the High Court Judges sat.

Consequently, that remarkable fraternity of the Bench and the Bar, of Judges and barristers, which is still organized in the same professional guilds and has its private offices grouped around the same courtyards as seven centuries ago, has from the beginning had an extraordinary influence upon the political life of the country, upon the formalities of the procedure of Parliament and upon its spirit also. For without the influence of the Bench and the Bar, there could hardly have arisen that reliance upon the authority of precedent, which has so dominated the growth of the British Constitution, and without the habit of constantly referring to a Common Law, none of which is written down, it would hardly have been possible to build up that Constitution, which is so supple that some of its most important features—the very existence of the Cabinet, for instance—have no written legal warranty whatever.

Before examining the political fabric of England, it may be well to see how its judicial system works. It is founded upon three main principles. The first is that of the equality of all men before the law, which, as I have said, is indispensable to securing full justice. In England there are no special courts or administrative tribunals, and all men are amenable to the ordinary law courts, the Minister of State equally with the private citizen. This equality is also secured by the fact that the judiciary is completely independent of the executive.

This independence of the Judges, the respect in which they are held and the great authority with which they are invested are also expressions of the second principle, which is that the law must be supreme. A Judge may summarily send a man to prison for what is called Contempt of Court, which means an endeavor to influence the course of justice and includes comment in a newspaper upon a case which is still under trial. No such comment—and calling the accused "the culprit," instead of "the prisoner," is taken as such—is allowed in England.

A Judge is chosen for his proved eminence, character and learning as a barrister; and it is held that this practice of appointing Judges from among the members of the Bar is the only one possible in England, where so much of the law is uncodified and even unwritten, and where knowledge of it can only be acquired by long working experience in the Courts. He is appointed for life, and is irremovable unless he commits a crime or becomes insane. He is highly paid, and is therefore above the temptation of monetary influence. He cannot be prosecuted for anything which he does in his office as a Judge. On the other hand, he cannot be a member of the Government, except in the case of the Lord Chancellor, who is not a permanent Judge, but who holds a political office and ceases to hold it when the Government to which he belongs comes to an end, even though he is at the head of the English judiciary as long as he does hold it.

The Lord Chancellor is usually a distinguished barrister who is also a politician, but his position must not be compared with that of Minister of Justice in other countries; for although he controls the nomination to the chief judicial appointments, he has no power whatever over the Judges, who can neither be degraded nor promoted by him or by any one else. It may be added incidentally, although this is irrelevant to the principle, that in England a Judge always sits alone, except at the lowest and the highest ends of the judicial scale —the Justices of the Peace and the Lords Justice of Appeal.

It is also in accordance with this second principle of the supremacy of the law that—except under war conditions—no man may be held in prison or punished except after due trial and conviction before a competent court of law. You have no doubt heard of the writ of Habeas Corpus, which furnishes protection against abuse in this matter.

The third principle is that legal proceedings must take place in public. In criminal matters, there is no preliminary questioning in private by an examining magistrate, and the police have no right to do more than arrest a man and tell him the crime with which he is charged. If he himself volunteers to say anything to the police, he must be warned that it will be taken down in writing, and may be brought in evidence at his trial.

In all serious cases of crime, the judges of fact are a jury of twelve members of the public, so that the trial is in a dual sense a public one; and although the presiding High Court Judge, at the end of the trial, sums up the facts as they appear to his trained legal mind, the jury are not bound by this summing up in making their decision on the question of fact. If they decide to acquit the prisoner, there is no appeal possible against this decision, although the prisoner may appeal if they have decided to convict him.

At the trial, all the evidence, both for the prosecution and for the defense, must be given orally, publicly, and upon oath, and it is the advocates for the prosecution and the defense respectively who bring out this evidence by questioning the witness. It is not the Judge, though the Judge occasionally inserts a question if he considers it desirable in the interest of elucidating the truth.

The barrister representing the party which has called the witness—either the prosecution or the defense—begins. It is his function to make the witness tell the story of which he himself has previously been informed. This is called the examination. Then the opposing barrister rises—they always refer to each other as "my learned friend"—and his object is to put questions which will shake the assurance of the witness or will demonstrate to the Court that his evidence depends upon an uncertain memory or a doubtful veracity. This is called the cross-examination. It may be added that the only evidence admitted is what the witness has himself seen or known. He is not allowed to repeat what somebody else has told him. After the evidence, the respective barristers address the Court—the defense always having the last word—and the Judge then sums up before the jury are locked up until they have unanimously agreed upon the verdict.

The barristers of the United Kingdom form a close and very ancient professional association, or group of associations —a trades union to use the term employed in the world of Labor. It is this group itself, or rather its governing body, the Bar Council, which holds the qualifying examination for admission to practice as a barrister, and it is not the Law Faculties at the Universities. These Faculties exist, and they grant university degrees in law, but such degrees are merely an academic distinction. Before being allowed to enter for the qualifying examination, the candidate has to put his name on the roll of one or other of what are called the Inns of Court, which are the ancient associations in question; and he has to attend a certain number of dinners in the common hall of the Inn which he has joined. This old custom is rather meaningless today, but it is a survival from the time when the student might meet experienced barristers at table and learn something of his profession from their talk; and its spirit survives in the practice of senior barristers taking pupils into their offices—or "Chambers," as they are called—so as to enable them to see the practical work while they are studying, and in the further practice of "devilling," that is to say, young barristers preparing part of the work for their seniors without payment and merely for the sake of experience.

The ladder of the judicial system begins, in criminal matters, with the Court of the Justices of the Peace. In towns, this Bench of lay Justices is replaced by a professional magistrate, known as a Police Magistrate. Next in importance comes the Court of Quarter Sessions, covering a larger district and dealing with more important cases, but still composed of a bench of lay Justices, although they have a professional lawyer as their chairman. Serious criminal cases, after a preliminary examination before the lay Justices, are referred to the Assizes of the visiting Judges in the case of the country or to the Central Criminal Court in the case of London; and there the real trial takes place before a Judge and jury. The minor cases are settled in the local Courts. Beyond the High Court trial, there is the Court of Criminal Appeal, and there is a possible further appeal to the House of Lords, sitting in its judicial capacity.

In civil matters, the lowest Court—which decides questions where the issue is of a value less than £100—is called a County Court. It is presided over by a professional County Court Judge. More important cases may either be tried locally by the visiting High Court Judge, when he arrives to hold his assizes, or else by the High Court of Justice in London. In either case, one or other of the parties has a right to demand a jury, who are then the sole judges of questions of fact and credibility. It is a feature of English civil justice that each party is expected to make a full disclosure to the other, and also to the Court, of all documents in his possession relating to the case, whether they are in his favor or not, and each party is entitled to inspect the documents of his opponent.

According to English legal practice, any person, who wishes to institute civil proceedings or defend himself in criminal ones, must address himself in the first place to a lawyer of the class called a solicitor. He cannot directly call upon a barrister, even if he knows him personally. It is the solicitor who must do that, and in theory it is even the solicitor who selects the barrister whom he will call upon, the client having no voice in the matter. The solicitor, who in England also deals with the kind of legal business which in other countries is covered by a notary, does the preliminary preparation of the case, and takes it to the barrister, who then decides when he will have a conference with the client, of course in the presence of the solicitor. It is the solicitor who collects all the fees from the client, and pays to the barrister those which are due to him—although the legal fiction is that the barrister receives no fees at all, and he cannot in fact sue the solicitor for payment, although the solicitor can sue the client. When the case is of so little importance that it can be heard at Petty Sessions—that is to say, before the Justices of the Peace—or else in the County Court, the solicitor can take charge of the whole business, without calling in the services of a barrister. But a solicitor cannot appear and plead before a Judge of the High Court. For this, a barrister is indispensable.

In most countries, Judges and advocates wear robes of some sort; but in England the ceremonial side of the administration of justice is carried a good deal further. Not only do Judges of the High Court and barristers wear robes—black embroidered with gold for Judges; red, trimmed with white fur, for Judges of Appeal; and black for barristers—and white neck bands, but they also wear white, or rather gray, horsehair wigs, which they cannot take off and place on the desk in front of them, as the judges in some other countries can with their official caps or toques. In the case of an ordinary barrister, this wig is short, with a little pigtail; but if he has reached the distinction of becoming a King's Counsel—in which case he is addressed on envelopes with the letter K.C. after his name, and never appears in Court without a junior counsel to assist him—he not only dons a silk gown (hence the expression "taking the silk" to describe his promotion) but wears what is called a full-bottomed wig, with two long flaps falling down upon his chest on each side of his face.

The full-bottomed wig is also worn by a High Court Judge, who lays upon it a little square of black velvet, when the moment comes, after a conviction for murder, for him to sentence the culprit to death. "His Lordship then assumed the Black Cap," say the accounts of such trials in the newspapers.

The newspaper describes the Judge as "His Lordship." When the barristers engaged in a case address him in the course of the proceedings, it is always as "My Lord"—traditionally pronounced "M'Lud" for this purpose. The historical reason for so addressing some one who is not a Peer of the Realm is that the High Court of Justice, in which he sits, is still theoretically a part of the High Court of Parliament, in which the Judges are still theoretically lords. Even now, they are summoned to the House of Lords by "writs of assistance"; but they long ago lost the right to vote in the Upper House, and do not now take their places there, except in the two following cases, which are no doubt survivals of the time when they belonged to it as of right. One is that the chairman of the House of Lords is the Lord Chancellor, the highest legal dignitary in the land, and the other is that the seven Law Lords, or "Lords of Appeal in Ordinary," are members of the House of Lords for life.

These examples of the close historical link between Justice and Parliament bring us to the examination of the English system of Government in itself.

The expression, "Parliamentary Government" is to some extent a misnomer. Parliament does not itself govern, although the members of the Government are members of Parliament. Its two main functions are, first, to authorize taxation and, second, to make laws; but in the exercise of the first of these functions, it can in fact control the Government. The business of administration could not be carried on if revenue could not be collected; and therefore no Government could live if Parliament refused its authority to collect revenue. Consequently a Government must in practice be able to command a majority in Parliament, and it must effectively represent the majority of Parliament. As it is the House of Commons which alone controls financial business, it is in the House of Commons that this majority must be found; and as the House of Commons is selected by the nation, the Government may therefore be said to be the expression of the national will.

However, there are Governments in other countries which may be said, in their way, to represent the national will. The Government of a totalitarian State may have been chosen by the representatives of the people in Parliament or otherwise. It may even have been chosen by a direct plebiscite of the nation. In what would such a Government differ from our own?

The essence of the matter was put in a few words some years ago by Mr. Winston Churchill, long before he became Prime Minister. "We claim the right," he said, "to choose our Government, to criticise our Government and to change our Government."

The right of criticising must be taken to include that of calling upon the Government publicly to explain and justify its action. The exercise of the right of choosing and changing must be assured by periodic and relatively frequent consultations of the people, which must be completely free to express its opinion. That is to say, there must be a normal machinery for changing the Government without a revolution.

Behind this normal machinery, and absolutely essential to its smooth working, lies the assumption that the majority, when it takes over the Government from what has become the minority, will act reasonably, fairly and without vindictiveness. It is only upon this assumption that the minority quietly accepts the change. It is an assumption which has never been belied. Even the Labor Party, which has today virtually replaced the Liberals as the alternative Government to the Conservatives, can be counted upon to play the game; for although it loyally defends the interests of the

British workmen who vote for it, it is not revolutionary.

I remember that, a good many years ago, when international communications were not as complete as they are today, I read about the description of a ministerial crisis in England, as given in a newspaper of what was still then a turbulent Balkan country. The Government, said the writer, had fallen, and its members had taken to the mountains. That seemed to him the normal thing for them to do, and he took it for granted that they had done it. It is to the credit of England and it is her pride, that for more than two hundred years, changes of Government have taken place without violence, and that not only today, but throughout the whole of living memory, nothing more uncomfortable need happen to departing Ministers than to form the parliamentary Opposition, or else to retire into private life—unless, of course, they were to be guilty of crimes punishable under the ordinary law, which has never in fact happened. Of how many countries in the world could the same thing be said?

These conditions are assured in England by the instinct for liberty, the instinct for accommodation and the ingrained tolerance of the people. Let us examine how they are expressed in what is called the English Constitution.

It may almost be said that the most important thing to understand about the English Constitution is that it does not exist. There is no document, there are no tables of the law, to which reference can be made to discover whether any particular act is constitutional or not. We speak with reverence of Magna Charta, that imposing list of derogations from the arbitrary powers of the Crown, which was extorted from King John by his barons at the beginning of the thirteenth century. But Magna Charta, although still theoretically in force, is in fact quite obsolete, and is only interesting historically. Since then, there have been many laws, which are constitutional laws in the sense that they deal with the organization of Government, with the royal prerogative and with the liberty of the subject. But they have not been passed in any different manner from other laws, nor with any greater solemnity; and they could at any moment be annulled or amended by the same process as that by which they were passed, that is to say, the ordinary form of parliamentary legislation.

Moreover, many of what are universally regarded as essential features of the Constitution rest upon no legal authority whatever. The most important of these is the chief political body in the country, the very instrument through which the Government of the country is carried on, that is to say, the Cabinet. As far as the law of England is concerned, the Cabinet has no existence, and need never meet. Its consent is not legally required for any kind of Government action or measure, for all of them are executed in the name of the King. There are no rules of law which prescribe who shall be admitted to its membership, what business shall be laid before it or what its quorum shall be; and it is entitled to keep its deliberations secret from every official body or person, even from the King; for its very being is not officially recognized.

In fact, a great part of the English Constitution has been built up like a great part of English law—that part which is known as Common Law. It has grown with practice and with custom, and has never been written down. This gives it an elasticity, which has enabled it to evolve and to be modified in accordance with changing needs and a changing public conscience. It has also enabled it to be based upon the instinctive combination of justice, liberty and practical efficiency, which inspires the mass of the English people.

In all government which is not mere irresponsible tyranny, the central problem has always been to construct a system which will reconcile what may be called policy with what may be called law, what may be called the dynamic with what may be called the static, public interests with private rights, or—

to put the issue in its simplest form—efficiency with liberty.

In the totalitarian States, even in peace time, everything is sacrificed to the former of the two. Efficiency is supreme. In war time, efficiency is bound to be temporarily supreme even in democratic States; but in peace time, the aim of these democratic States is to strike a proper balance.

The theorists of the eighteenth century conceived that this balance could best be obtained by what was called the "separation of powers." The legislature was to be entirely independent of the executive, and the administration of the law was to be independent of both.

This latter independence, that of the Judges, was secured in England as early as the beginning of the eighteenth century, and I have already explained how it operates today. It lies at the very foundation of the liberties of the private citizen. It is because the Judges are the jealous guardians of those liberties that the private citizen can neither be taxed without parliamentary authority nor imprisoned without trial by jury, and that he enjoys the freedom of expressing his political and religious opinions in speech and writing.

However, the mutual independence of the executive and the legislature is another matter. It is not towards such a goal that the evolution of our form of government has tended. On the contrary, as our great Constitutional authority, Bagehot, has written, "the efficient secret of the English Constitution may be described as the close union and nearly complete fusion of the executive and legislative powers." It is by co-operation, and not by an opposition which might have ended in deadlock, that the legislature has maintained those individual and representative rights and liberties, which were no doubt first won by conflict.

This co-operation eventually found its expression in the gradual evolution of what has become the system of Cabinet government; and when once this system had been created, there was still less danger that there would ever be irreconciliable opposition between the executive and the legislature. For one of its conditions is that the members of the Cabinet must be members of Parliament and collectively responsible to the majority of the House of Commons; and there is little danger that Cabinet Ministers of this political formation, who desire to be re-elected and are anxious above all to retain the allegiance of their party and promote its fortunes, will defy the House of Commons and the electorate. Besides, co-operation between the executive and the legislature is in accord with the political genius of the people. It fits in with the popular instinct for settling important and controversial matters by quiet discussion and consultation, as well as with the instinct for political compromise, for preferring the maximum of consent for a half way measure to the triumph, but also the bitterness, of complete victory by a narrow margin. It is in agreement with the general disinclination to reopen a political issue once decided. In fact it is one more expression of that feeling for law and orderliness to whose importance in English life I have already drawn attention.

The existence of Cabinet Government means that although all the executive acts of the State are performed in the name of the King, they are really decided upon by the Cabinet. That is to say, the ruling principle of each important action is settled by the Cabinet, which in practice delegates part of its powers to the political chiefs of the principal Departments of State, the most important of whom are members of the Cabinet; and it is they who in fact make many of the decisions, independently of the Cabinet. Consequently, when a Minister gives an order, he does so in form as the representative of the King, but he does so in fact as the delegate of the Cabinet of which he is a member. What has happened is that the powers of the Crown have been put into commission, and that the commission is held by the Cabinet, a relatively small body of men, which has delegated part of its collective powers to its individual members. The Cabinet represents the dominant political party in that Parliament, to which, by the unwritten law of tradition, its members must belong, for they must be present to answer questions in Parliament; and, through Parliament, it represents the dominant political party in the country.

This representation means that the Cabinet itself and its members in their capacity as heads of the Departments of State, only hold office so long as they represent that dominant political party, or so long as that political party remains dominant. While it is in office, however, the Cabinet is, in practice, the chief executive authority in what is officially known as the "United Kingdom of Great Britain and Northern Ireland"—remember that this authority does not extend to the self-governing Dominions of the British Commonwealth of Nations, which are completely autonomous, and have their own Governments and their own Parliaments.

The first thing to notice is that the authority is collectively that of the Cabinet and not of the Prime Minister, exceptionally powerful though he is by reason of his office, and great as his personal prestige may be. The decisions are those of the Cabinet. If any member does not agree, he can individually resign; but if he does not resign, he takes his share in the responsibility for a measure which he may privately have opposed before it was adopted. Indeed, this principle of collective responsibility is at the bottom of the jealous preservation of the secrecy of Cabinet deliberations; for a Minister might be charged with inconsistency if he afterwards defended a measure to which he was known to have objected at first—and he is expected by tradition to defend it publicly, and not merely to acquiesce silently in its adoption. He stands or falls with the Cabinet, and, as Lord Morley has written, "an excellent Home Secretary may suffer from the blunders of a stupid Minister of War."

The second point is that as a result of this delegation of the authority of the Crown to the Cabinet, the King, in modern times, takes no part in politics. He does not preside over meetings of the Cabinet in the way that the President of the French Republic, until the present reorganization of the French form of government, presided over the Council of Ministers. As I have already said, he has no right to be told what happens at Cabinet meetings. He has, however, the right to be told by the Prime Minister of the decisions of the Cabinet and the general policy of the Government, and he has the right to give the Prime Minister his opinion, which may be valuable from his impartial position and from his experience. He has, as it has been well put, the right "to be informed, to advise and to warn." There his power in the daily conduct of Government business ends. There is only one political decision which he can take independently and on his own personal judgment. That is the choice of the politician whom he will entrust with the duty of forming a new Government, when the last one has either been placed in a minority in the House of Commons or has been defeated in the country in a general Election, and has therefore been obliged to resign.

These are the limitations upon the direct power of the King in modern England; but it would be entirely mistaken to conclude that he is a mere figurehead. His moral influence is immense; and the respect, affection and even veneration in which the persons of the King and Queen are held enable them to give leadership and encouragement which are of inestimable value. The affection between the King and his people has been described as being of a family nature, and the description is good. It is a family link which binds him to all his subjects in Great Britain and the Empire.

I have said that the King can exercise his discretion in the choice of the man who will try to form the next Government. That is not quite the same thing as saying that the King can choose the next Prime Minister; for the man whom he has selected may fail to form a Government, or he and his Government may fail to secure a majority in the House of Commons, in which case he must resign. Nor does the King choose any of his Ministers. They kiss his hands ceremonially on receiving from him their formal appointment; but it is the Prime Minister alone who invites them to join the Government.

It is also the Prime Minister alone who decides which of his Ministers shall belong to the Cabinet. He can make the Cabinet small or large, according to his choice. He could hardly leave out the ministerial holders of certain important offices, but every Minister is by no means necessarily a member of the Cabinet, and it never happens that all the Ministers are. Nor does it ever happen that the political Under Secretaries in the several Departments of State are members of the Cabinet. The Cabinet is in fact the Board of Directors of the business. Its members are also the departmental managers in that business; but not all the departmental managers are on the Board of Directors. Both as directors and as departmental managers, they can constantly be called to account by the representatives of the general body of the shareholders, that is to say by Parliament, representing the electorate.

The examination of the list of the offices whose holders compose the Government of the United Kingdom will present one of the many examples to be found in English public and private life of the persistence of tradition and the reverence for precedent. It is not that evolution and change are not constantly going on in England. They are, as they must in any living organism; but they go on behind the mask of permanence. The transition is thus accomplished with less friction, and by the time that most people realize that it has taken place, what is new has acquired some of the prestige as well as the appearance of what is old. In fact, England, in defiance of the parable, is constantly putting new wines into old bottles.

One of the most typical anachronisms in the Government is that of the office usually held by the Prime Minister himself. It is called First Lord of the Treasury. Now the Treasury is the name, in England, of what would elsewhere be called the Ministry of Finance; but the First Lord of the Treasury has nothing to do with finance. He is, in theory, chairman of the Treasury Board, which has also, in theory, inherited the powers of a now extinct officer, the Lord High Treasurer; but the Treasury Board never meets, and the real Minister of Finance is another member of it, who is called the Chancellor of the Exchequer. There are also four or five Junior Lords of the Treasury, who belong to the Board which never meets, but whose real duties have nothing to do with finance either. These duties are to discipline and to whip up the members of the Government party in the House of Commons, and to see that they are in attendance to vote in divisions. The Junior Lords are consequently called Whips, and there are other Whips on the side of the Opposition, so that arrangements are made for the temporary release, in each party, of members, who are then described as being "paired." On the other hand, the Financial Secretary to the Treasury, who is really the second in command to the Chancellor of the Exchequer, and holds a very important financial office, is not a member of the Treasury Board at all.

There are, in connection with the Government, three other Boards, which have only a nominal existence, and never meet. These are the Board of Education, the Board of Trade and the Board of Works. These three Boards even give their names to what are in fact Ministries; and the men who in other countries would be called the Minister of Education, the Minister of Commerce and the Minister of Public Works, are known in England as the President of the Board of Education, the President of the Board of Trade and the First Commissioner of Works. The way in which the English rather enjoy the humor of these anachronisms is illustrated by a story of a question being asked in the House of Commons as to whether the Archbishop of Canterbury was regular in his attendance at one of these Boards—no doubt the Board of Education—of which he was nominally a member. The Minister responsible solemnly replied that he was happy to be able to say that His Grace had attended on every occasion on which he had been summoned. The same rather affectionate attitude of mockery—this time aimed at no less important an institution than the House of Lords itself—is expressed in some lines which the nineteenth-century humorist, W. S. Gilbert, introduced into one of his many comic operas:

> "The House of Lords, throughout the War,
>   Did nothing in particular,
>   And did it very well."

The Prime Minister does not usually hold any office in addition to that of First Lord of the Treasury, so that he is in effect a Minister without portfolio. But there have been exceptions. Mr. Winston Churchill is at present Minister of Defense, and coordinates the services of the Army, the Navy and the Air Force, which, however, have each their separate Ministers; but this is a War measure, which may perhaps be regarded as exceptional. There have, however, been occasions, within living memory, of a Prime Minister assuming a Departmental office. Mr. Ramsay MacDonald took on the duties of Foreign Secretary, as well as those of Prime Minister, in 1924, and the late Lord Salisbury did the same in two Governments towards the end of the nineteenth century. Earlier still, Mr. Gladstone was once Chancellor of the Exchequer as well as Prime Minister.

There are two other members of the Government who are virtually Ministers without portfolio. These are the Lord Privy Seal, who in ancient days was responsible for sealing public documents, and the Lord President of the Council.

The Council over which the latter is supposed to preside but hardly ever does, is not the Cabinet, at which the chair is taken by the Prime Minister, but the King's Privy Council, a body which meets as a whole only at the death of the Sovereign to declare the accession of his successor, and otherwise has a mainly historical and decorative existence, although the Judicial Committee of it is the final Court of Appeal from legal decisions in the Dominions and the Colonies. However, membership of the Privy Council, which is shared by Ministers with a number of other dignitaries, is the qualification for being addressed as "The Right Honorable" on the envelopes of letters. To these two Ministers, one might almost add the Chancellor of the Duchy of Lancaster, whose departmental duties relating to the administration of the Crown properties and jurisdiction in Lancashire, although they do exist, are not onerous. Moreover, it is possible, though not usual, definitely to nominate a Minister without portfolio, and there is one, Mr. Arthur Greenwood, in the present War Cabinet, which, as it also includes the Lord President of the Council and the Lord Privy Seal, has three of its eight members who have no departmental responsibilities.

In addition to the Premier, there are certain other Ministers, who may be described as ex-officio members of the Cabinet. They are never left out in time of peace. These are the Chancellor of the Exchequer, who is generally regarded as the second in command to the Prime Minister, and represents the Government in the House of Commons when the Prime Minister is absent, the Lord Chancellor, the Lord Privy Seal, the Lord President of the Council, the First Lord of the Admiralty—who in most other countries would be called Minister of Marine—and "His Majesty's Principal Secretaries of State," of whom there are eight. These are the Secretaries of State for Foreign Affairs, the Dominions, the Colonies, War, Air, India and Scotland, and finally the

Home Secretary, who is what would elsewhere be known as Minister of the Interior.

Other Ministers, whom the Premier may or may not include in the Cabinet, are the Ministers of Agriculture, Labor, Transport and Health (the office of the last of whom used to have the rather more explanatory title of Local Government Board), the Presidents of the Board of Trade and the Board of Education, the First Commissioner of Works, the Postmaster General, the Paymaster General, the Chancellor of the Duchy of Lancaster, the Attorney General and the Solicitor General, who may be called the legal advisers and representatives of the Government—the Solicitor General is, illogically enough, not a solicitor but a barrister—and the Lord Advocate and the Solicitor General for Scotland, both of whom theoretically fulfil the same functions with regard to that country.

These Ministers number twenty-eight in all, and in War time they are supplemented by others, the Minister of Aircraft Production, the Minister of Supply, the Minister of National Security, the Minister of Food, the Minister of Information, the Minister of Shipping and the Minister of Economic Warfare, who bring the total up to thirty-six. When it is said that no Cabinet has ever numbered more than twenty-one—and that figure has been attained only in recent years—it will be seen that there are always some Ministers who are not Cabinet Ministers. At present, the War Cabinet, as I have said, numbers only eight; but that again is exceptional.

In addition, there are junior members of the Government —Under-Secretaries of State, Financial and Parliamentary Secretaries, a Civil Lord of the Admiralty, Junior Lords of the Treasury and so forth, who may all be said, in a general way, to belong to the Ministry, but who cannot be described as Ministers, as they all have departmental heads over them.

A word should be said about the First Lord of the Admiralty. He is not a lord in the aristocratic or titular sense (unless he happens to be one by private family right) any more than the Civil Lord of the Admiralty and the Junior Lords of the Treasury are lords. Indeed, they are all almost invariably commoners. What is interesting about the First Lord of the Admiralty is that he represents a Board of Admiralty, which, in distinction from the other Boards which I have mentioned, really does meet. It includes two other political members, the Civil Lord and the Parliamentary Secretary, and also four Sea Lords, who are admirals and do not go out of office with the Government.

In order to understand the general working of the system of Government in the United Kingdom, two important facts should be borne in mind. The first is that local administration in Great Britain is more independent of interference from the central Government than is that of many other countries. The central Government has no local representatives or administrators. There are no provincial governors, no prefects. Local Government is carried on by the independent parishes or communes and by the independent municipalities, and it is not centralized beyond the grouping of the parishes into rural districts, and these into counties. The counties and the municipalities administer their own affairs, and raise their own local revenues for the purpose. They have their own separate police forces. There are inspectors from Whitehall, who report upon the observance or otherwise of certain regulations which have become law, but it is entirely upon the local authorities that rests the responsibility for enforcing those regulations.

The second point is that the Ministers and Under-Secretaries whom I have indicated above are absolutely the only officials who vacate their posts when the Government is defeated by a vote in Parliament or at a General Election, and goes out of office. All the other members of the Administration are permanent Civil Servants. Political influence may sometimes enter to a small extent into the appointment of an ambassador; but even so, very little, for such appointments are usually the final step of promotion in a professional career which has lasted a lifetime. In all the lower appointments and promotions, political influence enters not at all. Entrance into the Civil Service, both in the higher and in the lower grades, is by competitive examination, and has been so ever since the middle of the nineteenth century. Civil servants are outside of politics. They are not allowed to be parliamentary candidates, and, although they may vote, they must not take part in political conflicts or discussions. On the other hand, they cannot, even the highest of them, be made responsible to Parliament. That responsibility must be borne by the political chief of the Department concerned, even if the mismanagement or error in question was committed without his instructions, and perhaps without his knowledge.

I have purposely tried to explain the system of Government in Great Britain before touching upon Parliament, because what I have said about the manner in which the country is ruled will already have told something of the spirit which animates its parliamentary system.

Parliament consists of the King, the House of Lords and the House of Commons—which was first so called, not because it consisted of commoners as distinct from the aristocracy, but because it represented the "communes" or parishes and municipalities of the whole country. I have already referred to that most significant event of its early history, which was that the "knights of the shire," who might naturally have been expected to ally themselves to the nobles, to whose class they socially belonged, threw in their lot with the burgesses of the towns and consequently with the commercial interests of the nation. It must also be remembered that Parliament has never consisted of the Three Estates of the Realm; for the clergy abstained, almost from the beginning, from being directly represented in the House of Commons, and have ever since had a place in Parliament only through the twenty-four bishops who sit in the House of Lords. These two facts are of the utmost importance; for the alliance between the townspeople and the country gentry explains the partly aristocratic and partly democratic character of the power which the House of Commons acquired, while the absence of the clergy explains the rapid rise to influence of the lawyers, who at once became the most educated class present in the assembly.

Since the beginning of Parliament, the basis of representation in the House of Commons has been progressively broadened, so that today practically every man or woman who is of full age and a British subject has the vote. The qualification for being elected to the House of Commons is almost as wide—there are several women who can write M.P. (Member of Parliament) after their names, and there has been one woman Minister—but there are certain exceptions. These include the civil and military servants of the Crown, the clergy of the Church of England, the Church of Scotland and the Catholic Church, bankrupts, criminals and Peers of the Realm. Members were unpaid until the beginning of the present century, for the aristocratic tradition long was that membership should be enjoyed only by gentlemen of means; but there is now a salary of £600 a year.

The House of Commons at present contains 615 members, of whom 528 come from England and Wales, 74 from Scotland and 13 from Northern Ireland—for it must be remembered that when Southern Ireland, or Eire, became a self-governing Dominion, Northern Ireland remained attached to Great Britain.

The meetings of the House of Commons are held in a long rectangular chamber with a table and an open space down the middle. This space is flanked by benches lengthways and facing each other, with a small number of cross

benches at the end farthest removed from the chairman. The
chairman is called the Speaker, and he sits on a chair raised
upon a dais at the top end of the table. The dais is the only
elevated part of the Chamber, and members make their
speeches from the floor level. They do so generally from
their places, wherever they may be; but the members of the
Government and the leading members of the Opposition,
who sit on the two long front benches facing each other, ap-
proach the table when they speak.

These physical features of the House of Commons are
not without importance. In most parliaments of other countries, the Chamber is an amphitheatre, and the orator walks
up some steps to a raised platform below the President's seat
in order to address his audience, the whole of which he has
in front of him in tiers. The members of such a Chamber,
being seated in a semicircle, may be arranged in a political
gradation, which gently fades from the President's Right,
through the Center to the Left.

In the British House of Commons there can be no center,
or Right Center or Left Center. There is the Government
side, and there is the Opposition side, and that is all, except
for the cross benches at the back. I do not say that this formation is entirely responsible for the long prevalence of the
two-party system in England, because we have more than
two parties today; but I think that it is partly responsible
for the attitude of mind which makes an English politician
definitely take his place either for the Government or against
it, and perhaps also for that other attitude of mind, so shocking to logical Latins, which makes all Englishmen satisfied,
in every kind of vote or election, with the rough and ready
arbitrament of a bare majority when there are more than
two parties or candidates, without insisting upon a second
ballot in order that an absolute majority may be reached.

Moreover, I do think that the shape of the House of
Commons is largely responsible for the character of British

parliamentary discussion—I say discussion, for it is that rather than oratory. I have sometimes seen printed in a newspaper in a Latin country, "The British Prime Minister then stepped up into the tribune." Well, he never does, because there is no tribune. He just gets up from his seat, and lays his hand on one of the large brass-bound boxes in front of him on the table, at the end of which sits the Clerk of Parliament in his barrister's wig, and along which lies the heavy brass and silver mace, which has been ceremoniously carried into the House when the Speaker opened the sitting. And he then conversationally addresses the Speaker, who is sitting a couple of yards away on his throne, wearing Court dress— that is to say, silk knee breeches and stockings—and with robes and a wig very like those of a Judge.

He addresses the Speaker, because a member of the House of Commons is not supposed to be directing his observations to the House, but to its President, whom he calls "Mr. Speaker." This is part of the exact procedure, whose complication is such a terror to the young parliamentarian. The Englishman in his private life is all for simplicity and directness. He is, indeed, careful about his manners; but, apart from the general principle that good behavior means consideration for others, and the particular rule that one must not talk too much, manners for him mean chiefly table manners—not eating peas with a knife or soup with a noise, asking your neighbor to pass the salt instead of stretching out your hand for it and abstaining from the use of a toothpick in public. He rather affects to despise the elaborate politeness of the Frenchman in speech and writing. In his public life, however, he has a passion for form and ceremonial and a genius for carrying them out well. What he loves in them is very little their picturesqueness, and only so much of their historical association as gives him the comfortable feeling that the past is being carried on into the present without abrupt change. What chiefly endears ceremonial to him is the sense

of security it gives that while he is performing it in the orderly manner which it requires, he is not likely to lose his
head or get excited or to make any rapid commitment which
he might afterwards regret.

Thus he surrounds all his public acts with forms of procedure. In the House of Commons, he addresses the Speaker.
In order to make a speech, he must "catch the Speaker's eye,"
and he cannot begin unless the Speaker calls upon him. He
must know what constituency is represented by any member
to whom he wishes to refer in the course of his speech, for he
cannot do so by his name. He must say "the honorable member for So and So." If he refers to a Minister or ex-Minister,
he must say "the right honorable member" or "the right honorable gentleman." A retired military officer is "the honorable and gallant member." The House of Lords must never
be spoken of except as "another place." Applause in the sense
of the clapping of hands is not permitted in the House of
Commons, and is never heard, while any kind of demonstration in the public galleries, of which there is a separate one
for ladies, is immediately suppressed. Members signify their
approbation by interpolated ejaculations which are reported
in the Press as "hear, hear," but which actually sound rather
like a discreet murmur. This becomes a continuous groan of
" 'ear, 'ear, 'ear" when a speech is followed by what the
newspapers describe as "loud and prolonged cheering." There
are occasions when a member has to make a remark with his
hat on his head; and one night, a couple of years ago, Lady
Astor, who is a Member of Parliament, rose to speak, and
suddenly remembered that she was bareheaded. She snatched
the top hat of a male colleague at her side, and put it on over
her elegant coiffure. There are other occasions when the
member must not rise from his seat, and others again when
he must bow to the Speaker. If, in any of these matters, he
makes a slip, he is immediately greeted by loud cries of "Order, Order." No wonder that the new member often waits a

long time before he makes what is called his maiden speech. I may add that votes in the British Parliament are taken by the members walking into one or other of the "Division Lobbies" and consequently require the physical presence of the voter.

The members of the Government sit on the front bench on the Speaker's right. There is also a similar Government bench in the House of Lords; but a Minister can sit only in the Chamber to which he belongs, and he can address only the Chamber to which he belongs. There is no Minister's bench on which any member of the Government can appear in either Chamber. Consequently, in order that the Government shall be represented in both houses, the Prime Minister appoints a "Leader of the House" to speak in his name in that Chamber to which he does not belong—usually the House of Lords, for in modern times the Prime Minister is nearly always in the House of Commons—and it is the practice that the Under-Secretary in each Government Department belongs to the House to which the Minister does not.

Parliament is the supreme authority in the United Kingdom. It has power to overthrow Governments, to render impossible the existence of any Government of which it does not approve, to make or repeal all laws, and, as it has been said, to do everything except to change a man into a woman. It can delegate its own powers, and virtually turn the Government of the country into a dictatorship, as it has temporarily done during the present war.

In practice, Parliament exercises its power by publicly asking questions, by voting resolutions and by making laws. It can force a Government to resign by passing a vote of censure on its conduct or by defeating any major measure which the Government has introduced. It is, however, not the habit in England for the Government to announce beforehand that it will make the vote on any particular matter a question of confidence.

A sitting of the House of Commons always opens with prayers, which are read by its chaplain, and the business then begins with the asking of questions, previously communicated to the Ministers concerned, and now answered by them. The House then passes to debate, either upon a resolution or upon some stage of a Bill, or proposed law. The decision as to what matters shall be discussed and how much time shall be given to each theoretically rests with the House as a whole, and is determined by its vote; but it is in fact in the hands of the Leader of the House, who is usually the Prime Minister, and it is reached after he has consulted the Leader of the Opposition, who sits opposite to him.

The Leader of the Opposition is the leader of the party which is opposed to the Government, or of the most important of two or more parties which may be opposed to the Government, and he holds a position which has long been more or less official. He is referred to as "Leader of His Majesty's Opposition," and he is in constant consultation with the Prime Minister, not only over the allocation of parliamentary time, but over such business as is, by tacit consent, allowed to go through unopposed. A few years ago, it was even decided that he should draw a salary almost equal to that of a Minister.

In order to become law, a measure must be passed by both Houses of Parliament and receive the assent of the King, which is never refused. In theory, a Bill may be initiated in either House—except in the case of those involving the collection or spending of public money, which must be introduced in the Commons and by the Government—but in practice it is nearly always what is called the Lower House which votes the Bill first and then sends it to the Upper.

In theory also, a Bill may be introduced by any member, but in fact one which has not received Government backing has little chance of getting through all its stages in the Session of a single year—and it must do this, for in a new Session it cannot be taken up at the point at which it was left.

The stages through which a Bill has to pass are these. It is not examined or discussed by any parliamentary committee before being brought in, but after it has been drafted by the legal experts of the Government Department concerned, its introducers present it to the House for a First Reading, which is a mere formality, and is always accorded without discussion. The next stage is that of the Second Reading, when the principle of the measure is discussed, and then accepted or rejected, but when the Bill is not examined in detail. Then follows what is called the Committee stage, when detailed amendments are adopted or not. This Committee stage, in the case of mainly uncontroversial and technical measures, is proceeded with in one or other of the Committees of the House which deals with specialized matters, and not on the floor of the House itself; but in the case of an important Government proposal, the whole House "goes into Committee," as it is called, under the presidency of the Chairman of Committees instead of the Speaker, and the detailed discussion is undertaken, the chief difference in procedure being that when the Speaker presides, a member can address the House only once, whereas "in Committee" he can do so several times. Finally, the Bill, as amended, comes back to the House for Third Reading, and may then be rejected also, though this does not often happen.

When the Bill reaches the House of Lords, the same three stages are followed, but the powers of the House of Lords are limited today. Not only must financial measures be introduced in the Commons, which has been the case for hundreds of years, but the Lords can now neither amend nor reject them, and such a measure automatically becomes law at the end of the Session, if the House of Lords has failed to pass it. A similar automatic passage must also be given to a

Bill which is not a financial measure, on condition that it is sent up by the Commons to the Lords in three successive Sessions and rejected by them.

These provisions, which are those of the Parliament Act of 1911, will probably never actually be enforced, for the House of Lords will accept the inevitable, as it did in accepting the Parliament Act; but they will make it unnecessary ever again to bring into action the one expedient to which the Crown—that is to say, the Government—could previously resort in order to break a deadlock between the two Houses. This was the creation of a sufficient number of Peers to secure a majority.

This expedient has never actually been employed since 1711, when twelve Peers were made in order to confirm the Treaty of Utrecht; but the threat of using it has twice forced the House of Lords to submit—at the time of the Reform Bill of 1832 and the Parliament Act of 1911. Its existence emphasizes the entirely different theoretical basis of the House of Lords from that of the House of Commons. The great majority of the members of the House of Lords sit in it, not because they represent the nation or any part of it, or because they are elected by anybody, but because they are themselves important persons and are members of the House of Lords by individual right. Their importance has been consecrated by the fact that they, or one of their ancestors, have been ennobled by the Crown, that is to say that they hold hereditary Peerages. Over seven hundred Peers of the United Kingdom sit in the House of Lords by this hereditary title; but women cannot take their seat there, although, in certain circumstances they can be Peers in their own right. In addition, there are sixteen Scottish Peers, who are not Peers of the United Kingdom, but are elected by the whole body of Scottish Peers to represent them, and there can be twenty-eight Irish Peers, chosen in the same way—there are in fact only sixteen who have actually been elected. Then there are the life members of the House, who are the two archbishops and twenty-four bishops, as well as the seven Lords of Appeal in Ordinary, as they are called.

There are Constitutional provisions which determine the life of any one Parliament, that is to say the dissolution of the House of Commons and a new General Election. The House of Commons is dissolved by the King, if the Prime Minister makes the request. The Constitutional tradition is that he should do so only if he not only finds himself in a minority in the House of Commons but no alternative Government could find a majority. It may be that the existing Prime Minister asks for this dissolution in order to secure a new mandate from the country, or that he first resigns and then his successor immediately asks for a dissolution before meeting the House of Commons. In practice, the threat of dissolution with its consequent return of every Member of Parliament to his constituency, to face the expense and uncertainty of an election, places in the hands of the Prime Minister a power over the House which does not exist in countries where the life of each Parliament is fixed, and where the Popular Chamber cannot be, or in practice is not, dissolved during that period. The life of a British Parliament is limited also—it was seven years before 1911, but was then reduced to five by the Parliament Act. The important fact, however, is that the Prime Minister can threaten to cut it short at any moment by challenging the majority to vote against him. The challenge sometimes brings the majority to heel; but when public opinion has turned against a Government, it is difficult for even the most obedient House of Commons to vote for it, and it is significant that it rarely happens that a legislature lives out its full term.

Let us sum up the essential features of the political system of England. It is an organism, for it has never ceased growing, and it has never been crystallized. Yet it has never discarded its past, so that it preserves much of the spirit of an aristocracy, though it has become a democracy. It is permeated by the habit of tolerance and by the practical instinct for getting something done, at the expense of compromise, rather than creating a deadlock for the sake of principle. Above all, its guiding spirit is a combination of the passion for liberty with the love of justice, law and order.

⊙ ⊙ ⊙ ⊙ ⊙ ⊙ ⊙ ⊙ ⊙

Chapter III

⊙ ⊙ ⊙ ⊙ ⊙ ⊙ ⊙ ⊙ ⊙

THE SOCIAL STRUCTURE OF ENGLAND

Two THINGS should be remembered about the social structure of England. The first is that, although the great majority of the total population of the British Isles today lives in towns, the Englishman remains at heart a countryman. The second is that, although England is today a democracy, it is still socially an aristocracy in spirit.

Consequently, much of the foundation of English life will be explained by first examining that part of it which is most traditional and most permanent. Take the English village.

Before you reach the village itself, you will be able to notice several things about the appearance of the countryside which will tell you something of the habits of the people. The villages are close to one another, and there are many houses which are not in the villages, so that it is hardly ever possible to look at a stretch of landscape without seeing human dwellings of some sort. Some of these isolated buildings are farm houses, for these are not grouped near each other in the village street, as they are in so many countries of Europe. Each is more or less in the center of the land, which is worked by the farmer.

For two centuries England has not known war, civil or other, within her own borders, and it is longer still since British farmers have felt the need for congregating together and seeking the protection of each other against marauders. This sense of security affects the appearance of the farm buildings themselves. They are not surrounded by high walls or barred doors, and although the gates will be closed against animals, human beings can easily climb over them or open them. Moreover, there is, in the country, an aspect not only of security, but of permanence. The fields, whether pasture or arable, are all separated from each other by old and well-grown hedges and by gates; and these hedges would hardly exist if the land were frequently changing hands and therefore liable to be divided up.

The existence of the hedges and gates indicates another very characteristic trait of English country life—the exclusiveness of the man who holds land. He does not want any stranger to go on to his territory, even for an inoffensive walk; and you will frequently see a board put up, with the notice "trespassers will be prosecuted." At the same time, tradition, which tolerates this exclusiveness, does also give certain rights to the pedestrian. There are footpaths, which are known as "rights of way," because they have been used for generations; and these footpaths will go across private fields, and will pass from one field to another by means of what are called "stiles"—steps to help the walker over a wooden fence —or a wicket gate which can be opened only sufficiently to give passage to a human being and not to an animal or a cart, or else again a turnstile, which is much the same thing.

One more evidence of local tradition is the winding nature of nearly all the roads. When they were made, long ago, they had to go round the field of one man and then round the field of another; and no central authority has since intervened to insist upon straightening them out.

The English farmer is nearly always the tenant of a big landowner, and he is a fairly large tenant. There are no peasant farmers, doing a great part of the heavy work themselves, with the assistance of their wives and children and perhaps one laborer. For there are no peasants who own small farms, and there are not even any peasants who rent small farms. Consequently, the farms are big and the fields are big. The farmer does not put his hand to the plough himself. He organizes and directs his agricultural laborers. The landed proprietor, who is his landlord, would no doubt not admit that he and his tenant are of the same social class, nor perhaps would the village as a whole; but the farmer is almost a gentleman. When you call upon him, the door is opened by a parlor maid in a black dress and a white apron, and you are asked to wait in the drawing room.

The principal landowner of the village would until recent years have been, and in many places still is, called the squire. He lives in what the village generally refers to as "the big house," and the house is surrounded, first of all by a garden, almost always with its clump of trees, as well as its lawns, its flowers and its walled enclosure for vegetables, and, beyond the garden, by a park, in which trees and pasture are agreeably mixed in a sort of ordered naturalness. The park is bounded by a fence or a hedge, and the road through it and up to the house begins with park gates and the lodge of the gatekeeper, who is very often also the gamekeeper—for the landed proprietor retains the shooting rights over the land which he rents to his farmers, and the shooting of partridges, pheasants and hares, in the autumn and winter, is the principal distraction, not only of himself, but of his friends whom he invites down for week-ends. To be sure, he may be a hunting man, in which case he and his friends will go out on horseback with the foxhounds twice a week or more; but even then he is pretty sure to have some shooting as well.

The squire in the big house is the center of the upper class social life of the village; but he is far from being its only gentleman, and his is very rarely the only important property. There are sure to be a certain number of people of means who may not be great landowners, but possess large country houses, with parks not perhaps so big as that of the squire, but imposing enough. There will be manufacturers, businessmen, professional men, who spend their days working in London or some other large town, but who come back every evening to live and sleep in the country. Some of them will have houses with no park at all, and no keeper's lodge at the park gates, but always with a garden and always with an entrance gate and a drive, which twists ingeniously through the trees so that the house cannot be seen from the road. There will be the village doctor. There will perhaps be an artist or a novelist. Finally, there will be the parson of the established Anglican Protestant Church and his family, which is usually large, for country parsons have a way of being blessed with many children.

All these people belong to more or less the same social class. That is to say, they do so today; for it is not so long ago that the artist would certainly not have been admitted, and the parson would only have been let in on sufferance. The barrister has always had the right to call himself a gentleman, but not so—until quite recent times—the solicitor, or notary, and certainly not any one who was in trade. But those times have passed. Today, there are virtually three social strata in the English village—at the bottom the working man, then the small shopkeeper and the schoolmaster, and finally the gentleman; and there are certain old maids, always badly dressed and riding bicycles about the village in a dignified manner, who obviously belong to the highest of these strata. You cannot make any mistake about them. They are ladies.

The existence of this upper-class society in a country village is possible only because English people of all classes prefer to live in the country if they can—and that not only in the fine weather and the summer months, but all through the year.

The City of London—that is to say the central and most ancient part of London as a whole—is a hive of activity all day and a desert at night. Its empty streets then re-echo only to the tramp of the dozen soldiers and their officer, who march down from Wellington Barracks to mount guard over the Bank of England until daybreak. Hardly anybody sleeps in the City. The principal reason is no doubt that the houses in its narrow streets command such enormous rents as offices that no one could afford to live there, and no doubt many of its workers have their homes in other parts of London; but many live in the suburbs and even in the country, and go back there every evening—no business people go home in the middle of the day in London, but have their lunch in clubs, restaurants or tea shops, according to their means.

These London workers live in the country, partly because rents are cheaper there, but very often because they prefer to live in the country. The people who do so are not only the clerks and smaller employees, who have little houses in the outer suburbs, where the daily fare to London is cheap, but also the employers and the managers, who could well afford houses in the West-End of the town, but go farther out still, so as to enjoy the pleasures of country air, country sport and, above all, a country garden, for which they willingly sacrifice extra time every day on the journey.

Even the clerk is willing to give a little more time and a little more money, if it will bring him to his own house and his own patch of garden, where he can plant his flowers with loving care and pass the mowing machine and the roller over his little lawn every evening.

It is the patch of garden which really counts. A little house to himself he could probably find in a modest quarter of the town; for, in London, separate houses—though they touch one another—have not yet been generally superseded by flats, although the change is proceeding. To find the patch of garden, he must go into the suburbs.

The traveller who approaches London by train or road can see thousands of these little houses—usually "semidetached," that is to say, touching the next door house on one side only —with, in front of them, but particularly behind them, their thousands of little flower gardens, separated from the neighbors by a fence that you can only just look over, and so carefully kept that the occasional one which is neglected is an eyesore.

Out in the country he could see larger houses with larger gardens; but even here the cottages of the agricultural laborers in the villages, with their little flower gardens in front and their vegetable garden at the back, which the workman keeps in trim after what is often a heavy day on the farm, show that with Englishmen gardening is a passion.

For these reasons, all classes of society are to be found in an English village, and nowhere better can be seen in full bloom that peculiar and rather petty, but really not entirely unamiable characteristic of the English, which is called snobbishness. In the sense in which the word is understood in England, snobbishness means, generally, the desire to frequent a class which is socially superior to your own, and, particularly, the effort to make your friends believe that not only do you frequent that class, but also that you belong to it.

Snobbishness is perhaps inseparable from the aristocratic organization of society, and no doubt the fact that it certainly still flourishes in England is as good a proof as any that the aristocratic tradition still reigns over the English spirit. Snobbishness implies what is almost veneration for the aristocracy, as well as a passionate desire to belong to it—a desire which is, however, *quite without envy*.

The aristocracy itself half consciously but cleverly keeps alive both the veneration and the ambition to get into the charmed circle. Neither would probably have survived so long if the society of what are called the upper classes had either been rigorously closed or haughtily aloof. It is neither. The aristocracy is constantly reinvigorating itself by the introduction of plebeian blood. It also reinvigorates itself by constantly admitting non-aristocratic elements into association with it. It is true that the legend that it is difficult to get into the best society is carefully kept alive; and it represents a certain reality. It *is* difficult to get into the best society, and money alone cannot do it. But the thing is not impossible. As for aloofness, the English aristocracy knows well enough how to put on, when necessary, the look of a duchess who thinks she is about to be insulted by a waiter; but it knows also how to be condescending with simplicity and gracious with cordiality, which the middle class in England unfortunately does not. Most important of all, it generally possesses that supreme gift of good manners, which consists of being able to put every one at his ease with an appearance of familiarity and equality. That touches the heart of the real snob; and I can remember a country vicar's wife enthusiastically describing some one as "son of a lord, too, though he very properly never mentions the fact." It also touches the heart of simple people, and it is chiefly because an Englishman of good breeding has the capacity for comradeship with men of a class inferior to his own that the English soldier has always preferred to be officered by gentlemen, even if they were not brilliant, and has always been so officered until modern times, when soldiering has become such a highly mechanized business that only technical capacity can count.

This good comradeship between classes, which is fusing the aristocratic spirit of yesterday with the democratic spirit of today, has been created largely by the habit of the upper and middle classes of living in the country and particularly of considering it to be part of their public duty to take an active share in organizing the communal life of the working classes in the country. The old sense that aristocracy has its duties as well as its privileges, the feudal sense in fact, has always survived in rural England. It is now merged in the more modern consciousness of civic duty, which is a communal feeling and not merely aristocratic, but which still retains a certain aristocratic color.

One of the most typical expressions in country life of this fusion of the old spirit with the new is the village cricket match. It takes place on a Saturday afternoon—when the residents who work in town are at home for their weekly half holiday, and the village workers have a half holiday also. It is true that nowadays games are also played on Sunday, which sabbatarian conventions would have made impossible hardly more than a generation ago; but in a country village the inhabitants have not yet got so far as to hold cricket matches on that day.

Later on I shall tell you something about the game of cricket. It is sufficient here to say that the village match is played on an open field by two teams, each team usually representing a locality or some other corporate unit, and that quite a lot of local patriotism is aroused by the contest. Included in the village side on a basis of absolute equality with one another may be the squire's son, his footman, the parson —who will have all the more influence as a parson if he is a good cricketer—a small tradesman and even a farmhand. When I say, "on a basis of absolute equality," I mean in the game only. None of the players has the smallest illusion that this temporary levelling makes any alteration in the social hierarchy; but for the moment it exists.

The Boy Scout movement also expresses the feeling of class comradeship, as indeed it expresses many other things which are typical of the English spirit in the nineteenth and twentieth centuries. It may almost be said that more may be learned about that spirit by studying the Boy Scout movement than in any other way. It is a remarkable fact that within the single lifetime of Lord Baden-Powell, the distinguished general and creator of the movement, the idea which he launched was enthusiastically taken up by boys in every country of the world. The essence of the idea is that all boys have a healthy and natural instinct for playing at romantic adventure, for the rules of a game, for the open-air life, for the inventive use of their hands, for fidelity to their leaders and for loyalty to their comrades, and that this instinct can easily be dramatized into a picturesque game, which will direct it towards good citizenship and public duty. In the village there is pretty sure to be a Boy Scout troop, to which boys of all classes will belong.

There are many other expressions of the good feeling between classes, which exists side by side with definite class distinctions.

In every big country house, at this moment, those women who cannot get away to take up employment as nurses in hospitals or to do other jobs, are at work making garments for the troops or for people who have been rendered homeless by bombardment. They usually furnish the materials themselves, thus giving one more example of the many forms of voluntary self-taxation, which people of means are imposing upon *themselves*. They do this work every day, for they have the leisure to give to it; but—and here is the example of class cooperation—on two days a week, poor women from the village, who have little time to give, join the working party.

The same feeling finds its expression in other ways, in the country and in towns.

The King and the Queen are regarded with such a curious combination of reverence and simple affection that they can take part in the games in a Boy Scouts' camp, and can visit the bombed quarters of London with no further escort than a couple of motorcyclists. Poor school children evacuated from London can be and have been distributed among homes of all classes in the country. Labor conflicts, severe though they often are as economic struggles, have never had the same bitter and violent character as in some other countries. Even the general strike of 1926 ended, to the astonishment of the world, without bloodshed; and the workers have long since acquired by mutual agreement with the employers advantages which they have yet to win under Governments which would generally be described as more democratic than that of Great Britain.

I know that there are also other reasons for the last of these things—the general British tendency to come to terms rather than be irreconcilable, the instinct of the governing class for accepting reform before it is thrust upon them, the genius of the nation for wrapping up change and progress in the cloak of permanence and continuity; but I believe that the chief reason why the aristocratic class continues to hold and is still allowed to hold the influence in the country which it does, continues to occupy the key posts in the Government, in the Civil Service and in the Army and the Navy, is that the people as a whole have grown to believe that it is inspired by a sense of public duty and of private honesty and this conviction has been formed chiefly in consequence of the share which the upper and middle classes have always taken and continue to take in the life of every village.

As far as politics are concerned, the fact that the aristocracy has never ceased to regard them as the occupation of a gentleman and has never ceased to take part in them has been largely responsible for the high standard of public life which has obtained in England ever since the corrupt eighteenth century was left behind and the relatively modern ideal of the conduct of a gentleman was gradually formulated. As regards the public services, the fact that the law of primogeniture induced relatively penniless younger sons of aristocratic families to seek careers in them has caused them to be well paid—for the elder sons who were in politics saw to that. England then discovered that a highly paid public service means an honest public service—"En Angleterre," a Frenchman once said to me, "vous avez des salaires. Nous n'avons que des pourboires." It was also discovered that it was worth while, not only to pay public servants well, but to give them good pensions, so that, on retirement, they did not drop out of the class in which they had lived.

The result is that, at least as far as the highest posts are concerned, a British official is relieved of monetary anxiety for the rest of his life, and is almost as independent of monetary considerations as if he had a private fortune. A Judge draws his salary of £5000 a year until he dies. The Prime Minister receives £10,000 a year when in office and a pension of £2000 a year. The salary of each of the other Ministers is £5000 a year. Salaries on a corresponding scale are paid to the holders of other responsible posts, and although junior officers in the army and junior members of the diplomatic service can hardly live on the social scale to which they are expected to conform in peace time unless they also have means of their own, even they are better paid than they would be in most other countries.

Few of the men of means, who acquire houses in the neighborhood of country villages and settle down there, imagine that they have the right to enjoy their parks and gardens, without doing anything more for the community than merely spending their money. If they nourish this illusion, they soon find that they are, if not ostracized, at least regarded with a certain coolness. In any case, new arrivals in a district always have to wait until the established local people call upon them before they can take part in the social life of the place, and this calling will largely depend upon their readiness to contribute to the local well-being. Moreover, what is expected from each of them is not merely subscribing money to local charities, clubs and other organizations. That they will have to do as a matter of course in a country where even the hospitals, in most cases, are "supported entirely by voluntary contributions," as they advertise in their appeals for funds. These rich men, and particularly their wives and daughters, will find that they must take an active part in promoting the welfare of the poorer people.

At bottom, this obligation is, as I have said, a survival of the old feudal tradition that the lord had duties towards his tenants as well as rights over them, and indeed that the tenants had a right to demand help from him without any of the sense of shame of being beggars. I do not pretend that every owner of a modern country house imagines himself to be a feudal lord; but he wants to be considered to be the social equal of the feudal lord, and one of the ways of succeeding in this ambition—here, once more, snobbishness is of use to the community—is to shoulder some of the feudal responsibilities. The head of the family will perhaps do this by belonging to the unpaid magistracy of the Commission of the Peace, whose functions are described in another chapter—that is, he will do so if he has the good fortune to be nominated, which he certainly will not be when he first arrives. The female members of his family will do it in other ways.

A couple of generations ago, they would have been to see the wife of the village parson, and offered to help her in "visiting the poor." The parson and his wife were then the principal channel through which the poor received any assistance other than that granted by the severe and sometimes harsh official administration of the Poor Law, which the poor themselves regarded it as surrender to accept. At the vicarage, once a week, was held the Mothers' Meeting, at which a certain amount of sewing was done, many cups of tea were drunk and winter blankets and other things were distributed. There was the annual "school treat"—games, tea, cake and gifts— for the children of the Sunday school attached to the church; and there were the visits of the benevolent ladies in their pair-horsed carriages.

All this charity had, however, taken on an air of patronage, and had lost its early feudal character of something to which the poor had a right. The parson himself was obliged to limit his aid to the followers of the Established Church, and to exclude those of the Nonconformist sects, one or other of which probably had a small chapel in the village. In politics, the Established Church was Conservative, while the Nonconformists were Radical. The fact is of interest as showing that the tradition of the parties of the Left in England is not anti-religious, but it put the clergymen of the Established Church into the position of being almost the agent of a political party.

The whole atmosphere is changed today. The village, as a community, has taken over the management of its charitable, as well as its social services. The village Institute, where there is a workmen's club and newspaper reading room, and the Women's Institute, which is the successor of the Mothers' Meeting, are conducted without religious distinctions. The parson is still an important figure, but patronage has become cooperation, and the parson himself is sometimes a Radical and even a Socialist. It is far less to the Church than to the village that the wealthy lady of today will offer her subscriptions and her services. She may work at the Women's Institute or the Cottage Hospital, or she may help the Girl Guides, the feminine counterpart of the Boy Scouts. She will feel bound to work for the village in some way, and the village will expect her to do so.

There is another aristocratic tradition, which is not quite the same as the capacity for putting social inferiors at their ease, nor the same as the old feudal obligation to give protection and assistance to inferiors in return for their recognition of superiority, although it partakes of both. This is the feeling which any decent employer or officer or landlord must have that it is his duty to show a certain consideration for those who are working for him, or obeying his orders or paying him rent. He must not press them too hard. He must not exact from them everything that the law or his agreement with them allows. He must even deliberately relax these con-

ditions from time to time, although they may be readily and
loyally observed. Such consideration is not only human, but
it is even good policy, for it creates personal attachment,
which is the only basis upon which effective service is ever
rendered.

There is a long tradition in the upper and middle classes
in England of this sort of consideration. It comes out in
the army. It comes out in industry. It comes out perhaps
most of all in relations with domestic servants. These relations tend to be difficult in all countries today. In all, there
are bad masters and bad servants; in England, as elsewhere,
bad servants have taken advantage of the difficulty of finding
servants at all in order to make unreasonable exactions. But
a certain experience of other countries has shown me that
while there is none in which the relations between master—
or mistress—and servant are less familiar and so apparently
frigid, there is also none where such consideration is shown
to servants as in England. For instance, hardly an upper or
middle class family anywhere, in the country or in town,
does not make it a rule on Sunday evenings to have a cold
supper laid on the table instead of having dinner served, in
order that the staff shall have no work to do and be able to
go out. There is hardly a mistress who is not constantly doing
her servants unexpected kindnesses, which are quite outside
her strict obligations. She will bring them little presents
when she comes back from a journey, to say nothing of a new
dress at Christmas. She will find all sorts of other ways of
making her relations with them sympathetic and human.

In the upper middle class and aristocratic society, which
lives in the country, there are constant exchanges of visits. It
is true that afternoon calls have gone out of fashion in London, where ladies no longer have their "at home" days, and
no longer wait behind a tray of teacups in their drawing
rooms on the appointed day of the week for their friends to
arrive, and perform what used to be given the depressing

name of "social duties"—calling after a dinner party and so forth. But in the country, though there are no "at home" days, people still call at about four in the afternoon, and are always given tea, and there are still tea parties. Let me describe one of them to you.

It will take place in the drawing room, which almost certainly has long windows opening on to the garden lawn. Its comfortably padded chairs and sofa will have loose coverings, made of cheerful-looking, glazed, flowered chintz, and ending towards the ground with pleated flounces, which suggest that each piece of furniture has been given a skirt, so that there shall be no risk of the impropriety of its legs being seen. The armchairs will have antimacassars thrown over the tops of their padded backs—the origin of the word being the name of a certain Macassar, who sold a hair oil very much in use at the beginning of the nineteenth century, and the purpose of the thing being to protect the chintz from any record of the men's heads having been leaned upon it. Between the chairs will be little tables of the kind called occasional in England, perhaps because they are only occasionally steady enough to hold anything securely. It certainly requires a good deal of practice to be able to move between them without knocking them over. On the walls will be pictures in heavy gold frames. Among them will perhaps be portraits in oil of the hostess and her husband—fortunately for portrait painters, the tradition of each generation adding to the family portraits still obtains in many well-to-do families. There will also be water-colors representing pheasants and partridges or hunting and shooting in England, or else landscapes in Italy—rarely will an English country house show a picture representing landscape in England, for what reason I do not know, but perhaps because Italy is supposed to be more romantic.

Such is the setting for the ceremony. The ceremony itself is not a religious observance, as tea drinking is or was in

Japan, but its ritual is almost as precise and as immutable.

The parlor maid enters the room, and places a low table before the hostess, who is seated in her armchair. On this table she spreads a white cloth. She brings in a big tray—preferably of silver—on which are the teapot, the milk jug, the sugar basin, with its tongs, and the tea caddy—of silver also—as well as the teacups and a small bowl called the slop basin. She sets upon the middle of the tray the large silver hot-water urn and lights the spirit lamp beneath it, so that the water shall always be kept at boiling point. She finally carries in a little three-tiered stand, of which each tier contains a plate. In the top one, which has a cover over it, are hot, buttered, sweet tea-cakes, or, in more old-fashioned houses, muffins—which are soft, very lightly toasted, oozing melted butter, but not sweet. In the second plate are cold slices of buttered bread, cut very thin. In the third are a round cake and a knife, so that each person's slice may be freshly cut.

The parlor maid then retires. For it is not she who will pass the cups of tea to the guests and offer them the food, which they will delicately put on the edge of their saucers, for they will not be given plates—or very rarely. It is not even the unmarried girls present, as it would be in France. It is the men, especially the young men—and very awkwardly do they usually perform the task, for social ease is not one of the accomplishments of the Englishman, at any rate in youth.

When the parlor maid has gone, the hostess first warms the teapot with a little boiling water, which she pours away into the slop basin. She then puts in the prescribed number of teaspoonfuls of tea, while she says the ritual phrase over to herself, or perhaps out loud— "One for each person and one for the pot." She waits the two or three minutes necessary for the tea to "draw," as it is called—that is to say, for the infusion to take place. After this, she asks each guest how many lumps of sugar he or she takes, and she places them in the cup. She then pours in the tea, and asks each guest to tell her when she shall stop adding milk. Later on, when the guest takes his second cup—and everybody takes two cups—the hostess will begin by emptying the dregs, including one or two tea leaves, into the slop basin, for she naturally could not permit herself to pour the second cupful on to the top of them, and a strainer for the tea leaves is rarely added to the teapot in England. There are special refinements, such as offering slices of lemon as the alternative to milk, or making entirely fresh tea for the second round, since the original tea may have become bitter; but they are not general—the health of English people would be improved if the second of them were more frequently adopted, for many digestions are ruined by the tannic acid of tea which has been allowed to stand too long.

You will perhaps think that all this is very small beer —though tea and not beer is in question—but it is not without its importance as showing how rigorously fixed are certain minor social observances in England.

Dressing in the evening is one of the sheet anchors of gentility. In London, the habit of dressing for the theatre has been maintained, in regard to the most expensive seats. As for dinner, a hostess, in sending out invitations to an informal dinner party, may add two words "black tie," to indicate that the men need wear only dinner jackets; but if she says nothing the "white tie," with tail coat, must be taken for granted. It is only very rarely that she will say "Do not dress." You dress for dinner also in the country. You will remember Kipling's story of the Indian Civil Servant, alone in an up-country station, who always dressed to maintain his self-respect and the respect of the natives around him. Perhaps it is something of the same spirit which keeps up dressing in the country in England.

Among the observances of the dinner table, which always

surprise visitors from abroad, is the habit of concluding the meal with what is called a savory, that is to say a tit-bit of fish or cheese, hot, well salted and peppered and served on a small square of buttered toast. It even comes after the sweet dish, and to any amateur of good cooking it is a shocking anticlimax. Unfortunately, however, there is no disguising the fact that amateurs of good cooking are rare in England, and consequently good cooking is rare also, though excellent plain food is not rare at all. At the same time, amateurs of good wine are much less rare. Hence the savory. It dates from the period when men took their wine, not at dinner but afterwards, as they still do in the universities of Oxford and Cambridge, where tradition dies hard; and its purpose was to excite a proper thirst for the wine to come. It is typical of the survival of old forms in England that the savory remains, although wine is now taken all through the meal.

With this tradition of drinking wine after dinner is connected the following observance. After the savory the hostess will look round the table at the other ladies, and, when she has "collected eyes," as the saying is, they will all rise and go to the drawing room, the man nearest the door opening it for them. In former times, the men were thus left to get drunk by themselves. Nowadays, they no longer get drunk, but they are still left alone at the end of dinner, and the survival of the practice is not only a question of the wine, but touches a profound and perhaps not entirely gallant social instinct of the Englishman, the separation of the sexes for relaxation. The same instinct is at the bottom of the English club habit and even of the English devotion to golf. The men want to be in male society. In Latin countries, a wife feels certain, when her husband is not with her, that he is with another woman, and she is frequently right. The English wife may have similar doubts, but it is quite as likely that her husband really is at his club.

The club habit is not merely misogynist. It is not only that a man wants to get away from women, but also from those men whom he does not like, or whom he does not consider to be his social equals. Aristocratic tradition and snobbish ambitions have had a lot to do with club candidatures, elections and exclusions. Belonging to a club means not only associating with men who are congenial, but avoiding association with men who are not congenial, and the real clubs in the traditional sense are those which are exclusive, those whose members do not hesitate to "black ball" the sort of candidate who is not considered to be socially admissible or who has not the talent for being popular. There is a curiously silent unanimity in England about that sort of man, and the way in which he is ignored and "cold-shouldered" is implacable. There is a story of one such who had managed to get into a good club, and came up indignantly to a fellow member one day with a letter in his hand. "It is an insult," he said. "This scoundrel has the impudence to offer me fifty pounds if I resign from the club." "Hold on, and he will make it a hundred," said the other coldly.

It is true that London clubs are not what they were, which is perhaps one of the many signs that social barriers are breaking down. The glorious days when every window in Piccadilly, overlooking the Green Park, was the window of a club with a long waiting list of candidates for membership are past, although the clubs are still there. No longer is the club the stronghold of comfortably middle-aged gentlemen, nor are there many of them to snore over *The Times* in easy chairs in the writing room, where all conversation is forbidden. The reason is not that Englishmen have become more conversational. They will never be very talkative, I think. But they have less desire to be protected from women, to say nothing of other men. There are more and more clubs with members of both sexes. There are more and more, even of the male clubs, which admit women as guests into certain rooms and into a special dining room, all of which would have been unheard of a generation ago.

The separation of the sexes is even disappearing from some dinner parties, where the ladies remain' with the men until the end. ·The men do not have to wait until they are gone in order to smoke, as the ladies smoke also. It is obviously impossible at restaurant dinner parties, which people give nowadays, but which would have struck a host of the last generation as almost an insult to his guests. It survives in many houses, however, especially in the country. When the ladies are gone, the host, who has been sitting at the end of the table farthest from his wife, takes what was her place, and sends round the wine again—it must always circulate in the direction of the sun, and it passes from hand to hand, each man serving the neighbor on his left. There are two wines—port and claret, claret being the English name for the red wine of Bordeaux. These have been the traditional after-dinner wines in England for over two hundred years, and many an English country house has an excellent cellar of both.

The Englishman is ready and even casual with his hospitality. When he invites a friend to dinner, to take pot luck, he does not mean that phrase to be a falsely modest cover for a carefully prepared menu, but is quite ready to ask his guest to share the meal which he would have had himself—a thing which a man belonging to a country where hospitality is a more ceremonial matter would be ashamed to do. It may even be said that today, more the society is distinguished, more are its manners casual. Many of us can recall a period when there was no social occasion without elaborate introductions. Nowadays that sort of thing is middle-class and provincial. People give parties without introducing their guests to one another; and even when there are only a few people, an introduction is hardly more than "of course you know So and So."

Ready and casual are invitations to meals, and almost equally ready and casual are invitations to week-ends, which are a great feature of country-house hospitality. I know that the expression "week-end" has been adopted into more than one foreign language, but never in the sense which it has in England. Sometimes it is made to mean no more than closing down on Saturday afternoons for the half holiday. Sometimes it is interpreted as going away from Saturday to Monday to stay in a hotel. Only very rarely is it understood as going to stay with friends, which is nearly always what it means in England.

A man I knew once wrote a book about France, which he began with the phrase "France is the country of no spare bedrooms." He might have written "one of the countries." In England, at any rate, a town house or flat without a spare bedroom is rare, and a country house without one would be unthinkable. There are many country houses, where not a Sunday is allowed to pass—even in winter, or perhaps particularly in winter, for that is the shooting season—without one or two friends being invited to stay. In big houses, the one or two become half a dozen or more. But there is little formality about these visits, except that you dress for dinner. You will be free to spend your day as you like and to go where you like, and your host and hostess will not feel obliged to look after you, or to accompany you if you prefer to be left alone.

As dinner time approaches, a warning gong will remind you that it is time to go and dress; and in your room you will find your evening clothes laid out on the bed and the studs already placed in your shirt. In the morning, you will be equally well looked after. A cup of morning tea will be brought to you in your room, and you can take one or two biscuits from the silver box which had already been placed on your bed table, in case you should be hungry in the night. The footman will bring you back your day suit, which he had taken away to brush, and will arrange it neatly on a chair with your day underclothes and your shoes, which have been cleaned. You will find that you have been supplied with soap, which you are not expected to bring with you.

The cup of early tea, with dry biscuits, which the visitor has had in his room, is merely a preliminary introduction to his real breakfast, which he takes in company of the whole house-party in the dining room. Nobody waits for anybody else, however, and when he arrives, he will probably find that, after a few casual greetings, he will be left to look after himself. He will see nothing but racks of toast and dishes of butter and orange marmalade on the table, but his hostess, after pouring his tea or his coffee out for him, will invite him to go to the sideboard and fetch whatever he wants. There he will find an imposing array of dishes, hot and cold. He can begin with some oatmeal porridge. Then he can have some fish—perhaps a bloater, as the herring salted and cured in the particular Yarmouth way is called. After that, he may be tempted by some bacon and eggs, or some sausages, or some kedjuree—an Indian dish of rice and fish—or a helping of omelet, or merely a boiled egg. He can then finish up with some cold partridge or ham or tongue, before putting on the final touch with the inevitable toast and marmalade— or else some fruit. When I was an undergraduate at Oxford, it was considered that a breakfast was not really complete unless a glass of strong beer crowned all; but I can hardly recommend the practice to the dyspeptic. In any case, you will not be offered beer at breakfast in a country house.

In the summer, every family of any importance in the village gives its garden party, which is held on the lawn. It is difficult for any one who has never been to England to imagine what a perfect lawn is like or to understand the importance which is attached to it. To begin with, the tennis court is on a lawn, for in England lawn tennis—real tennis is a different and more ancient game—is nearly always played on grass courts, and rarely on any others. The great Wimbledon championships are always fought out on grass courts. However, in a private garden, it will not be on the tennis lawn that the garden party will be given; for the tennis court has a lawn to itself, remote from the decorative part of the garden and from trees, which would throw disturbing shadows on the game. Big trees, however, form a great part of the beauty of the lawn which adjoins the house, and it is in their shade that the garden party will be held. This lawn is kept merely for the pleasant appearance of its greensward, and for the foreground which it supplies to the flower beds which surround it. Yet its carpet is so fine and so close, the grass is so carefully weeded, is cut so short and is rolled so often that it can safely be walked upon, and even the smallest of ladies' heels make no impression upon it. You probably know the story of the gardener of one of the older Oxford colleges, who told an enquiring visitor that, to make a really good lawn you must roll it for three hundred years. I myself knew a man who had a splendid lawn, of which he was justly proud. He used to weed it carefully himself, so that it should contain nothing but pure grass. One day, he became paralyzed in the legs, and had to be wheeled about in an invalid chair. Nothing daunted, he had the lawn lifted, piece by piece, and the pieces, one after the other, placed in a tray on his knees. There he removed the weeds with the aid of a magnifying glass, and had the turf put back into the ground.

The street of an English village usually has an inviting look, with quite a lot of gaiety and variety and color. This effect is partly created by the fact that the low fences and gates which admit to the little front gardens of the cottages are often painted white or some bright color, but chiefly by the front gardens themselves, which are nearly always packed with flowers, and sometimes by flower boxes on the window sills. The thatched roofs, which used to be universal except upon important houses, are growing rare, and the trade of the thatcher is one which is disappearing from our villages. New cottages are consequently less picturesque than they used to be; but there are still a good many of the old ones left, and there are many landlords today who have sufficient taste to make even the new cottages which they build for agricultural laborers attractive—for, of course, most of the cottages in a village are rented by a landlord to the laborers whom he employs.

There will be a village shop, and, if there is only one, it is most likely to be arranged on the model of two counters, at one of which groceries and ironmongery are sold, while the one opposite is for drapery, haberdashery, shoes and hats and stationery. On the other hand, they have a way in English villages of selling things in places where you would least expect to find them. You will get eggs at the Post Office, butter from the butcher, and so forth, while the carrier will fetch anything else from the nearest town, unless you go in and get it yourself on market day.

Then there will be the public house. The public house is what in any Latin country would be called a café. Neither name indicates its real function, which is to sell what are officially described as "alcoholic beverages." The place may be an inn as well, but it is not by letting rooms that the money is made. Nor is it by supplying food, for, although the law requires every public house to serve bread and cheese, if it is asked for, even that is very little in demand, and it is virtually impossible to get anything to eat in an English village. It is equally impossible to get wine, which probably millions of English working men have never tasted, except for those who have had an occasional glass of port at a bar in town— certainly not in the country. The working man can sometimes, but not always, have spirits—whisky, rum or gin—if he asks for them; but usually, and almost always in the country, his staple drink is beer—except in those western counties where he drinks cider. For readers who do not know English beer, I may add that it is stronger and more bitter than that which is made in other countries.

Now the official attitude towards the drinking of beer in England is a curious one. It starts from the principle that it is a sin. This principle is that of the severe moralists, represented typically by what we call the Nonconformist Conscience, but it has been taken over by the legislature. It has never been carried so far as prohibition. The Englishman is allowed to indulge in his sin; but the legislator has made it as uncomfortable and as expensive as possible for him to do. First of all, the number of places at which he can buy beer—which he must generally drink "on the premises"—is severely limited. The moral purpose of the limitation is to reduce beer drinking; but its practical effect is to make the trade an enormous and powerful monopoly, the public-house landlord being in nearly every case no more than the servant of the brewer. Then the hours during which beer can be obtained are limited also, with the same ostensible moral purpose. Finally, the State heavily increases the price by making the drinker pay in taxes most of what his glass or, more usually his pewter tankard, costs him. The rich consumer used to get round the restriction as to hours by using his club. With the same end in view, the workmen started clubs in towns, and brought about the result that restricted hours are now applied to clubs of every kind.

However, these inconveniences have not prevented the public house from being the nerve center of working-class discussion and opinion in every village. It is a center frequented only by the men—the separation of the sexes again—and here, of an evening, the farm laborer, having escaped from family cares, throws darts at a target in the game which has become the rage of working-class England, takes his beer and airs his views. He does not take such a tremendous lot of beer, though sometimes he would like you to think he does. There is a story of a man who rode up to an inn, and, without dismounting from his horse, called for a gallon of ale. He drained it at a draught, called for another, and swallowed that, after which he said, "Good, I will get down and drink some of that beer." It is stories of this kind which give the Englishman a bad reputation.

Once a year, in the late summer, the village holds what in any other country would be its annual fête. In England it is called the Flower Show. What I have said about the composition of the village society will help you to understand what happens. A field has been lent by one of the chief landed proprietors, and at the gate there are a few flags and a table at which the modest entrance fee is collected. There are two marquees in the field, a large one for the exhibits and a rather smaller one for refreshments. There is a band, and, later in the evening there will probably be dancing on the grass— very solemn, as English village dancing usually is. There will perhaps be fireworks after the prizes have publicly been distributed by the squire's wife at the end of a speech by a political bigwig of the locality, perhaps the M.P. for the constituency.

The public are admitted after lunch, and they enter the large tent, where the judges have been at work throughout the morning. The awards—First Prize, Second Prize or Highly Commended—are indicated by cards pinned on to the flowers and fruits and vegetables which have been successful. It will be remarked that there are two classes of exhibitor. The cottagers show both flowers and vegetables, which they have themselves grown, and the little girls from the village school show nosegays of wild flowers, which they have picked. In the other class, the competitors are the people who live in the big houses, or rather; their gardeners. On a collection of magnificent peaches, for instance, is a card which announces that it is shown by "Mr. John Smith, gardener to William Robinson, Esquire."

The whole aristocratic fabric of rural England is expressed in this card. Why is the gardener's employer described as William Robinson, Esquire, and the gardener as Mr. John Smith? Simply to show that the former is a gentleman and the latter is not. Any one from a country whose people are more preoccupied with asserting the rights of equality than are the English might say that this is most insulting to the gardener. He does not take it like that. To him, the thing is perfectly natural. He has an assured and important position, but he makes no claim to call himself a gentleman.

Every one in the village is accustomed to a precisely similar distinction every day on the envelopes of letters, and so is every one in London. A tradesman—your tailor, for instance—has always received letters which are addressed to him as "Mr.—abbreviation for Mister—So-and-So," and he thinks nothing of the matter. On the other hand, a member of one of the liberal professions would consider it to be a deliberate slur if his name were preceded by "Mr.," instead of being followed by "Esquire." At the same time, the tailor, if he is a leading and prosperous tailor, would almost certainly expect his butcher, in sending the monthly bill to his private house, to address him as "So-and-So, Esq."—abbreviation for Esquire—while, in sending the check, he would not give the butcher any more than "Mr."

There was a time—and that not so very long ago—when the right to be addressed as Esquire, which in chivalry was the squire to a knight, was as definitely limited as the right to be called a gentleman, for it meant the same thing. I have already explained how the membership of certain professions was held to give this right; but apart from that, one had to be *armiger*, which Latin word meant entitled to carry a coat of arms. Nobody today would think of restricting the right to these claims of old family, which could be established only by reference to the College of Heralds. On the contrary, the tendency is all towards abolishing class distinctions. It is curious to notice, however, that such is the ineradicable snobbishness of the English that this tendency does not operate in the direction of addressing everybody on envelopes as "Mr.," as they do in the United States, but in that of addressing everybody as "Esq."

And yet it is perhaps not entirely a question of snobbishness. Perhaps it is one more expression of the English instinct for making a transition with the least possible shock and for investing the new with some of the prestige of the old. When everybody has become esquire, everybody will be a gentleman, and will have inherited his share of a great tradition and a great responsibility.

At the same time, I doubt whether there is a single Englishman who imagines that such a complete change will ever take place. Some people in other countries think of the English as a nation of boors, but others speak of them as gentlemen, meaning that they are all gentlemen. An Englishman can have no such comprehensive conception. For him, gentlemen are the minority, and I do not think that he can imagine that they will ever be other than the minority, the élite. That does not prevent him from having a perfectly conscious pride and satisfaction in his own position, like the squire's gardener, without in the least pretending that it is the position of a gentleman. There is a story of Mr. Lloyd George, when he was Prime Minister, discussing the claims of an applicant for a certain appointment in a committee, of which one of the members was a public works contractor recently raised to the peerage. "An able man, certainly," said some one else speaking of the applicant. "But is he quite—well quite a gentleman?" "What on earth does that matter?" said Mr. Lloyd George. "I am not a gentleman. Lord —— here is not a gentleman." This outspoken way of dealing with the matter must have shocked, not only the man who had so tentatively made the suggestion, but all the other members of the committee. For the word "gentleman" rarely comes into the conversation of an Englishman, though the idea is never far from his thoughts. No Englishman, indeed, would claim to be a gentleman. Either he is one, and he knows that it is not necessary to mention the matter, or he is not, and he knows it, and knows that every one else knows it.

Every Englishman, in fact, can recognize a gentleman when he sees one; but hardly any would be able to define him. Many definitions have been attempted. Some have sought refuge in epigram. "A gentleman is a man who is rude only on purpose." That is well enough as a definition of the manners of a gentleman, who knows how to behave, and is rude only when he means to be rude; but being a gentleman is not solely a question of manners, or even of instinctive discretion and consideration for others. If it had been, the rather ironical expression "nature's gentleman," would not have been invented. Nor is it entirely a question of education. Birth and antecedents enter in also. "A gentleman is a man who can tell you who his grandfather was" expresses pretty well the minimum of family qualification, which thus extends two generations back. But even that is not a complete definition.

One might almost say that a gentleman is a man who, from family tradition and from education, knows the right thing to do without thinking about it, and does it without effort; but perhaps this definition is too exclusive. For it would leave out hundreds of thousands of admirable people, who always do the right thing, but are anxiously thinking about it all the time, who indeed live under the perpetual tyranny of the right thing, and the anxiety of not recognizing it until too late. It would leave out the clergyman's wife in Galsworthy's novel, who "always wore the expression of one who was resolved to do her duty, her rather painful duty." It would in fact leave out the whole of the middle class, whom

Bernard Shaw describes in the Hades scene of his "Man and Superman" as boring themselves to eternity in Heaven, by listening to celestial music which did not amuse them, just as they had bored themselves through life, by going to classical concerts because they had thought it was the proper thing to do. Nevertheless, I am not sure that the definition is not the right one.

There is perhaps less that is typically English in the outward aspects of town life than in that of the country. Towns all over the world tend to look more and more like one another, and so do industrial districts. Perhaps the first peculiarity which any one from the Continent of Europe would notice about the town workers in England is that hardly any of them go home for the midday meal. You will frequently see a laborer set out in the morning carrying this meal in a pudding basin, wrapped up in a handkerchief, usually a red one with white spots. Others have their meal in the factory canteen. What are known in England as the black-coated workers—that is to say, clerks, salesmen and saleswomen and other members of shop and office staffs—will take their lunch in tea rooms, of which there are many in all the big towns. In these tea rooms, customers of both sexes can sit down and be served with simple hot or cold dishes; but they cannot drink anything but tea, coffee, milk or mineral waters. There do exist occasional restaurants, at which beer and spirits can be served with the food; but they are usually beyond the purse of the modest worker, who indeed generally has the habit of drinking tea with his meals, even at home. The principal evening meal, in all except the upper classes, is always known as tea and not dinner, which latter name is reserved for what the upper classes would call lunch in the middle of the day. Consequently, the clerk is probably satisfied with the existing conditions. If he wants what in English is universally understood by "a drink," he takes it out of meal times at a public house.

The British urban worker's idea of a holiday is usually what he would call an outing; and if you asked him what he meant by that, he would say a drive into the country. His chief purpose is to get away. Now that is perfectly normal. Nearly every human being imagines that he would be happier somewhere else, and considers that the first condition of relaxation is to go somewhere else. Consequently it is quite natural that the workman who lives in town should want to get away from town. Moreover, if he is an Englishman, he may also be moved by that basic and instinctive love of the country to which I referred at the beginning of this chapter. He wants to get away from town for his holiday, and he also wants to get away from it on Sunday, if he can.

For this second desire there is another reason. English towns are depressing places on Sundays. In the morning, absolutely everything is closed except the churches. There is hardly any traffic in the streets. The daily papers do not appear—this is quite illogical from the point of view of the observance of the Sabbath, which was the origin of the custom, because the papers which appear on Monday oblige every one who is connected with them to work on Sunday; but nothing illogical is surprising in England. It is true that there are special Sunday papers, enormous in size, but they have an air of being something illicit and surreptitious, especially as none of the ordinary newspaper stalls are open, for they have put up their shutters like the shops. After midday, those who have been to church, and a good many who have not, walk up and down in the Park in their best clothes, before going home to the heavy Sunday lunch, of which the traditional dish is a large roast joint of beef, accompanied by roast potatoes and crisply fried slices of batter, called Yorkshire pudding.

In the afternoon, the air of yawning boredom which has so often been described as typical of the English Sunday has been modified to some extent in recent years. Although theatrical entertainments are still forbidden by law at any hour on Sunday, concerts can be given, on condition that the music is serious, and cinemas may be opened—once more, quite illogical if theatres are closed. The fact is that the law in this matter lags behind public opinion, which has quite decided that people ought to be able to amuse themselves on Sunday if they want to; and those who do not want to amuse themselves escape into the country.

Unfortunately, they do not find many opportunities for amusement in the country, unless they play golf or lawn tennis, or unless they row or swim; so that for many the escape resolves itself into merely going into the country and coming home again.

Glasgow was once described as an excellent place to live in because there are so many facilities for getting away from it. Such facilities are now to be found in any industrial town. They consist principally of motor coaches, which nominally take passengers to visit "beauty spots" some miles away in the country, but in fact do little more than carry them to a succession of "drinks." However, lest it be thought that the Englishman always takes his pleasures sadly, as the French used to accuse him of doing, or that these pleasures are merely alcoholic, I hasten to add that these outings, especially when they take on a corporate character, are very often the occasion for a great deal of gaiety. Every factory or workshop has its annual "beanfeast," as it is called, and the feast is always held somewhere which has to be reached by a drive.

The annual beanfeast is a single-day affair, but the annual holiday, to which under modern social legislation all workers are entitled, is a longer business. For an Englishman, a holiday nearly always means a stay at the seaside, if he can get there—and that is generally fairly easy, as there is no place in England more than a hundred kilometres from the coast.

The result is that almost every village on the sea in England and Wales—and there are many—has become what is called a seaside resort. What the young male holiday maker does when he gets there is to bathe in the morning, to lie on the beach with his hat over his face most of the afternoon, and in the evening to walk up and down the "parade," to the sound of the band, and ogle the girls, who giggle in reply. Thus acquaintance is struck up, and romance is started.

But there are some seaside resorts where the amusements are more active. Particularly is this the case with those which are frequented by the Lancashire mill hands. Lancashire people are very thrifty for fifty-one weeks in the year. That is perhaps why their idea of a holiday is to spend money like water during the fifty-second. The most favored place for these really quite innocent debauches is Blackpool, the whole of whose extended sea front is an enormous fair throughout the summer. There are great dancing halls, where the music never stops. There are scenic railways, swings, merry-go-rounds, shooting galleries and ingenious mechanical elaborations of them all; and there never ceases to be an enormous crowd, happily and noisily spending the money that it has been carefully saving up for the whole year. There is no taking of pleasures sadly in Blackpool.

When the middle-class English, unmarried or in family parties, go for their seaside holiday, it is only rarely at a hotel that they put up. There are few hotels and hardly any small and inexpensive ones. What most people do is to go into lodgings. These lodgings are let by couples who are very often retired domestic servants. They have invested their savings in a seaside house, and by sleeping under the kitchen table and working very hard in the summer, they make enough money to live comfortably for the rest of the year in the better rooms. The wife does the cooking, and by a tradition which has become mellowed through generations of music-hall jokes, she is a grasping and domineering person, while her husband is a timid little man who cleans the boots. Needless to say, they are not always like that.

It is also in lodgings that the young, unmarried workman will live in town during the rest of the year. I have already said that in London there are more people who have little houses than those who have flats. This is even more true of working class than of more prosperous districts. But the little single-story house, of which a fairly well-paid workman—say a foreman—is the tenant, is generally large enough, not only for him and his family, but for a spare bedroom as well. So his wife puts a card into the parlor window to announce that she is willing to take a boarder.

The mention of the parlor demands a digression. It is the front room on the ground floor, and when you have opened the house door into the absurdly narrow passage, it is to the parlor that the first door in that passage will lead. The door will generally be locked, for the room is hardly ever used, except on quite ceremonial occasions. It contains the best furniture, possibly including a piano which is never played upon, and its real purpose is to create an impression of social grandeur. For the sake of this grandeur, the family lives in the kitchen at the back, and the precious space of the parlor is wasted.

The habit of families taking in these young men as lodgers has no little influence on the social life of the working and lower middle classes. The lodger is in a position which is neither that of the impersonal occupant of a furnished room in an hotel or an unfurnished room elsewhere, nor even that of one amongst several lodgers in a seaside boarding house. He is alone with the family; and as the woman who has let him the room generally "does for him," as the saying is—that is, gives him his meals—he almost inevitably becomes one of the family. The result in many cases is that he leads quite a different sort of life from that which he would have followed under other circumstances. He acquires family habits.

The duties, training and general attitude of the policeman in large towns, and especially in London, are an indication of many of the social instincts of the English lower classes. I am not thinking of the way in which he has taught the whole world to direct traffic with serenity and effectiveness, but rather of his attitude towards individuals. He is aloof and Olympian, but he is also kindly. In his stolid way he is everybody's friend. He helps the very old and the very young across the street, he is always condescendingly ready to answer questions, and one imagines that, even when he arrests a burglar, he must do it in a benevolent sort of way. At night, he walks along every street of his beat, tries every door to see that it is properly locked, and throws the flash of his bull's-eye lamp at every window to make sure that it is fastened. There is a legend that there is always the cook of some house or other who asks him in to a little cold supper at her master's expense, but that is a libel.

He is large and bland, and whether he is dealing with crowds or individuals, his first movement is to restore good humor and to introduce an atmosphere of calm. He will generally begin operations with some such questions as "Now, what is all this about?" At the same time, he is quite capable of quickly changing his tone to one of quiet but curt, firm and unmistakable finality. I remember a little man volubly protesting against an order that had been given to him to "move on," which is the consecrated police version of "go away." The policeman glanced down at him, and his reply was laconic. It consisted of two words, "you 'eard."

The London police have a long tradition of tolerance, but when action is required, it is short, rapid and decisive. This can be seen any Sunday afternoon just inside Hyde Park at the Marble Arch, where, for generations, fanatics of all kinds—religious, scientific and political—have been allowed to stand on little boxes and air their views to any audience that cares to listen to them. The official attitude in England about this sort of thing has long been to adopt the principle of the safety valve, and it is applied to many things besides the speeches of ragged and half-mad Hyde Park orators. Repression, it is argued, only sends discontent and opposition underground. Let them come out, and people will see how absurd they are. Let the surplus steam be let off.

Well, the policemen in Hyde Park are instructed to deal with the Sunday afternoon speakers on this principle. They stand by, half smiling, while the most revolutionary arguments are advanced—that is to say, revolutionary in theory, revolutionary by the use of normal political methods. But if a word is said in the nature of incitement to armed rebellion or to physical violence towards any one, official or not—then suddenly, almost before you know that it has happened, the orator has disappeared from off his box, and has been run out of the park gates.

Hyde Park is only one of many parks in London, and it is perhaps characteristic of the Englishman's love of the country that in this great, grimy town, so much green grass and trees have been preserved. To some extent, perhaps, they enable the Londoner to look at town life with the eyes of a countryman.

There will no doubt be those who will say that in presenting the whole of English social life through the eyes of some one living in a country house in the pleasantest part of England, I have given an entirely false picture. The villages in the North, I shall be told, are not like that. I admit that they are not. Their dark gray stone houses, their stone walls instead of hedges are cold and forbidding. It is true also that little of the landscape of Northern England is smiling, even when it is not industrial, though much of its moorland is hauntingly beautiful. As for the industrial landscape, it is certainly not pretty or picturesque, though there is a certain fierce grandeur in blast furnaces and a poetry in smoke stacks. I shall be told that the many millions who form the predominantly industrial, maritime and mining population of Great Britain are not in the least like the docile agricultural laborers whose relations with the parson and the squire I have been describing.

I shall be told, above all, that the aristocratic view of English life is entirely out of date, that the aristocracy no longer counts and that quite different ideals are now animating the English of today.

All of this is true up to a point. A profound evolution is going on in English social life, and the sort of village that I have described is no longer typical of the whole country. But it is still typical of a great many villages, and the spirit which it illustrates remains, even today, the foundation of the social instincts of the people. Much that is new has been and will be built upon it; but the rock will still be there.

Chapter IV

WOMEN, CHILDREN AND HOME LIFE

To UNDERSTAND the English home of today and the men and women and children who live in it, three different aspects must be considered; for each one of them is indispensable to a comprehension of the whole. First, one must know the bedrock of social tradition, upon which all the developments of today are based; that is to say one must know the home of the late nineteenth and early twentieth centuries, which is still the home of a great part of the English people. Second, it is necessary to see what modifications, of a more or less permanent nature, have often been made in that home through the operation of changed social and economic conditions. Third, the picture is not complete unless it includes the great but temporary upheaval which has taken place in the home in consequence of the war.

It used to be said that the Englishman's home is his castle. In so far as this saying creates the impression that there is something defensive and inhospitable about the Englishman's home, it is quite misleading; for there is no country where family life has always been more readily thrown open to friends, and even to strangers, than England. It represents a certain truth, however, in the sense that the Englishman hates to be interfered with, and prefers to live without too close a contact with his neighbors. He likes to be able

94

to keep himself to himself if he wants to. He is clubbable, but he is not gregarious. That is to say, he readily associates with those who are sympathetic to him, but has no love for the kind of communal life which brings him into constant touch with everybody and anybody.

Hence his preference for living in a house to living in a flat, if he can. I say, "if he can," because for the town dweller this is becoming more and more difficult. Blocks of flats are gradually replacing private houses everywhere. Nevertheless, there are still many private houses in all the big towns —large for those who can afford them, and smaller for those of more limited means, down to the diminutive ones, which touch one another in long and dreary rows in the working-class districts, but give their occupiers the satisfaction that even though they may have no real privacy and none of the communal comforts and conveniences which flats would afford, nevertheless each man has his own front door on to the street. The personal front door also enters into the calculations of the man of the lower middle class, who takes a little house in the suburbs rather than a flat in town, although, as I have explained elsewhere, the desire to have a garden is a still more important factor.

Long after almost the whole of upper and middle class families in the other capitals of Europe had taken to living in flats, those of London continued to inhabit their rather gloomy but usually solid and imposing town houses, and many of them still continue to do so. These houses have at least the advantage of a certain spaciousness. In cases where the house is small, it is true that the rooms themselves are not large; but there are always a good many of them, distributed on the several floors, and the house with small rooms is an exception.

The arrangement of these rooms is almost invariable. First there is the basement, whose windows—entirely or partly below the level of the street—look out upon a small, sunk yard, protected by tall iron railings at the top. Here are the kitchen and accompanying offices, which, in a house of some importance, will include what is called the servants' hall, where the servants have their meals, presided over by the butler, if there is one, and, if not, by the cook, and seated in strict order of precedence, for the hierarchy is severe. On the ground floor, the front door opens into an entrance hall. The typically English thing about the front door is that it always has a letter box attached to the inside of it, and a slit through which the postman drops the letters, announcing that he has done so by the peculiar double "rat-tat" with the door knocker, which it is difficult for a non-professional to imitate, and is in any case reserved as his particular signal. Every house has its door knocker, but the door is not likely to be opened to any one who merely uses it, without ringing the bell also. In houses which are now a little old-fashioned, there are two bells, one marked "visitors" and the other "servants," presumably in order that the maid may be warned in advance whether she must put on her black dress, white apron and cap before going to open. Many houses have their special servants' entrances in the basement, reached by a steep flight of stone steps into the sunk yard, or "area."

The entrance hall—which is more frequently a passage—has one typically English piece of furniture. This is the hat-stand, a rack of pegs for men's coats and hats, with a little shelf on which letters are laid, and a bowl to receive the cards of visitors—although leaving cards has very much gone out of fashion nowadays—a drawer for gloves and a receptacle for the umbrellas so indispensable in the English climate.

Opening out of the entrance hall is the dining room, which tends to have a heavy table and heavy chairs and a sideboard, like dining rooms all over the world, but whose almost invariable mirror over the chimney piece is perhaps peculiarly English, especially in its long and low shape. Behind the dining room is a small room, which would have been called the smoking room in the Early Victorian days, when it was not considered seemly to smoke except rather furtively, and certainly not in any room entered by ladies (indeed I can remember a certain country house where the men could smoke only in the kitchen after the servants and the ladies had gone to bed). Today, conditions are so entirely changed in the matter of smoking that not only is it no longer necessary to avoid the ladies in order to be able to smoke, but the ladies themselves smoke even more than the men, many of whom have given it up since their wives and daughters have taken to it. So that, at present, the room behind the dining room may be called the master's study or anything else; but it certainly will not be called the smoking room.

The first floor will be entirely devoted to the drawing room, or rather to the two drawing rooms opening out of one another. The town drawing room varies little from the country drawing room, which I have already described. Perhaps the most English characteristic of both is the presence of several very large and comfortably padded chairs, which it is quite difficult to get out of when once you are ensconced in them. They remove from the whole room the air of formality which drawing rooms generally—and no doubt should —possess.

Above the drawing room comes the principal bedroom floor, after that the children's floor, with its day nursery and its night nursery, and after that again a floor with bedrooms for servants.

This is what may be called the normal distribution. A large house might have a billiard room and a library on the ground floor, a morning room on the first, and, of course, additional bedrooms and bathrooms, although no house built before 1910 would have more than one bathroom, in spite of the Englishman's reputed concern for his ablutions.

These larger houses, most of which date from about the

middle of the nineteenth century, were built for families
with a number of children, families who entertained regularly and employed many servants. Even those who lived in
houses of medium size, and did not aspire to the social
importance of engaging menservants, would have at least a
cook, a kitchen maid and a scullery maid in the kitchen, a
parlor maid and one or two house maids, probably a ladies'
maid, a nurse and possibly a nursery maid for the children,
and perhaps a genteel governess to educate the daughters of
the house as they grew up.

In well-to-do houses of the upper classes, this staff—with
the exception of the governess and perhaps the nursery maid
—remains typical today, menservants being left to the really
wealthy, and being of course suppressed in war time. For
English servants in families of any social pretensions refuse
ever to depart from their strictly limited attributions, or to
do work which does not fall into their particular department.
"I know my place," as they are fond of saying. Moreover,
the system provides for the automatic training of young
servants in their duties. The kitchen maid learns to become
a cook, and so on.

Of course, smaller houses are run with fewer servants than
this; but it would hardly be possible to find one where there
are less than two—at least none which would have any claim
to gentility. It would only be quite humble folk who would
be content with a "general"—that is to say, one servant.

Naturally, under war conditions, the high standard of
living of the separate house has to be abandoned; and one of
the most remarkable things about the present situation is the
cheerfulness with which people who have been used to comforts have given them up. Some houses have been closed,
while their former occupants have thrown in their lot with
those of others, thus ensuring valuable economy of time
and labor in housekeeping and particularly obtaining provisions. Every one is ready to camp out, just as every one is

ready to fill up his leisure with every sort of voluntary war service.

Even under conditions which were not those of war, it was becoming more and more difficult, in 1939, for any one who was not already living in a separate house to find one. No new private houses were being built. Many of those which existed already were being pulled down to make way for blocks of flats, and the larger ones were being divided up into separate floors and let out as flats also—even sometimes including the basements. In fact Londoners were being obliged to drop the house habit and adopt that of the flat.

There are several reasons for this. One is that modern families are smaller, and need less accommodation. Another is that in modern London women spend a much greater part of their day away from their homes—either in offices where they are employed, or in clubs or restaurants where they eat, spend their leisure and even entertain; and as the home of a town-dwelling man is in any case merely the place where he sleeps, it is women who count in the matter. Another again is that wealth is, on the whole, more evenly distributed than it was, and there are fewer people who can afford to keep up a considerable establishment. Finally, and probably most important, there is the difficulty in finding servants nowadays, and the consequent greater temptation to live in a flat where there are no stairs, where hot water can be obtained by merely turning on a tap, where the rooms are heated from a communal furnace in the basement, and where service can be drastically cut down to what is barely necessary to keep up appearances before visitors—for no middle-class Englishwoman would surrender the last trench of gentility which consists in having a maid in white cap and apron to open the front door. It is possible that the difficulty of finding servants will produce other important social results. It may kill the big country house, whose owner, even when he has the means to keep it up, may have to close it if he cannot find the staff to run it. In any case, it is killing the big private house in town. The country girl will not enter domestic service, even though it would be comfortable and well paid, because she wants to get to town; and the town girl prefers work in a factory to domestic service, because the work in a factory, although monotonous in itself, is done in the company of many others, and has the crowning attraction that it leaves all the evenings free.

Therefore, home life—for the town dweller at least—is gradually becoming flat life; and what used to be an important part of home life, that is to say entertaining friends, takes place elsewhere, in clubs and restaurants, while even the recreations of members of the family chiefly consist of going out. They go out to the cinema, they go out to the theatre, they go out to the country for week-ends, they go out to play golf or lawn tennis, or merely for a drive in the car—the car having almost taken the place of the home as the principal interest of many a family.

Home life is still further reduced by the fact that in an English town the head of the family does not return for lunch. He certainly has his breakfast with his wife and his children, if they are old enough not to have theirs in the nursery; and it is a meal taken in the dining room. But breakfast—at least on week days—is not a very conversational meal in England. Father reads his newspaper, which is propped up in front of him on the table. Mother probably does the same; and the children are not encouraged to be chatty. Besides, every one probably has to hurry off to be in time for business.

Home life on ordinary days therefore means dinner in the evening and the hour or two before and after it; and the hour before dinner is probably the only time when a busy man sees his younger children, for they are not allowed to "sit up" for the evening meal, but have their tea in the nursery and are put to bed early.

On Saturday afternoon and on Sunday, the family is—or

at least can be—more united; but I have already pointed out that they are not likely to be at home.

When people live in the suburbs or the country, the picture will probably be quite a different one. If they want to receive their friends, they must do so at home; for there are no restaurants to which they can invite them. Besides, the garden is likely to have enabled the home to recover its importance. It may induce the head of the family to spend his leisure there, if his hobby is gardening, which it very likely is. In any case, the house and the garden together will have more personality than can ever be acquired by the town flat.

The position of women in the middle-class English home is in some ways different from what it would be in a Latin country. I have already suggested that perhaps the innate shyness of the English character prevents husbands and wives from easily becoming the familiar associates—almost the business partners—which they so often are elsewhere. Perhaps the reason is partly that English husbands think it is unfair to burden their wives with their office worries. In any case, I fancy that it frequently happens that a wife knows little of her husband's affairs; and the jest about her being able to say no more about his occupation than that "he is something in the City" is not entirely an absurdity. She has been brought up to regard marriage rather as a romantic adventure than as a contract, and her husband is often inclined to encourage the assumption that all the responsibilities are his and none of them hers.

Some people might be tempted, after being present at an English wedding, to imagine that we also treat the whole thing rather as something comic. Throwing rice over the bride and bridegroom as they leave the church has a certain air of carnival although it is really a very ancient custom. Tying a satin shoe to the back of the carriage in which they are driven away is also justified by tradition; but no such excuse can be found for the practical joke of adding a card with a large capital letter "L," as they do on motor cars, which are being driven by learners, who have not yet obtained their driving license.

However, it need hardly be said that although marriages are never arranged in England by parents, nor is there any close bargaining over marriage portions and allowances, and although the great majority of girls who marry in England have no dowry at all, and are not expected by their husbands to bring one, there are young Englishmen who are fortune hunters, and there are plenty of English girls, as well as men, who take a realistic view of the situation, and plenty more who are quite aware that a wife has duties as well as privileges.

This is especially the case since so many young women are now independently earning their living before they marry—since, in fact, the revolution in the social, economic and political status of women, which began about 1900, but reached its full development only after the other war.

Towards the end of the nineteenth century, when large families were already disappearing, the old tradition of the middle-class wife as competent mistress and organizer of her household was gradually dying also. I can remember my grandmother walking about the house in the morning with a bunch of keys at her girdle, keeping a firm hold over her store cupboard and her linen chest, and actively superintending the work of the kitchen and the pantry. Shops did not then sell preserved foods, and still less freshly prepared ones, and there were no big laundries. So everything had to be done at home; and the mother of the family had to see that it was done. That was the period when mistresses trained their servants, and worked with them.

Then came the time when everything was left to the servants, and the middle-class wife became a drone. She was no longer competent to issue detailed instructions to her staff, and indeed the cook would probably have given notice at once if the mistress had set her foot in the kitchen. On the other hand, she had not yet acquired the economic and intellectual consciousness of independence, which enables her to-day to live with her husband as an equal and an associate.

The evolution which has brought her to this point has its counterpart in most countries; but in no European country—unless Turkey can be called European—has it been so great and so rapid as in England. This is partly because in no European country had middle-class women fallen so far behind. Those of France and Germany, for instance, had never lost their skill in the domestic arts, as Englishwomen had. Again, the unmarried girls of the United States had long enjoyed a social freedom which has been imitated by those of England only in relatively recent years.

Many of us can remember the time when no middle-class mother would dream of allowing her daughter to go out into the streets unless she were accompanied by a maid or else by a member of her own family, and the idea that she might go out alone with a young man would have seemed inconceivable. When girls went to dances, they were always accompanied by their mothers, as chaperons, and these unfortunate ladies used to sit round the ballroom until the small hours of the morning, while their daughters were dancing on the floor.

Even when, after many years of struggle, girls were allowed a right to higher education, and were admitted as students to the universities, first of Cambridge, in 1873, and later of Oxford, the social tradition that they must never be allowed to meet young men except under supervision was maintained. They were housed in colleges, which were at first built at a considerable distance from the town, so that they had to cover several miles daily to attend university lectures. Nor were they allowed to do so alone, or even in groups, unless each group was in the charge of an elderly lady to "chaperon" it. At the lectures themselves, they sat apart, and I can remember, as an undergraduate, seeing these young women eagerly taking down notes on some such subject as political economy, while the chaperons drowsed at their posts of guard. Even now women cannot be said to have won complete sex equality in both of the two principal universities; for, although they can obtain degrees at Oxford, Cambridge, while allowing them to enter for examinations, will grant them no more than certificates to the effect that they have reached the necessary standard for a degree, and limits the total number of women students in the university to five hundred.

It was higher education which first broke down the barriers which had placed women within a sort of social and intellectual pale. Hardly more than a generation ago, many mothers and fathers would have considered it unseemly and dangerous to allow their daughters to be educated anywhere but in the home. That was the day of the resident governess, whose polite and ladylike, but sketchy and limited educational competence was only supplemented by a special teacher or so, who came to the house once a week for an hour. But the resident governess has disappeared—partly because there is no room for her in the flat, but chiefly because the education which she gave was quite insufficient for a girl who aspired to go to the university. So girls were sent to secondary schools—sometimes to schools which they attended by day and left to come home in the evenings, but also to boarding schools, like their brothers; and these schools were like the schools of their brothers, not only in the fact that they prepared their pupils for the university, but also because they made athletic exercises and games a regular part of the curriculum—for the time is now past when this sort of physical development was considered, even by certain doctors, to be unnecessary and perhaps harmful for the future mothers of the nation. The extent of the revolution which has taken place will be realized when it is said that there are now not far short of a quarter of a million girls in Secondary Schools —mostly day schools—as against thirty-three thousand in 1902.

The education of women was naturally accompanied by the employment of women. Indeed, it was no doubt the fact that many women found themselves obliged to seek employment which largely created the demand for higher education.

They were obliged to seek employment because they found it more and more difficult to enter the one profession which had previously been considered to be appropriate for them—that is to say, marriage. Various causes had led to an excess of females over males in England. One was the emigration of males, who were not accompanied by females—or at any rate by anything like a corresponding number of females. Another was the high rate of infant mortality, which falls heavier on males than on females, for infant boys are more delicate than infant girls. This unequal balance is gradually being corrected, partly because the better nursing of babies under modern conditions is saving the boys who died off, partly because there is less emigration and also partly because, when there is competition among women for husbands, it is the more sexually attractive women who get them, and the children of a married couple tend to be boys when the mother is the more sexually developed of the two parents.

When the equilibrium is restored, certain social results may follow, and the great freedom which has recently been allowed to unmarried girls by their parents may be restricted. There is always a swing of the pendulum in these matters, and we may be in for a period of moral severity, which will take us back to early Victorianism. Already, just before the war, there was a tendency, in the higher circles of London society, to revive the custom of the chaperon at dances. Nevertheless, whatever these social reactions may be, the place of women in the professions and in industry will by then long since have been established.

As far as industry and even commerce are concerned, the employment of women has not been brought about solely by the superfluity of the unmarried. It is largely the result of mechanical progress. In factories, human intervention has been reduced to such simple movements that they can be performed after very little training, and, for business offices, young women can soon learn to manipulate a typewriter.

Therefore women are employed in each case, because they do the work as well or even better than men—certainly better and quicker in the case of typewriting and in that of certain deft movements of machine minding—and also because women are nearly always paid less than men for any particular work. They are paid less because they are willing to accept less, and they accept less for two reasons. The first is that at the age at which they begin, they do not depend upon their employment for their living, or at least the whole of their living, as they are generally still at home with their parents. They also accept less, because they regard their employment as merely a provisional affair until they are married—for at that age they assume that they are going to get married. Indeed, they usually do get married, and they usually give up working when they marry. This produces the further result that the great majority of employed women are young. It has been calculated that whereas 80 per cent of the girlhood of England between the ages of eighteen and twenty is earning money in some way, the percentage drops sharply to 65 between the ages of twenty-one and twenty-four and still farther later on. Those who disappear are replaced by another generation of young girls.

I have said that these young girls accept relatively small salaries; but in fact they are not badly paid for the work they do, and probably many boys of their age would be glad to be paid as well. Most boys, however, would hesitate to accept a job which is never likely to lead to anything better; and the field is left open to the young women, of whom there is always a great mass in employment. In the business quarters of the City of London, the whole aspect of the streets has been entirely changed, in hardly more than a generation, by the influx of girl clerks and typists. What was an exclusively male preserve, with hardly a woman to be seen, has become a crowd, in which—at least at the hours when employees arrive and depart—the feminine note predominates.

The disappearance of these women when they marry is not always voluntary on their part. It is often the deliberate policy of the employers to dismiss women on marriage, not because they become less competent, but because they are supposed then to be supported by their husbands, and no longer need to earn any money; and the married woman is obliged to give up her job, in order that it may be passed to an unmarried girl who is out of work. This policy is adopted by the Civil Service and by other public authorities, such as Education Committees with regard to school teachers, and private employers are encouraged to follow it.

In the industrial North of England, female labor dates much farther back, back to a period when nobody thought of protecting the girl mill-hand from the competition of the married woman; and in the textile industry, even today, nearly half of the women employed are married. However, in factories of other kinds, the practice of not retaining women after their marriage has been established.

This invasion of commerce and industry by what may be called the rank and file of the army of women workers has been accompanied by the entrance of women into the higher as well as the lower branches of the Civil Service and also into several of the liberal professions. It is that of medicine which has attracted the greatest number, and it is there that women have attained the highest distinction. Medicine is also the first profession into which women succeeded in gaining admittance. This happened as long ago as 1870, when the London School of Medicine for Women was founded; but for many years, women doctors were few. Even now, when they are accepted as students in most of the London hospitals, there are one or two which still refuse to take them. The great majority allow them to study and to qualify, however, and in 1918 there was a military hospital in France, where the only males were the soldier patients, all the staff—doctors, surgeons and nurses—being women.

Women can now become barristers in England, but only since 1920, while in France they have been able to do so since 1900. They can also be solicitors; but in neither branch of the law has any woman yet risen to any considerable practice. They have been far more successful as architects, as decorators and also as expert designers of kitchens; and in literature, journalism, painting, sculpture and the theatre they have achieved success and more. They have won fame. Some of them had indeed done so more than a hundred years before any feminist movement was thought of; but it is only in our own time that the number of women successfully practicing any of the arts has been such that the rise to eminence of one of them is no longer a rare phenomenon.

It is also only in our own time that women in England have achieved the full rights of citizenship—that is to say, the right to vote, on an equality with men, at parliamentary and municipal elections, the right to be elected as members of the House of Commons, and the right not to be disqualified, by reason of their sex, from the exercise of any public function. The pressure of demand for these rights became insistent at the same time as the feminine pressure upon the employment market, that is to say, at the beginning of the present century; and it was the result of the same set of circumstances, the excess in numbers of women over men and the consequent mass of unmarried women. The rights were granted immediately after the other war—the parliamentary suffrage in 1918 and the eligibility to the House of Commons a year later—there are now fourteen women members of that Chamber. It was also in 1919 that was passed the Act abolishing the sex disqualification for any Government post. Even now, however, the exercise of these rights in practice cannot be said to be complete. Although a woman can be a member of the House of Commons, it has been decided that she cannot sit in the House of Lords, even when she is a peeress in her own right; and although a woman might in theory be made a Judge or an Ambassador, it is highly unlikely that such an appointment will be made in our time. Nor are we likely to see women in the Army.

That is to say, we are not likely to see women in the Army as active combatants; but already in the other war and again in this one there have been hundreds of thousands of women who have been enrolled in the auxiliary services of the Navy, the Army and the Air Force, and are now wearing uniform as members of those services. In this capacity they have done heavy and dangerous work as air pilots to deliver machines from factory to aerodrome, as motor drivers of cars and also of lorries and ambulances, as air-raid wardens, as assistants to the Fire Brigades and as fire spotters during enemy raids, as cooks and bakers, as messengers and porters, as clerks, paymasters and telephonists, and in many other employments, to say nothing of their virtual monopoly of the nursing and subsidiary hospital services, to which has been added, in this war, the staffing of the numerous First Aid Posts for the treatment of air-raid casualties. Women are also employed as aeroplane spotters in anti-aircraft batteries, and it is said that they do the work better than men.

Apart from these direct war services, there are thousands of girls and women who have volunteered for work in the armament and munition factories. There are the women who organize the evacuation of children from urban danger zones into houses in the country—to say nothing of the women who receive and care for these children in their homes. Finally, there is the Women's Land Army, an organization which existed during the other war, and has been revived for this one. The members of this body wear uniform—which, I fancy, for the English girl, is one of the attractions of belonging to it—but they are employed on all kinds of farm work, chiefly in mobile units, which are sent wherever emergency assistance is required.

This catalogue of the business and professional activities of the modern middle-class Englishwoman, the public rights which she has won and the public duties which she has undertaken, shows that modern women are very much out and about. One natural result of this is that women now have their clubs, like men; and it must be supposed that women take life more seriously than men, for their clubs are not such idle places as men's clubs. There is always something going on to improve the mind—a debate, a lecture or an exhibition of books or pictures. This seriousness also extends to the Women's Institutes for working women in the villages, to which I have referred elsewhere.

Away from her home, the middle-class Englishwoman of today is therefore no longer the drone that she was a generation or a couple of generations ago; and it is only rarely that she is so any longer when she is within it.

Suppose that she is a town dweller, and that her home is a small flat. Necessity has probably made her study the problem of preparing meals, as the scarcity of servants may at any moment oblige her to do it herself; and she has no doubt secured a number of the labor-saving appliances which modern ingenuity has devised to make cooking easy.

Unfortunately, the most obvious and the easiest way of saving labor on cooking is not to do any—that is to say, to buy food which is either entirely cooked already, or is half-cooked and needs only warming up. Shops where freshly cooked food can be bought are not very numerous, even in

London, though they are becoming more so, and they are virtually unknown in provincial towns. Tinned foods can, however, be purchased almost anywhere, and it is to them that far too many housewives of the middle class resort—to say nothing of working-class wives, for whom tinned foods are an almost perpetual stand-by.

In most other countries a young woman of the middle class has been brought up to know something about cooking, but this is rarely the case in England, where, moreover, few have the taste for it—I mean the taste in a double sense, first, in that of taking an interest in the processes of cooking, and then in that of being able to appreciate it when it is good. Excellent food can be obtained in England, that is to say, excellent raw material. But few English housewives will take the trouble themselves to go to market and choose what is best. Nor will their cooks, when they have cooks. Besides, even if either one or the other did go, they rarely possess the knowledge which is necessary for choosing. So they telephone the order, and accept what the tradesman sends. As the tradesman has little imagination, one of the results is that when green peas are in season, you have green peas every day, when asparagus is in season you have nothing else, and so on.

Even with the most sincere sense of patriotic pride, it is impossible to advise any one who has lived in another European country that he will find good cooking in England. He will have excellent grilled and roast meat. If he can get hold of a real Yorkshire or Wiltshire ham—which is not easy to do, even in peace time—he will have something delicious. A fine Stilton cheese is incomparable. So is plain boiled Scotch salmon. So is the best fried bacon—and frying bacon for breakfast is one of the things that the English cook can really do, for it is not difficult. But beyond that, it is best not to expect much.

One of the bad habits of the English cook is not to use

salt in cooking, whether roasting or boiling. So the Englishman always helps himself liberally to salt on the side of his
plate. There is an old story of a French chef, who was engaged by an English family, and distressed them by making
his cooking more and more salt. At last the mistress summoned up courage to speak to him about it. "Madame," he
replied, "I thought you considered that my cooking was not
salt enough; for I always found salt on the edge of the plates
when they came back."

There is another story of an English family, who went to
live in Paris, and proudly announced to their friends there
that they had persuaded their old cook to accompany them.
"And we shall be able to have real blanc mange," they said.
Those who have tasted that peculiar mixture of gelatine
and cornflower will alone appreciate the real horror of the
situation.

However, sheer necessity is gradually forcing the modern
English housewife to teach herself something about cookery;
for food must be provided, and the English are hearty eaters.
Breakfast, as I have explained elsewhere in talking of the
country house, is a full meal. It may consist merely of bacon
and eggs, but it may run into several courses. Luncheon,
which is hardly ever taken before one o'clock, is a meal also,
but not, except in the working classes, the most important
meal of the day. This is dinner, for which the hour nowadays
is eight or half past eight in the evening—in the seventeenth
century it was three in the afternoon, and it has been moving
later ever since.

Between lunch and dinner, however, comes tea, and that
is almost a meal also. The Englishman's tea is sacred. In
every business office in London, tea is made at half past four
in the afternoon by one of the typists, and a cup of tea, dosed
with milk and sugar, is served to all, including any one who
may have dropped in to see the head of the firm on business.
It is accompanied by symbolic dry biscuits, to replace the

muffins and other cakes that there would be at home; but it is never omitted. The workingman makes his tea into his evening meal, and he always has it, even though he may drink beer at all other times of the day except in the early morning. If it is too hot for him, he will pour it from the cup into the saucer to drink it.

These four meals the housewife must furnish somehow; and although she will probably not see the men of her family at lunch or even at tea, she will have her children at the one and perhaps friends at the other. The fact that she appreciates the need for learning what she was not taught at school or at home, and probably does not really care much about, except as a duty, is proved by the success of the cookery and domestic-economy classes for girls and young women, which have recently come into being. They evidently fill a want.

Englishwomen of the upper classes nearly always look more distinguished in the evening than the women of any other country; but the Englishwomen in general who could afford to dress really well in the daytime can hardly be said to do so. They do not dress so well as most women in the United States, and not nearly so well as women of their class in France. The trouble is much the same as it is with cooking. They do not take enough interest in it to give it their full care and attention. Especially is this true with regard to their way of wearing their clothes, even when they are well made, and also with regard to the details and accessories, which go to the composition of a harmonious whole. In the more or less exceptional cases, when they do take an interest, the result is only too often that they give rein to individual fancy in a way which shocks the conformists of fashion; and this is particularly true of certain elderly ladies, whose aggressively personal styles could be matched in no other country.

The chief reasons why the average well-bred Englishman

has the reputation of being the best-dressed man in the world are three. First, he takes the trouble to groom himself well. Second, he usually has a long and lean figure, which goes well with modern male clothing. Third, and most important, he is always severely conformist. He strictly follows what his tailor tells him, checked up against what he learns himself about the right thing to wear. The chief reason why men of other nations are hardly ever well dressed is that they are too individualist. They cannot resist the little touch of color or fantasy. They do not conform. It is in just the same way that the Englishwoman, when she takes trouble about her dressing at all, is inclined to err. She does not conform, as the Frenchwoman, for instance, always does.

And yet there are occasions even in the daytime when an Englishwoman looks so appropriately dressed that you can almost say that she is well dressed, and that she also has the distinction which is hers when she is at her best in the evening. This is when she is dressed for any kind of sport. Women of other countries nearly always tend just to overdress the part. The Englishwoman does not. When it is a question of dressing for sport, she is on safe ground. She conforms.

With regard to the lower middle-class girl and the working girl in England, it may be said that today they look after their appearance with a care, a neatness and a smartness which make them at least the equal of the corresponding class anywhere else. It was not always so, especially with regard to the working girl in the industrial districts. The Lancashire and Yorkshire mill-hand used to be content to cover her head and shoulders with a woollen shawl and to wear wooden-soled clogs or pattens on her feet. Now she will have a tailored costume—ready-made, of course—and high-heeled shoes. As for the London typist or shop girl, she is not only well dressed, but well manicured, and her hair has nearly always been given a "perm." All of this is no doubt partly due to the fact that these girls are earning what is good money for their age; but increased self-respect and conscious care also enter into the matter.

England has been described as the paradise of the child; and certainly the English were the first people to realize that one of our first duties towards children is to give them an opportunity for having a happy time, and to let them have it in their own way: to allow them to develop as children before insisting that they shall follow the path which will lead them to becoming men and women. Perhaps one of the reasons is that Englishmen, as I have said, preserve the mentality of children to a later age than men of most other nations, and that sometimes they never lose it at all. Englishmen, as well as Englishwomen, enjoy playing with children, and the importance of children in the household has been a long tradition of English upper and middle class families. It will be remembered that I have said that in a comfortably appointed house, there will be the night nursery, where the children sleep, and also the day nursery, where they play and have most of their food. There will be a nurse to look after them, and perhaps a nursery maid as well.

Some people may ask why, if the English are so fond of their children, they are prepared to be separated from them for so great a part of the time. The children do not spend very much of their lives with their parents. They do not appear at dinner in the evening, and hardly ever at any meal when guests are present; nor do the smaller ones even appear at breakfast in the morning. The boys are sent to a boarding school at the age of nine, and are never at home, except for the holidays, until they are grown up. The girls go to school also, and many of them even to boarding school, though at rather a later age. In any case, they do not take part in the social life of their parents until they also are grown up, and they "come out," as the saying is. Until then, they are either at school or in the nursery, which may change its name and be called the schoolroom as the children get older.

Many mothers in other countries would not consent thus to delegate to others the bringing up of their children, and would particularly not consent to be separated from them so long. The English answer, I think, would be that it is more in the interest of the children that they should not grow up too much in the company of their elders, and that they are also happier if they are left more to themselves.

This preoccupation about the happiness of the children is a relatively modern attitude. The Victorian mother took a great deal of trouble about the upbringing of her family, and looked after much of it herself—especially as the girls did not go to school—but she was very severe. As for the Victorian father, he recognized the existence of his offspring only when he was called in to administer corporal punishment to them—boys and girls alike—and became a sort of remote figure of vengeance. Children were taught not to speak until they were spoken to. The little girls had to curtsey to their parents, and the boys had to address their father as "Sir." This strictness made for discipline, as is illustrated by the story of a mother who came into the nursery and found that her youngest boy had fallen out of the dormer window and was sliding down the roof. "John," she said severely, and the little boy—or so the story goes—slowly slid up again.

However, if there was not much cordiality between parents and children at this period, the children were able to make their own world, for they had their own part of the house; and as families were usually large, that world was often an active and a happy one.

Today, the scene is entirely changed. There are no longer any large families, to begin with. Then, in the small modern flat, there is rarely room for a day nursery; nor, in many cases, can a mother easily find a suitable person to act as nurse, even if she has the accommodation to lodge her. The result is that the mother often brings up her one child—or at most two children—herself, until they are old enough to be sent to an infant day school, soon after the age of two, and looks after them herself when they are at home. There is certainly more frankness of intercourse, more comradeship between parents and children than there was in an earlier generation.

One reason why the modern mother probably looks after her children herself is that she has almost certainly studied the theory of the whole question, even before she was married. More attention is being given to the science of what is called mothercraft than ever before; and, all over the country Infant Welfare Centers are teaching mothers of all classes how to rear and feed their children, and are giving them practical help in doing so. The concentration of effort on this matter since the beginning of the century had already produced the result in 1930 that in the previous twenty-five years the infant death rate, as well as the death rate of the mothers in childbirth, had been reduced by 50 per cent.

The modern middle-class mother is consequently much less ignorant about all these matters than her own mother was. She knows something about the necessary varieties in children's diet, so as to supply them with the right proportion of the several vitamins. She has perhaps learned a little about child psychology. She is usually armed with certain precepts, which she is ready to put into practice.

The new freedom of association between parents and children has produced certain results which might have been expected. Most noticeable is a conversational frankness on the part of the young towards their elders, which would profoundly have shocked those of even a generation ago. Forms of respect have been replaced by familiarity; and this familiarity is even encouraged, up to a point, by parents, who no doubt remember how difficult it was to establish with their own fathers, if not with their mothers, any relations not hampered by constraint.

Fathers of today make praiseworthy efforts to throw a bridge over the gap which must inevitably exist between them and their boys, and try to convince them of their desire to be comrades and "pals"; while mothers do their best to encourage the confidence of their girls.

These easier contacts within the home do not, however, mean that English children are no longer taught to show good manners outside of it. Very early in their little lives they learn, not only the self-reliance which is to accompany them through life, but the self-control which, to more spontaneous and less inarticulate peoples, sometimes gives the impression that they are reserved and secretive and even that they are little prigs. They are studiously polite, even to other children, until they know them and all restraint suddenly breaks down, which happens very quickly; and, as for their meetings with grown-up people, they rarely forget such rules as the one about not making personal remarks. I have even heard a little girl say to another, "Excuse me, but I do like your dress," just as a grown-up young woman would have said to another grown-up young woman—for in the English middle class, the compliment would certainly have been preceded by a similar apology.

As for the little boys, one cannot say that they are very polite. They would like to be, but they generally succeed only in being awkward; and they take little pains to conceal their obvious relief when they can get away, and resume being noisy. Their noisiness is, of course, not an English monopoly. What, I think, is particularly characteristic of English little boys—and it may be a clue to the English spirit in general—is the early development in them of the team instinct. In all their games they tend to form "sides"—opposing parties, each of which has a captain, loyally obeyed by his followers, and the individual members of each of which naturally fall into the tradition of working for the success of his "side," as well as, perhaps even more than, his personal distinction.

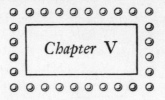

SCHOOLS AND UNIVERSITIES

It MAY be said that today a democratic system of education exists in England.

There is a public elementary school within reach of every child in the country, each school being really three schools, one for infants, one for girls and one for boys. Education in these schools is free. That is to say, it is provided at the expense of the community. It is also compulsory. That is to say, every child must attend school between the ages of five and fourteen—it will be fifteen after the war, for a law to this effect has been passed, and was to have come into operation in September, 1939, but its application has been postponed.

The public authorities have also created Secondary and Technical schools, into which children who reach a certain standard in the elementary schools can pass at the age of eleven and remain until nearly the age of seventeen. About 13.7 per cent of the elementary school children do so. Education in these schools is not entirely free, but the fees are graded according to the means of the parents, and in fact no fees at all are paid for nearly half of the pupils. The community may therefore be said to undertake the charge of the greater part of this stage of education also.

Finally, pupils from the State Secondary schools, most of whom have passed up from the public elementary schools, can and do compete for what are called open scholarships in the universities of Oxford and Cambridge, and have won as many as one third of them. These scholarships are money prizes, which cover about half the expenses of a student during his four years' course. They are not provided from public funds, but from various private endowments at the universities. However, they complete the series of steps by which a clever boy or girl, without means or influence, can reach full academic honors.

That these facilities have been created does no little credit to the adaptability of English institutions and English character to the circumstances of contemporary life.

Nevertheless, it would be a great mistake to suppose that they cover the whole of the English educational field, or even give expression to what is most typically English in it.

The steps which lead from the elementary school to the university are there, and they will remain; but they have been cut across a rock of aristocratic tradition which remains also. They have equally been cut through a tangle of sectarian religious conflict, which has not yet been entirely uprooted.

Moreover, the realization by the State in England that among its duties is the provision, in some form or other, for the instruction of the people is relatively recent. Scotland felt the obligation much sooner; and in 1696 the Scottish Parliament, eleven years before it was merged in that of England, passed an Act which required every parish to establish a school at its own expense. The Scottish conception is indeed much nearer to the true spirit of democracy, for it has long been a commonplace in Scotland that every man, be he never so poor, has the right, not only to the elementary education which will be of practical use to him, but to the higher education, which, in the situation that he will occupy, will perhaps be no more than an ornament to his mind.

In England, such a sense of communal responsibility is

a very recent thing. No public authority did anything at all about education until 1833, and all that was done then, and for the next forty years, was to vote increasing parliamentary subsidies to a private organization, which was carrying on what should have been a public service, and carrying it on more with the desire to inculcate the religious principles of the Anglican Established Church into the minds of the children, than with any sense of the duty of giving them mental instruction. It was only in 1870 that schools directly provided out of public funds, as well as being supported by them, came into existence to fill in the gaps left by sectarian voluntary effort, and not until 1880 that attendance at elementary schools became compulsory.

Even then, there still survived the conception of popular education as a sort of charity to the poor, something whose quality, like that of blankets given away at Christmas, need not be high, and whose price must in any case be low.

Eventually, in the first year of the present century, what is called the Board of Education was created, and its President, who holds a political post as a member of the Government, is now what in other countries would be called Minister of Education.

However, his powers are very different from what most people in other countries would assume to be those of a Minister of Education. There, he would have a firm hold over the Universities, which would live on Government subsidies. He would appoint the professors. The granting of degrees would be in his hands. The organization, personnel and programs of both the elementary and the secondary schools would be under his direction.

The President of the Board of Education can do none of these things. The Board has no control whatever over the Universities. Nor does it finance them, except for a special grant for scientific installations and apparatus. They live independently on the income derived from the considerable properties with which they have been endowed by their past benefactors and on the fees paid by their students. The Board has no control over the granting of University degrees, nor over the examinations which qualify for them. It has no control over the large upper and middle class boarding schools, of which I shall speak in a moment, nor over the private preparatory schools, which feed them; for these large boarding schools are also corporations, which own property and are financially independent, and the preparatory schools are conducted by individuals for their own profit.

The Board has no control even over the publicly administered elementary, secondary and technical schools to which it does give financial assistance. That is to say, such control as it exercises is quite indirect, and is limited to the power, hardly ever put into practice, of withholding the State subsidy from the local authority, which does directly control the schools, their organization and their curriculum.

The authority in question is the locally elected Council, which manages this among other affairs of a large municipality or else of a County—the County being an administrative area, of which there are forty-eight in England.

The inspectors sent out by the Board of Education report upon the way in which the Local Education Authorities, as they are officially called, are carrying out the provisions of the various Acts of Parliament concerning education; and they give advice to these Local Education Authorities, and consult with them. But they can give them no orders. Indeed, the money which is granted to these Local Education Authorities by the State represents only half of what they receive altogether from public funds. The other half they raise themselves by local rates.

It must be added that, although the secular education in all the elementary schools of the country is directed and paid for by the County and Borough Councils, half of the total number of the buildings in which this education is given still belong to the two voluntary organizations which originally collected the money to build them, and only the other half are "Council Schools," that is to say publicly owned. "The National Society for promoting religious education in accordance with the principles of the Church of England," to give it its full title, is the proprietor of the greater part of the .privately owned buildings, while the remainder—about one seventh—belong to the Catholic Church. In most cases, they still look what they used to be called—Church Schools. In villages, they will nearly always be found close to the church, which continues to pay for their upkeep in order to retain the right of giving religious instruction in certain hours.

From all this it will be seen that the elementary, secondary and technical schools, to which the Board of Education distributes Government money, but which are managed by the local authorities, compose a system which is still rather hybrid, and still has about it, to some extent, the aristocratic air of patronage belonging to an earlier time. This is, however, gradually disappearing as efficiency increases. Buildings which no longer conform to the requirements of recent legislation are being taken over from the Churches by the local authorities, and the proportion of "Council schools" is constantly growing.

One of the increases in efficiency is represented by the creation of a new category of elementary school, to take children between the ages of eleven and fourteen—or fifteen, as it will be later. When this reorganization is complete—and it is complete already with regard to 63 per cent of the pupils— a child will go to the Infant School from the ages of five to seven, this school taking infants of both sexes. From the ages of seven to eleven there will be two schools, called Junior Schools, one for girls and one for boys. There will then be two Senior Schools for the older children—or at least for such of them as have not passed into the Secondary Schools. Other improvements relate to health. The local authorities now have power to provide milk and even meals to poor children, and to charge the cost to public funds when the children's parents cannot pay even the half price that is asked—54 per cent of the children receive milk in this way. There are voluntary School Care Committees, as they are called, which interest themselves in children who are in need of clothing. It has become the duty of the local authorities to look after the "health and physical condition" of the children, and there are 2400 school clinics, in which this work is carried on by 730 full-time doctors and 800 dentists. These reforms are no doubt partly responsible for the facts that three pounds have been aded to the average weight of elementary school children, and that, at the beginning of the present war, 84 per cent of the men examined for army service were classed in Grade I, whereas in 1919 only 33 per cent were declared really healthy.

It has been estimated that 93.5 per cent of the children between the ages of 5 and 14 in the country are educated in the elementary or secondary schools controlled by the public authorities. What happens to the remaining 6.5 per cent? They are not left without education, for they belong to the highest and in a general way the wealthiest classes in the country. The inspectors who supervise the application of the law of compulsory school attendance from the age of five will not knock at their parents' doors, for it will be assumed that their education is being looked after. At an early age, they will probably be taught at home. Later, they will be found in schools outside of the State system, the girls in private elementary and secondary schools, and the boys in private preparatory schools, and afterwards in what are called the Public Schools, which are the oldest and most characteristically English expression of educational principles.

Here enter the class isolation and the class consciousness which are still characteristic of the education of the children of those parents who have any pretensions to gentility. Although the education in the State secondary schools is now probably as good as—perhaps it is sometimes better than— that which can be obtained in a school which is not in the State system, these parents will not send their children there, in the way that the parents of children in most other countries send their children to the State secondary schools. They want the social prestige of the schools for "sons and daughters of gentlemen."

Thus, although there is a direct bridge from the Public Elementary School to the State secondary school, and another, even if it is rather narrow, from the State secondary school to the University, there is none from the Public Elementary School to the Public School, so called.

It need hardly be said that the Public School is not in the least public in the sense that it is open to every one. It is quite the reverse of public; first because, at least in the important schools, there are always more candidates for admission than there are places, and, second, because it is necessary to pass a social test which is nonetheless real for not being openly avowed—to say nothing of an educational test as well. These schools are called public merely to indicate that they are not the property of private individuals, conducting them for their own profit, as are the preparatory schools which lead up to them, but belong to associations or corporations, and are managed, each by a governing body.

The education of the upper and upper middle classes remains, therefore, a separate thing from that of the people as a whole. For good or for evil, it forms part of the aristocratic tradition of England, on to which democracy has been grafted, but which democracy has not yet replaced, although it is assuming a constantly increasing importance. While there does exist today a system of education which is democratic, and will tend to be the dominant system as time goes on, there still survives, side by side with it, a far older aristocratic system which has not yet been merged with it. This is the rock in which the aforementioned steps have been cut, and it is this which continues to set the note, everywhere recognized out of England, as that of a typically English education.

This note is the cause of a certain impatience among certain English democrats, who are not prepared to wait for the steady march of evolution, and would like to set a quicker pace to change. They speak scornfully of the spirit which they describe as that of "the old school tie."

They are referring, not so much to the aristocratic system of education in itself, as to what they consider to be the unfair prestige which still attaches in after life to those who have passed through it. There is no doubt that a man who has spent six or seven years at one of the principal "public schools" and then four years at one of a limited number of the separate Colleges which make up the two Universities of Oxford and Cambridge sets out with a social and even a professional advantage, which, in a country still impregnated with such aristocratic traditions as England, is undeniable. This is especially the case when his family origins and connections are such that he naturally drops into easy and casual intimacy with those whom he meets at these schools and Colleges, those whose fathers and perhaps grandfathers were there before them, those whose names were probably entered, on the very day of their birth, by their fathers, in the list for admission to the school in question, so as to make sure that when they arrived at the proper age, they would not be kept out by the always crowded list of applicants.

It matters little what academic distinction a man with such an educational past achieved at the end of his school and university career. It will indeed help him much more in after life if the honors which he did obtain were athletic rather than scholastic; and the fact that he can hang up in his dining

room the oar which he used in the university boat race, especially if accompanied by other oars used in other races, or
that he can place on the sideboard the silver cups and medals
which he won in athletic contests, will count in his career in
a way which is out of all proportion to any school prizes
which may be on his bookshelves, or any diplomas which
may be in his desk. In one of J. M. Barrie's plays, "The
Admirable Crichton," there is a desultory discussion among
a group of influential politicians as to who ought to be appointed to a vacant bishopric, and one candiate is considered
to be a strong one because he is "an excellent slow bowler"
(at the game of cricket). The irony is hardly underlined.

Moreover, although a man's years at public school and
university may not have been distinguished, either athlet-
ically or even academically, it is almost enough for him to
be able to say that he was there. As I have indicated, it is
best of all if he can say that he was at one of a limited number of schools and at one of an equally limited number of
Colleges at Oxford and Cambridge.

There are about a dozen public schools which can be
called first class. Eton, Harrow and Winchester, which are
the oldest, are indisputably in that class, and some would
say that they entirely compose it. This would really mean
that among just upwards of two thousand schoolboys are to
be found the greater number of those who will be the effective rulers of England in the next generation; for there are
a little over a thousand boys at Eton and about five hundred
at each of the other two.

In the early part of the nineteenth century, it could almost
certainly be said to be true that the real prestige was limited
to these three schools. There is even a story, which is told,
with a slight variation, by former pupils of each. It is said
that the captain of the cricket team of one of the lesser-known
schools aspired to arrange a match with, let us say, Winchester, and wrote a letter to that effect. The reply came as

follows: "Eton we know. Harrow we have heard of. But who are ye?"

Today, inclusion in the first class can perhaps be extended to a dozen or fifteen schools, which I shall certainly not attempt to name, for fear of bringing down upon my head the vengeance of the partisans of any that I may have left out. With an average of five hundred boys to each school, this would bring the privileged class up to about eight thousand. Altogether, there are just over thirty schools having belonged to which will entitle a man afterwards to say that he has had what is generally understood in England by a public-school education. Beyond these schools, there are more than a hundred which are public schools in the sense that they are owned and managed by disinterested and sometimes ancient corporate associations, and are not conducted for profit, but which have the importance or even the size to be called public schools in the usual acceptation of the term.

The Colleges of Oxford and Cambridge—of which, speaking only of the men's colleges, there are twenty-two at Oxford and seventeen at Cambridge—are divided into similar inner and outer circles. It is something, for instance, for any one to be able to say that he is an Oxford man; but it is much more for him to be able to add that he was at Magdalen or New College or Christ Church.

This gradation of importance gives a ready handle to those who denounce the old school tie; for it is nearly always the men who were in the outer circle who are constantly recalling the fact that they were within the pale at all. Not only do they never forget that they were at school—which I am afraid is common to many upper- and middle-class Englishmen—but they are either constantly reminding you where it was, or else they are suspiciously reticent as to where it was. Among the former are no doubt some who feel it necessary to draw attention to the fact that they have had "the education of a gentleman," presumably since they may be afraid that it will not be self-evident; and it is they who are likely constantly to be wearing a necktie, in diagonal stripes, of the colors of the cricket or some other club of their old school or college. It need hardly be said that in England all the combinations of two or three colors are registered as belonging to this or that club, that most people can recognize them and that no one who is not quite indifferent to being regarded as socially impossible would wear the tie of a club of which he is not a member.

The traditions, ideals and standard of conduct which were formed in the old public schools and universities—for the public schools and the universities must be taken together, and not separately—are, more or less consciously, the basis of the whole schoolboy code of honor in England, including that of the State secondary schools whose pupils are not exclusively, or even at all the sons of gentlemen. Loyalty, refusing to "sneak" or tell tales, team-work are commonplaces of decent conduct in schools, which are not in the least aristocratic; but they began as part of the public-school tradition of which the well-known novel, *Tom Brown's Schooldays*, though it is entirely out of date, gives some idea.

The first thing to remark about the tradition is that what are today its essential features do not date nearly so far back as is generally supposed. It is true that there were schools attached to several of the English cathedrals even before the tenth century, and those of Westminster and St. Paul's in London, which are still in existence and are now schools of the upper middle class, are two of them. But Westminster and St. Paul's have never been very typical "public schools," as the term is now understood; for they are mainly day schools, and not boarding schools, and one of the chief characteristics of the real public school is that the boys do not live at home, but come from all parts of the country and are lodged at the school.

Winchester College, the oldest and among the most famous of the real public schools, was founded by William of Wykeham, Bishop of Winchester, in 1382, and the quadrangle and chapel which were built by him at that time are still standing and in use. Eton College was established by King Henry VI near his castle of Windsor nearly sixty years later. It also has its original chapel. Harrow School, which is some fifteen miles out of London, dates from 1571, and it was one of a number of grammar schools, as they were called, which were founded and endowed by English Kings and other benefactors in the sixteenth century. Many of these grammar schools still exist, though some have fallen upon evil days; but they, like the cathedral schools, were principally day schools for local pupils of all classes; and it is only by chance that Harrow became one of the great upper- and middle-class boarding schools.

Moreover, Eton and Winchester, though they had resident scholars from the beginning and have long since had no other, were, at the time of their foundation and for long afterwards, nothing like what they are now. Their founders definitely established them to prepare poor boys as Latin scholars for the Universities of Oxford and Cambridge respectively, William of Wykeham for New College at Oxford, which he built at the same time as Winchester, and Henry VI for King's College at Cambridge; and although the Latinists thus formed no doubt subsequently passed into the service of the State, as well as the Church, there was certainly not yet any tradition of the governing class sending their boys to be educated there.

Indeed, the habit of sending their boys away from home at all to be educated did not become general among the upper classes until the eighteenth century was nearly ended. It was still later, in the middle of the nineteenth century, that the public-school tradition, as it has been and is still understood in our own time, was created; and its creation is not due to one of the three schools mentioned, but to the Headmaster of another, Doctor Arnold, of Rugby.

It is with the establishment of this tradition that *Tom Brown's Schooldays* deals.

Starting from the premise that the school was a boarding school and that the boys were consequently left to themselves for a large part of their time, the central feature of the system was the delegation of disciplinary powers, even including the right to inflict corporal punishment, to certain of the elder boys, specially nominated as "prefects." It was equally part of the system that none of the masters could give corporal punishment, except the Headmaster in certain rare cases. The "prefects" also had the right to send the smaller boys on errands, and each prefect could appoint two small boys as his "fags," a "fag" being in point of fact nothing more nor less than a personal servant: for the little fellow had to clean his "fagmaster's" boots, make his tea and so forth.

It is claimed in justification of this system that it gives a sense of responsibility to older boys, who might otherwise merely become bullies, while it teaches the smaller boys that before giving orders, one must learn to obey them.

Compulsory games are almost as integral a part of the public-school tradition as the Prefect system. This does not mean that any boy can play any game he likes. When there is a river, he can decide to devote the whole of his open-air time to rowing—of course, under instruction and with the ambition of being a member of the "Eight" of his school, or of his "house" within the school.

When there is no river, or if he does not want to row, he will be made to play football in the autumn term; to train for running or some other athletic contest in the spring term and to play cricket in the summer term. Of these exercises, rowing, football and cricket are considered to be particularly important because they call upon the team spirit and the sense of cooperation and individual sacrifice. The contests with other schools also foster school patriotism and enthusiasm and the group consciousness of unity.

Games are regarded as so indispensable to the whole school course that in every public school there is at least one "games master," who is engaged rather for his aptitude in advising, organizing and training in regard to games than for any academic qualifications which he may possess. He is generally given the lowest class—or "form," as it is called—to teach, and the most backward boys suffer accordingly. However, there are very few English schoolboys who would not prefer to get into the school football or cricket team to achieving any success at his books; and the members of these teams are looked up to with a veneration which is never shown towards the merely clever fellow who is at the top of the school in learning. So the games master is no less a hero if he is not intellectually brilliant.

The masters at the public schools and at the preparatory schools which send boys to them are all graduates of the Universities of Oxford or Cambridge, and are former public schoolboys themselves—often "old boys" of the schools in which they are now teaching. This gives a unity of spirit and tradition to the whole educational sequence, from private preparatory school, through public school, to University.

The University is, however, by no means an essential part of the sequence. There are only about four thousand male students at Oxford and less than five thousand at Cambridge; and a certain number of these students come from other sources than the public schools—from outlying parts of the Empire, from foreign countries, from the elementary schools through the State secondary schools, and so forth. It is therefore evident that less than half of the boys from the public schools go on to Oxford or Cambridge.

Although the public schools, together with the private

schools which lead up to them, and the universities to which they lead, are an upper- and middle-class preserve, into which only a slight breach has been made in regard to the universities alone, it is a remarkable thing that not only, as I have already pointed out, has the schoolboy code, which they have created, been adopted by schoolboys in all other schools, but that their special methods of organization have been introduced into the State secondary schools, which cannot be accused of any aristocratic prejudice.

As these schools prepare pupils to pass into the universities, it is not surprising that their curriculum should be so arranged that the subjects required in the universities should be included and taught in a way which would be considered satisfactory in the universities. It is also not surprising that these secondary schools should appoint an increasing number of university graduates as masters.

What is surprising is that they should imitate the old public schools in other ways, that they should, for instance, have taken over the prefect system, and that they should have imposed compulsory games, started "speech days" and even chosen school colors—the hated old-school tie. That they have done so really only demonstrates once more that in England the new is ever something which is a development of the old or at least is grafted on to it.

There is no doubt that the public schools have maintained class consciousness; but the English are not afraid of class consciousness. They do not consider it to be incompatible with liberty. What is certain is that the public schools produce a type of character which has been of great service to the State, as well as being admirable in itself. The system encourages the sense of responsibility; but it tames arrogance and induces modesty. It brings the capacity for practical judgment to early maturity; but it also develops the sense of fairness in general and justice to inferiors in particular.

It is a type peculiarly English, and one of which England may be proud.

To follow a little middle-class English boy through the various stages of his education will perhaps enable one to give a better picture of what the whole system means than any further exposition of theory.

We will assume that until his ninth birthday he has been brought up at home, or in an infant school and then at a day school, from which he has returned home every evening. The time has now come when his mother must be prepared to give him up—in a sense definitely, for although he will return home for the holidays, he will never again be hers in quite the same way.

About the 15th of September—always in September, for that is the beginning of the scholastic year—he is to be sent to his first boarding school, a preparatory, or "prep." school for one of the big public schools. His father and mother have probably heard of it from friends, whose boys are already there, and have promised to look after the "new chap" when he arrives. The parents have been down to see the school in the seaside town in which it will almost certainly be placed. At first sight, it looks like an ordinary though rather large private house, surrounded by trees and a garden; but a big wing has probably been built out to accommodate the dormitories and class rooms, and there may be the three walls of a fives court—fives being a game not unlike pelota on a small scale. Farther away, there will be the field on which cricket and football are played, the former in the summer and the latter in the winter.

The headmaster, who owns the school, is of course a University man. In this particular case, we will suppose that he comes from Oxford and that, before going to Oxford, he was at Winchester; and it is for passing entrance examination into Winchester, and also for obtaining scholarships at Winchester that he makes a specialty of preparing his boys. There will perhaps be forty or so of them, and he will be assisted in the work of teaching them by perhaps two other masters.

He will almost certainly be assisted also by his wife, on whom will fall the duty of providing the food of the boys, seeing that they wash and dress themselves properly and looking after their health. If the headmaster is not married, there will be a matron to do this work.

Father and mother inspect the school, mother examining carefully the large room—hardly big enough to be called a dormitory—in which her little boy will have a bed among five or six others; and then the couple return home to prepare the victim for the sacrifice.

His hair has probably been allowed to grow long. It must be cut. Instead of the knickers in which he has been accustomed to run about, he will have to wear trousers, except for playing games; and even then, although he will wear "shorts" for football, he must put on white flannel trousers and a white flannel shirt for cricket, as that forms almost part of the ritual of the game. He will probably have to wear an Eton jacket, at least for Sundays. In case you may not know what an Eton jacket is, I may say that it is the very short coat, with a tiny point at the back, in which boys in other countries sometimes appear on the day of their First Communion, and then never again.

On the appointed day in September, Johnnie, heroically succeeding in not twisting his little face into tears, is taken to the railway station; for of course he must make the journey alone, or rather in the company only of the other small boys who are going back to the school. He is introduced to those whose parents had promised that they would look after him, and they eye him stonily. Meanwhile, his trunk has been put into the luggage van, and with it a white deal box, with lock and key, which contains his personal treasures—cakes and sweetmeats and also such toys as he has not deliberately left behind as being too childish.

So he sets out, and his mother returns home with a heavy heart; for he will not return until just before Christmas. He will then have four weeks holiday, to be followed later by three at Easter and six from the beginning of August.

He will be very happy to get home for his first holidays. It must not be supposed, however, that he has been miserable —not, that is to say, if he is a normal little English boy. His mother has probably sent him several "hampers" of good things to eat, to console him; and he has doubtless been glad to get them, not only for the satisfaction of eating the things himself, but for the popularity which they have brought him when he has distributed them to friends under the supervision of the matron. However, it is more than probable that he has very quickly dropped into his new life, and that when he returns to the railway station after Christmas, it will be for a cheerful and boisterous journey back to school with his friends, one or two of whom he will probably get his mother to invite to stay at home during the holidays at Easter.

His parents will probably go down to see him at his school once during the term, but probably not more often; for such visits are rather discouraged. The boy must learn to stand on his own feet. Moreover, although he is of course glad to see them, he will hardly conceal his relief when they go and he can return to what have become the firm friends of his own age. The one occasion on which the parents almost certainly will appear will be the old boys' day in the summer term—old school tie again. On that day there will probably be a cricket match between a team representing the boys of the school and another composed of former pupils and the fathers of present ones; and Johnnie will no doubt be extremely anxious lest his father disgrace him by being "bowled out for a duck"—that is to say, without having scored any runs.

The time will come when Johnnie, at the age of thirteen, will perhaps enter for the scholarship examination at Winchester. That is to say, he will try to be chosen as one of the dozen or so of boys who win the right each year to be "on the Foundation," as it is called. These boys live in College, which is the ancient part of the school. They wear long cloth gowns. They are called "scholars," and their education is given to them theoretically for nothing, although in fact their parents have to pay certain fees. The large rooms in which they sleep and study and eat are of historic architectural beauty, but of limited comfort, and the boys have to learn to rough it. The mediæval tradition is still maintained of eating off square oak platters. Until a few years ago, these were used even for hot roast meats, and, as they are quite flat, the only way of retaining the gravy was rapidly to erect a rampart with the potatoes so that it did not escape. It is on record that the warden replied to the father of one boy who wrote to complain of the quality of the food by the words "I cannot understand your son not being satisfied with what is prepared in our beautiful fifteenth-century kitchen."

However, Johnnie may not obtain a scholarship, or he may not try, and his father may pay for him in the ordinary way as a "commoner." This will cost him £210 a year. Johnnie will then live, not in College, but in one of the twelve "Master's houses." These houses are scattered about the part of the town surrounding the grounds enclosed within the wall of the school, but not in the main part of the town, which is definitely "out of bounds" to all the schoolboys (or "men in the school," for it is one of the Winchester traditions that every one is a "man" and not a boy, and is so addressed, not only by his comrades, but by his masters).

There are many other traditions which Johnnie must learn when he first arrives. He will be given a fortnight in which to do it, after which he will get into trouble if he makes a mistake. The time is none too long; for apart from such rules as that you may not wear your jacket unbuttoned until you have been in the school two years, there are so many special words that they amount to a particular language, a language whose origins go back hundreds of years.

With regard to his clothes, he no longer wears an Eton jacket. He would have done so during his early years at Eton, if he had gone there, and would also have had to put on a top hat on all occasions when he was not dressed for playing games. At Winchester, he will, during his first two years, wear an ordinary short coat—black, of course—and later he will blossom out into a morning coat and a stand-up collar, instead of the turn-down collar which will have been his hitherto. For headgear, in summer and winter, he will have the regulation Winchester flat straw hat, normally white, but speckled black and white if he becomes a prefect. The hat will bear the ribbon of the colors of his "house."

Each master who has a "house" is in one respect much in the same position as the headmaster of a preparatory school; for he lodges and feeds the thirty to forty boys who are entrusted to him, and makes a profit out of doing so. Of course, classes are not held at the "house," but in the general classrooms in the school buildings; and, during school hours, the house master is there taking a class, like any master who has not yet been given a "house." Also, during school hours, he, like all the other masters, is in "cap and gown." That is to say, he wears the long black alpaca gown of a Master of Arts of Oxford or Cambridge, and on his head he puts the academic cap, or "mortar board," so called because its stiff, thin, flat, square top sticks out from his head on every side, like the board on which masons prepare their mortar, or, more exactly, plasterers their plaster. He is probably a clergyman, as five-sixths of the public-school masters are.

When Johnnie arrives at Winchester, he will have a little more privacy in the dormitory than he had at the "prep" school; for he will have a cubicle to himself. The privacy will, however, be only relative; for his neighbor can easily look over the partition at him; and besides, the dormitory is much larger than the room in which he used to sleep. For work, he will have what is called his "toys"—that is to say a desk and a small cupboard in a sort of little stall, of which there are many along both sides of a large room. It is only several years later, if he becomes one of the five "house" prefects, that he will get a little study and even a "fag" to clean it out for him. Meanwhile, he must be a "fag" himself, and he must also be ready to run at full speed to any prefect who shouts "here"; for the "man" who gets there last has to run the errand.

He will go down to school at seven in the morning, will troop into chapel with every one else at a quarter to eight and will come back to breakfast at eight. More school, and then football and then lunch, to be followed by school again in the afternoon.

That is for the winter. In the summer there will be cricket matches all the afternoon on the two half holidays, and practice before lunch every day—except, of course on Sunday, when there are no games at all, and the only distraction is a walk in the afternoon.

Apart from the compulsory games, there are also compulsory gymnastics in school hours. As for the supplementary or voluntary games, which are played in spare time, some of these are indicated by the buildings, which can be seen in the school grounds—racket courts, fives courts, squash racket courts and a swimming bath. Others include boxing and fencing, and also golf and lawn tennis, the last two of which are, however, rather outside of the public-school tradition, for they are individualist games. There will be an officers' training corps, whose course of instruction includes rifle shooting.

I have already drawn attention to the importance which is attached to athletic sports, both by the masters of the school and by the public opinion of the boys. One indication of it at Winchester is that although a "man" cannot become a "school prefect," having authority in the whole school, unless he is in the Sixth Form, he can be made a "house prefect" by his housemaster, if his athletic prestige stands high, and even though his scholastic position is quite modest.

It may also be said that the directly intellectual curriculum does not occupy the first place in a typical public-school education. When Doctor Arnold appointed the members of the highest class, that is to say the "Sixth Form," as prefects of the school, and announced to them that he depended upon their moral courage and loyalty as much as any general depends upon that of his officers, he used to tell them what he looked for in the boys. First, he said, he wanted religious and moral principles; second, gentlemanly conduct; and, only third, intellectual ability. These ideals may be said even now to be those at which public-school education aims. All the big public schools are definitely Church of England schools. Those which are Catholic or undenominational are not quite in the first flight. At the same time, facilities have been granted recently to admit boys of other religious opinions into most of the schools, though not into all.

The study of the Latin and Greek classics, of which almost the entire public-school curriculum used to be composed, and continued to be so until even thirty years ago, still occupies a large part of it. Latin remains a compulsory subject, although Greek is rarely so any longer. The two great Universities, which maintain the tradition that Latin and Greek grammar is the best training for the intelligence, and the substance of the Latin and Greek classics the soundest furniture of the mind, are no doubt responsible for their survival in the public schools. However, just as there are now faculties of Modern History, Science, Law and Modern Languages at Oxford and Cambridge, which rank equally and alternatively with "Literæ Humaniores"—Greek and Latin texts, history and philosophy—in the qualification for an ordinary degree, so, in the public schools, more and more time and attention are given to these modern subjects.

The pre-eminence which is accorded to athletic sports is not allowed to put intellectual attainments quite into the background; and the annual speech day at the end of the summer term is a great occasion. At this ceremony, the prizes won during the year are publicly distributed, complimentary speeches in Latin are made by the masters and the senior prefects, and other speeches, the recorded orations of English statesmen, are recited in the mother tongue by other prefects. The fathers, mothers and sisters of the prize-winners probably attend.

Nevertheless, speech day is not by far so great an occasion as the annual cricket match against whatever school is the traditional rival. In the case of Winchester, this match, which lasts two days, is played against Eton, and takes place on the home cricket ground of each school in alternate years. In the case of Eton and Harrow, the match is played on Lord's Cricket Ground in London, and is one of the great social events of the London season, ranking equally or even above the match between Oxford and Cambridge, which takes place on the same ground a few days later.

At the annual cricket match the spirit of the old school tie manifests itself in its most typical form. Elderly gentlemen, many of whom have since become clergymen while others have perhaps gone into business, make long journeys from the country every year to be present at the match, and would not miss it for worlds. They have probably kept up their subscriptions to the Old Pupils' Association of their school ever since they left; but even if they have not, their school partisanship has probably not only not diminished with the years. It has even increased.

The excitement which is aroused among these middle-aged spectators, as well as among the schoolboys, by a close

finish to the match is something which would be incredible
to a foreigner if he has not seen it. A few years ago, when
Eton—or was it Harrow?—won the match by a narrow margin in the very last moments before the close of the play
would have made it into a draw, or undecided contest, the
field was immediately invaded by a crowd of the partisans of
the winning team, and one could see respectable professional
men, and even Cabinet Ministers, throwing their top hats
into the air and trampling them underfoot as they fell, and
all to express their enthusiasm at this school triumph.

An even more imposing, but not so intimately characteristic demonstration of the old-school-tie spirit is the eight-
oared boat race between the Universities of Oxford and
Cambridge—known all over the British Empire simply as
"the Boat Race." It is rowed about Easter for four miles and
a quarter on the Thames in the neighborhood of London,
and it has become a sort of national festival. The banks of the
river, the bridges, the riverside buildings and all the approaches are thronged by an enormous crowd, every member
of which, male or female, is wearing a rosette, either of the
dark blue of Oxford or the light blue of Cambridge; and the
remarkable thing is that at least ninety-nine per cent of the
people who show what is equivalent to the old school tie on
this occasion have not the smallest connection with either
Oxford or Cambridge. "I am Oxford," says a little shop girl
with conviction; and when you try to find out why, all you
will get is either that in her family every one has always
"been" Oxford, or else that she preferred the faces of the
Oxford crew—whose photographs have, of course, been ap-
pearing for days in the papers—or simply that she likes dark
blue better than light. In any case, every one has "taken a
side." It would be difficult to imagine an Englishman or
woman being an onlooker at any contest of any kind without
taking a side, without being a partisan of one competitor or
the other.

However, I have been anticipating a little in regard to Johnnie's educational career. He has now passed his eighteenth birthday, and we must call him John; for he has perhaps become senior prefect of his house, and has had occasion to lay the supple wand of ground ash across the shoulders of smaller "men," as it was laid across his shoulders in earlier years—yes, across the shoulders and not the posterior, and there is a particular way of holding the back so that the shoulder blades do not get hurt too much. The time has come for him to leave the school. His father may want to take him into his business, instead of sending him to the University. Or he himself may want to become an officer in the army, in which case he will enter the examination for entrance into Sandhurst—cavalry and infantry—or Woolwich—engineers and artillery.

If he does go to the University, it will almost certainly be either to Oxford or to Cambridge. Until 1832, these were the only two Universities in England, and both of them date back to the end of the twelfth century. Since 1832, when Durham University was created, ten modern universities have been founded, chiefly in the great manufacturing towns of the Midlands; but some of them are little more than examination boards for the granting of degrees, as is London University, and although they are sometimes composed of separate colleges, they have none of the corporate unity or residential collegiate life of the two universities which are world-famous. One indication of the prestige of Oxford and Cambridge is that to the library of each of them must, by law, be sent one copy of every book printed, as one must to the library of the British Museum in London.

If his father decides to send him to Oxford or Cambridge, John will perhaps compete for a scholarship in order to pay part of his fees. Nearly every public school has a connection with some College or other at Oxford or Cambridge, and this College reserves a certain number of scholarships, which are not thrown entirely open, but are kept for candidates from the particular school in question. The connection of Winchester, is, as I have said, with New College at Oxford—really one of the oldest Colleges in the University, but there are so many things in the world which have acquired a talisman of long life by having originally been given the title of "new"—from the Pont Neuf in Paris to New York in the United States.

Perhaps John will win one of the New College scholarships reserved to Wykehamists, as "men" from Winchester are called. Perhaps he will simply go to New College as a commoner, in which case he will cost his father £250 a year and perhaps more.

If the father is a rich man, and gives his son a liberal allowance, the £250 can easily become £800; but although there is certainly a "gilded youth" set at Oxford, which spends money extravagantly, the display of wealth is not in the tradition of the place. Differences in income have not often prevented the formation of those lifelong friendships, which are perhaps the greatest treasures acquired by a university career.

However, for a man of modest means £250 a year—or even £200, if it can be kept down to that—is a serious outlay; for it must be remembered that the three University terms are only of eight weeks each—the long vacation is from the middle of June to the middle of October. This sum will therefore only enable a young man to live for less than half a year. Moreover, even if he holds a scholarship, its annual value is not likely to be more than £80, for nearly all the University scholarships have been scaled down to that amount. So, even then, his parents will have to find a considerable sum, unless he is lucky and clever enough to hold another scholarship, from another source, at the same time. If he had come from a State secondary school and had won an open scholarship at Oxford, he might have received a grant from the Local Education Authority as well; but naturally, such a grant would not be given to any one from a big public school.

In any case, let us assume that John has arrived at New College. When he gets there, he will find himself once more in a mediæval quadrangle; but it will be one of many other quadrangles in Oxford, which, if they are not all mediæval, are all ancient. For every college is built more or less on the same model, and there are only two colleges whose main buildings are less than two hundred years old.

A college is an almost entirely independent foundation within the university. Originally it was a lodging house for students who came to attend the lectures of the university. Gradually each college became what is now sometimes a very wealthy corporation, owning land and other property, which was given or bequeathed to it by men who had formerly been its members.

Most of these bequests were made for the purpose of the advancement of learning. The income arising from them was either to be given to poor scholars—hence the existence of scholarships of money value—or else to Fellows, or "Senior Members" of the college, in order that they should deliver certain lectures, or even merely pursue certain particular forms of study—hence the establishment of "Fellowships," the holder of each "Fellowship" being granted an annual sum of money.

Some of the Fellowships are what are called prize Fellowships, and of these I shall speak later; but most of the "Fellows" of the several colleges are what in other universities would be called professors. Although a few lectures are given in the university buildings, where examinations are held, by far the greater number are given in the colleges, by the Fellows—colloquially referred to as "dons"—and they are open to undergraduates from all the other colleges in the university (undergraduates being those who have not yet taken their degree, that is to say graduated).

In fact, the colleges, taken together, make up the university, which could hardly be said to have any existence without them. It should be noted, moreover, that each college contains undergraduates who may be engaged in various kinds of study, and that, at Oxford and Cambridge, there is no grouping by Faculties.

When a new student, who is called a "freshman," arrives, he may at once be given rooms in his college, or he may have to spend his first year in lodgings in the town. The practice varies according to the college.

In either case, he will find that he is under supervision, and must be prepared to lead a life which—as far as association with the other sex is concerned—may be described as monastic. None of the gay and careless bohemianism of university life in other countries. The gates of his college or the doors of his lodgings are closed at nine in the evening; and although he can get in up to midnight on payment of a small fine, woe betide him if he is later.

There is a special sort of university police—they are called bulldogs, and they are college servants in the daytime—who walk the streets of the town at night under the command of one of the "dons" in his cap and gown—the "dons" take it in turns to fill this not very pleasant office. The two dons, each of whom commands a patrol, are called Proctors. It is the chief business of the Proctors to see that the undergraduates are not in undesirable feminine company, or indeed in feminine company at all, and they can enter any house in Oxford, but not any college, for each college controls its own internal discipline. The transgressor is inexorably punished by being "sent down"—that is to say, he is dismissed from the university.

The minor task of Proctors is to take the name of any

undergraduate who is not in cap and gown himself, as he should be in the streets after sunset or in the daytime when he goes to lectures. Every undergraduate has his cap and gown. The cap is the "mortarboard," previously described, but it is undergraduate tradition to bend the cardboard stiffening until it is almost a shapeless mass. The gown is long for scholars—scholarship holders—and so short for commoners that it does not come down to the edge of the coat.

The meeting between Proctor and undergraduate on these nocturnal occasions is always scrupulously polite. The Proctor, raising his cap to the undergraduate, who has probably had a run for it and has been brought back, breathless, by the bulldogs: "Do you belong to this university, Sir?" "Yes, Sir." "Your name and college, please, Sir." "Robinson, of Brasenose, Sir." "Kindly call upon me, at Trinity, at 9 o'clock tomorrow morning. Good night, Sir"—raising his cap again. The undergraduate calls, and is fined a guinea; but the tradition that the whole affair is between gentlemen is carefully maintained.

If the rooms which have been allotted to John—a bedroom and a sitting room—are in college, he will be attended by a "scout," a manservant who looks after him, as well as the four or five other men on his staircase; for no female servant is allowed within the college precincts. His breakfast and his lunch will be brought to him on a tray from the college kitchen; but for dinner he must go, either to a restaurant in the town, or to the ancient and oak-panelled college dining hall—where, in any case, he must eat a certain number of dinners during term.

There, at the top end of the hall, he will see the High Table, at which are seated, always in evening clothes, the president of the college, the other dons and whatever guests —male, of course—they may have invited. He himself need not be in evening dress, but he must wear his gown.

In one respect his dinner will resemble that which is being

served at the High Table. It will include no wine. The dons and their guests, always taking their napkins with them, will retire after dinner to the Senior Common Room, there to sip their port or claret. Some of the undergraduates will repair, once a week, to the meeting of a Wine Club—some of these Wine Clubs are more than a century old. The meetings are held in turn in the room of one or other of the members. They also will take port and claret; but I am afraid they will not always be content with sipping it, and the evening will perhaps end riotously, with a certain amount of breaking of glass, including that of the windows of such undergraduates, and sometimes even of such dons, as do not happen to be popular.

However, the great occasion for a noisy undergraduate demonstration arises if the college eight has established its position as "Head of the river." In the middle of the "quad" there will be a bonfire—quite unauthorized, of course, but tolerated—and a certain amount of furniture of various kinds will be burned, and cheerfully paid for afterwards.

Being "Head of the river" is a distinction to which the oarsmen of every college will aspire; but as the eights of all the colleges start simultaneously, at a certain distance behind one another, and in the order in which they finished the year before, and as one place only can be gained on each of the six days of racing, it is a distinction which is usually exchanged between a few leading colleges.

John will probably find that if he is the kind of weight and figure for rowing, a certain amount of pressure will be put upon him to persuade him to do so, though he may not have rowed at school. It must not be supposed, however, that if he does row, or play football or cricket, he will have entered a sort of specialist class apart, even if he devotes himself keenly to any one of these exercises. All the men who "get their blue"—that is to say row in the " 'Varsity" boat or play in the 'Varsity football or cricket team—take their degree in the ordinary way, and many of them take it with honors.

In any case, John will not be obliged to row; for there are no compulsory games or athletics at the university, and the time of the day between luncheon and tea, which is devoted to them, may be occupied by the undergraduate in any way that he likes.

Indeed, there is nothing at all compulsory at Oxford, not even book work—or "reading" as it is called. There are two attributes of maturity which a young man arriving at the University will find are his for the first time in his life. One is privacy. He has his own bedroom and his own sitting room; and he can "sport his oak"—that is to say, close the outer oak door of his rooms, which cannot be opened from the outside —whenever he wants to study or merely to be left alone. The other is freedom, naturally with its attendant responsibility. John will therefore realize that, from now onward, his energy and success will depend entirely upon his own choice and decision.

One of the "dons" of his College will be what is called his tutor. He will advise him as to what lectures to attend, and will give him as much private help as he can in his "reading"; but John will remain free to take his course. He can read for Honors—that is to say, a First, Second or Third Class—or he may be satisfied with a "Pass," merely getting through. Officially, the degree, which he will obtain after examination at the end of his four years for Honors and three for "Pass" will give no indication of whether he obtained Honors or whether he tried to do so. He will simply be entitled to call himself a Bachelor of Arts, whether he has been in the First Class or merely scraped through; and he can become a Master of Arts after a few further years, but need enter for no further examination. Although a man can try only once for Honors, he may enter for the Pass degree for as many years as he likes, and be "ploughed" every time until he finally succeeds; and there is an old Oxford story of a man who went on trying when he had a wife and family, and of his little girl running down the street to her mother after looking at the results sheet, and crying gleefully, "Father's ploughed again."

Many of John's intellectual interests will not be academic. He may speak at the Union, that famous debating society, where so many statesmen have won their first oratorical spurs, and learned the elements of parliamentary procedure. He may act in the Shakespeare performances of the Dramatic Society, with a view to going on the stage. He may read papers at the various literary societies.

Eventually, if he has taken a brilliant "First" in the "Schools," as the examinations are called, he may decide to try to obtain a Fellowship. This will not necessarily mean becoming a "don"; for there are the Prize Fellowships, which enable a young man to draw the £200 a year or so that they are worth, and at the same time begin his professional career in London or elsewhere. What it will mean is his becoming a "Senior Member" of the College in question, which need not necessarily be his own College, and dining at its High Table when he is in Oxford.

There are various stories illustrating what used to be the mainly social and aristocratic qualities demanded of candidates for Fellowships. One is that they were expected to be "bene natus, bene vestitus, mediæ doctus"—well born, well dressed and reasonably learned. Another tells of a test of the candidate's good manners. He was invited as a guest to dine at High Table; and the butler, watching for a moment when he had his mouth full, suddenly whispered into his ear "The President will take a glass of wine with you, Sir." Upon whether or not the young man gulped down his food in his hurry to raise his glass in the President's direction, or calmly took his time, was said largely to depend his chances of election.

These stories indicate a state of mind which now belongs to the past; for democracy is quite rightly invading Oxford, as it has invaded everywhere else. Oxford, however, remains one of the last strongholds of the old régime, and of social and political conservatism. It was not until 1871 that were removed the religious tests, which excluded all but members of the Church of England. Even today, the forms, customs and procedure of Oxford remain to a great extent as mediæval as its buildings. Once more, it is upon the old that the new has been and is being grafted. Once more, England is proving that it is not entirely a mistake to put new wine into old bottles.

Naturally, this picture of the Oxford undergraduate represents that which obtains under peace conditions. During war, many things are altered. The buildings of some of the Colleges have been requisitioned for Government purposes; and the undergraduates from those Colleges have moved to join the members of others which have been left undisturbed, although they sometimes return to their own Colleges to attend lectures and see their tutors, as the Fellows have not been evicted, even when the Colleges have been taken over. At the same time, many tutors have departed to do war work of various kinds, and those who remain have pupils from several Colleges.

In those Colleges in which undergraduates still reside, meals are no longer served in the rooms, as all except dinner used to be, but must be taken communally in Hall; and there is a fixed charge of £4-4-0 a week for board, lodging and service. The lodging no longer means that every undergraduate has a set of rooms to himself, but sometimes has to share them with some one else, although this is the exception rather than the rule. Wine Clubs, private motor cars and other such luxuries are suspended; but athletics and games continue, although in most cases two Colleges combine to form a team or a boat, and the officers' Training Corps and the University Air Squadron take up much of the time which would formerly have been devoted to sports.

Perhaps the most surprising thing about war-time Oxford is that the number of undergraduates in residence has not diminished to a greater degree. There are about half of the normal number of 4000 male students, while the number of women, which formerly stood at 750, has hardly changed at all. This situation is very different from that of the last war, when the number of male students had fallen by four fifths at the end of a year; but it has been caused by the immediate recognition, on the part of the Government on this occasion, that it was in the national interest that medical and certain science students should not be called up for military service, but should continue their studies. One result of this measure is that the number of medical and science students, which in normal times is only one fourth of that of the others, is now equal to it. However, the number of ordinary students is to some extent maintained by the fact that any one reading for the special War Degree, which is now being granted after a shorter course than usual, need not enter the army until he is nearly twenty-one.

On the other hand, we shall probably see Oxford, after the war is over, filled with ex-officers, who will be allowed to pursue their university career at a later age, in order to make up for the lost years, just as they were allowed to do after the last war.

In the schools, the war has naturally caused an upheaval. Many public-school boys, who had not reached the leaving age, have stayed away in order to go into munition factories and do other war work. Many middle-class preparatory boarding schools have been moved to safer areas, and the children from many public elementary schools have been transferred to camp schools in temporary buildings on big estates in the country. No less than fifty of these schools are working, and have thus suddenly become people's boarding schools after having been day schools. Many children have been taken away from their schools and their homes, not only to farms and cottages in England, but to Scotland, to Canada and to the United States, and have virtually had to begin their education all over again. It is one of the inconveniences of war; but it has also been the occasion for such cheerful courage on the part of the children and their parents and for such goodwill and kindness on the part of those who have taken the children in, and have helped to carry on the teaching of them, that the balance does not perhaps show a loss.

Chapter VI

THE PRESS AND ITS INFLUENCE

THE PRESS can be the instrument of tyranny or the expression of freedom. The former the British Press has never been in its history, and that is to its credit and to the credit of England. As for the latter, it may be said that the liberty of the British Press has been in continuous existence for two centuries and a half; and even in time of war, when it is inevitably restricted with regard to the dissemination of news, the degree of freedom to criticize the Government which is tolerated today is shown by the fact that only after the present war had been proceeding for a year and a half was the decision made to suppress the Communist *Daily Worker*, which had constantly been attacking, not only the conduct of the war but its very prosecution.

In the seventeenth century, Oliver Cromwell, the only ruler of England in modern history to maintain his power by military force and not by consent, nevertheless showed a moral greatness and a liberality of mind so far in advance of his time that he permitted the publication of all opinions, a freedom which had previously been unknown anywhere in Europe except in Holland; and he allowed his State Secretary, the John Milton of *Paradise Lost*, to issue that *Areopagitica, or defence of the liberty of unlicensed printing*, which remains the classic and monumental vindication of the right of a man to publish what he thinks. The seed was therefore sown; and although the freedom of the Press was withdrawn for a time after Cromwell fell, it was definitely established before the beginning of the eighteenth century, long before it prevailed in any major European country— even France did not win it until 1830.

The freedom of the Press exists therefore in England to-day in so far as the right to print is concerned. There is no law which forbids a man to publish his opinions, and that is a great thing. The degree to which he can reach a wide audience in that publication has, in practice, certain limits; for the Press can also be the prisoner of money, and this, as we shall see, a portion of the British Press has become. Nevertheless, the legal freedom is there.

Although newspapers, which were at first called news letters, existed in England as early as the seventeenth century —the first weekly paper was published in London in 1622 and the first daily in 1695—it was not until the end of the eighteenth that they began to assume any real importance in the life of the country, and they then already possessed the three features which were to be characteristic of them throughout the nineteenth—news, political opinion and advertisements. Expressions of political opinion had, of course, long been circulated; but the printing which Milton defended was the printing of pamphlets, and for long after his day political opinion appeared in this form, or else, rather later, in the form of periodicals, which were also literary in character, but were never associated with news. In the nineteenth century, however, the political pamphleteers moved their platform to the newspapers, and have ever since occupied it there.

The eighteenth-century pamphlets were addressed to the only classes who could then read—that is to say, the upper and the middle; and it was for these classes that the newspapers of the greater part of the nineteenth century continued to be produced. The two-party political system was then firmly established in England, and every newspaper consistently supported one party or the other. A family would take its Tory paper or its Whig paper—later, its Conservative paper or its Liberal paper—and would probably never read the paper of the opposite side. Other periodicals were produced, some weekly, some monthly, some mainly political in character, some mainly literary, some addressed particularly to women, some to sportsmen, but always to people of the upper and middle classes. Although these periodicals were not, strictly speaking, newspapers, for they contained no news, they were often commercially very prosperous publications, not only for their circulation, although that was sometimes considerable, but also and even chiefly for their advertisements.

I have said that from the beginning of the nineteenth century advertisements were one of the three main features of English newspapers, and it is advertisements which have enabled the British Press to be and to remain, in most cases, independent of constant financial support in order to live. For, although English daily newspapers have always been political, it must not be supposed that they have generally been or are today the paid organs, either of political parties or of individual politicians, and still less that they exist on or ever receive subsidies from the Government in the way in which newspapers frequently do in certain other countries. No doubt a Liberal or a Conservative daily has sometimes been acquired by persons or groups of persons interested in propagating the Liberal or Conservative point of view; but, although such persons or groups have occasionally kept papers alive when they were losing money, the tradition has always been followed of leaving the editor a free hand in framing the policy of the paper on the general lines agreed upon with the proprietor, and he has never been subjected to the direction of a political party except in the fairly recent case of the *Daily Herald*, which, at the beginning of its existence, was the official organ of the Labor Party executive.

As for any newspaper merely being the interpreter of the views of the Government or receiving payment from the Government for doing so, this certainly occurred in the corrupt days of the eighteenth century, but has simply never happened since, difficult to believe as this may be in countries where other customs prevail. The *Times* has frequently been referred to in foreign papers as the organ of the City of London, as if it reflected, in some authorized and subsidized way, the views of leading financial circles. It does not, and has never done so. It has always expressed the opinions of its directors alone. I am far from pretending that British newspapers are not subject to financial pressure, which is applied in other ways, and tends to restrict their liberty; but, except in the case of a well-known trade organ, they are not direct financial, any more than they are direct political mouthpieces.

This relative independence cannot be attributed to any moral superiority. The explanation merely is that in England a newspaper is nearly always a profitable and is always a large business, which is conducted on business lines with the object of earning dividends for its owners or shareholders. In the case of a big daily, this business is so important that, on the one hand, no subsidy which even a Government would find it worth while to pay the paper would make much difference to its yearly balance, and, on the other, the directors would never be likely to pledge themselves to any policy which would tie their hands in doing what they considered to be most conducive to increasing the circulation, the prestige and the profits.

In the nineteenth century, they decided that what paid them best was to appoint an able journalist as editor, and to leave him free to create an anonymous personality for the paper by infusing his own into it. This meant principally into the long political articles, although literary and artistic criticism, both of which were printed at considerable length, were not forgotten, and it was also thought desirable to have a responsible political correspondent in each of the half dozen most important foreign capitals.

The tradition of the editor's discretionary power was so strong until the beginning of the present century, that it was considered a scandal that the *Pall Mall Gazette* should be acquired by a new proprietor, who changed its politics, and the sympathy with the editor, who immediately resigned, was such that capital was at once found to give him a new paper, the *Westminster Gazette*. There was like sympathy with Mr. Massingham, who resigned from the editorship of the *Daily Chronicle* on similar grounds, although by that time the old tradition that the proprietor should not interfere was beginning to be broken.

Such foreign news as was not reported by the paper's correspondents was taken from the one important news agency then existing—Reuter's, which, in spite of the fact that its founder was a German Jew, has always been an English organization since it was created in 1849.

Anonymity was observed so severely that not only were the articles never signed, but even the name of the editor was never announced, and was probably unknown to the great majority of the readers. Still less was the name of the proprietor made public. The paper had a policy, as the paper. This policy was often formed in nightly consultations between the principal members of the staff, and was by no means always imposed by the editor, though, naturally, it had to have his approval. The inspiration of it was collective, and not individual.

In this way was built up the circulation of a typical nineteenth-century London daily. Nearly all the readers of each paper were regular and not casual. They felt a certain loyalty towards it and a certain interest in its fortunes.

However, the success of a newspaper did not consist only

or even principally in its circulation. It was chiefly because the English public—private individuals as well as business firms —acquired the habit of advertising in the Press for all sorts of purposes that papers became the important business properties that they were and are. It was the large advertisement revenue of the newspapers which enabled them to enjoy the luxury of being independent—politically and in every other way.

I can even remember a case in which the advertisement revenue of a newspaper was so much the most important part of the property that the chief preoccupation of the directors was to keep the circulation from rising. This is how it happened.

I was at that time the editor of a weekly paper, which was to be found on the table, not only of every London club, but also of every well-to-do town and country house in England. This made it a valuable advertising medium for those who wished to appeal to this wealthy but limited class. The prices that could be and were charged for the advertisements indeed illustrated the fact that it is not the number of sold copies of a paper which governs these prices, but the kind of people who buy the copies; and advertisements in the *Times* command a higher rate than will be paid for papers whose circulation is ten times as much.

In the paper of which I am speaking, every number contained so many advertising pages that they almost swamped the pages of text, which latter were indeed always reduced to the minimum proportion required by the Post Office regulations to enable the paper to be posted at newspaper rate. Every copy cost more to print than the price that was received for it; but the advertising more than paid for the difference. However, as the cost of the paper contained in each copy was constant, increased circulation would have meant diminished profits and ultimately loss, unless the advertisers had been willing to pay more for their advertisements, which they were not, since the goods that they had to sell were not for the million, but for a limited wealthy public, which they already reached. As long as their advertisements were read by that public, they were satisfied; and they did not complain when all sorts of devices were employed by the proprietor for not allowing the demand for the paper to increase and for limiting the supply.

No doubt there is always a possible danger that advertisers may exercise a sort of blackmail on a paper, and seek to dominate its policy. In the postscript to his recent and excellent little book on the Press, Mr. Wickham Steed even declared that most of the London papers, in October, 1938, yielded to the threat of certain large advertising agents that advertisements would be withdrawn if the seriousness of the international situation were pointed out to the public, as this would be "bad for trade."

At the same time, a newspaper which is read by the public which the advertiser wants to touch ought, for that reason, to be able safely to defy such blackmail.

There is one London daily paper today which still maintains the form and presentation which was that of all the London dailies in the nineteenth century. This is the *Times*. The other papers did not then have, and do not have today so many pages as the *Times*, which was always and is still sold at twopence, whereas they were and are sold at a penny; but in those days their appearance was otherwise much the same.

On the front page, below the large type title of the paper and the Royal Arms, are nothing but small advertisements. You must open the paper to the center page to find the important matter. Here, on the right, you will see a summary of the news of the day, followed by three columns of "leading articles," unsigned, of course, and some letters, which important persons, whose signatures are given, have addressed to the editor on matters of public interest. On the left is the page of foreign news telegrams. Other pages contain law reports, obituary notices, social news, racing, football or cricket news, and literary, art and dramatic criticism—all in the places where readers are accustomed to find them. The last page but one is always devoted to finance, and the back page consists of advertisements once more.

This was the normal layout of any London daily paper in the later nineteenth century. Comment and opinion were given at least as much prominence as news, the news was presented with studious objectivity and without descriptive headlines, and everything—opinions and news messages—was anonymous.

Already, however, news "stories" of a more personal and sensational character were beginning to be printed in some papers. The names of distinguished war correspondents were given, as for instance that of Archibald Forbes of the *Daily News*, one of whose exploits was to ensure that his paper should be the only one to hear of a certain battle in time for the next day's issue, by monopolizing the single telegraph line for two hours in transmitting several chapters of the Bible after he had sent his message.

However, the real revolution in the English newspaper world took place only at the beginning of the nineteenth century, and the man who made it was Alfred Harmsworth, afterwards Lord Northcliffe.

The establishment of compulsory elementary education in 1880 gradually built up a new and very large class of superficially educated but voracious readers. The standard of what they demanded could not yet be high, but they wanted what was given to them to be informative. The first man to make a fortune in journalism out of this demand was George Newnes, with a weekly paper called *Tit-Bits*, whose title completely describes what it was, and still is. It contained no news, but all sorts of little pieces of information on nondescript subjects.

Harmsworth made another fortune out of a similar paper,

called *Answers;* and he proceeded to cater for the same public by what were in spirit much the same methods in a daily newspaper, when, towards the end of the century, he founded the *Daily Mail*. Its appeal was frankly popular. It was sold at a halfpenny, instead of a penny, which was the price of the other dailies. It introduced what old-fashioned people considered to be the vulgar journalistic methods of New York. Above all, it had to be crisp, concise, sensational and alive. The news was given as shortly as possible, and further summarized in headlines, which were sometimes carried across two or more columns—an incredible thing to the older editors. Well-known persons were interviewed and their opinions asked, not on the subjects in which they had made their reputations, but on things they knew nothing about, and these opinions were given prominence simply because the names were known. Signatures were introduced into the paper, not only for special articles, which were as flamboyant as could be, but for news messages, to make them definitely personal.

With the anonymity of the contributors disappeared the personality of the paper. No longer was its policy a collective thing, which the editor directed, but to which members of the staff contributed in consultation. The editor himself was indeed virtually extinguished. He was replaced by the proprietor, who interfered constantly in the conduct of the paper, sometimes capriciously and with little sense of continuity. Policy, indeed, no longer mattered. Nothing mattered except news, to which it was not policy alone which was sacrificed. "We don't want facts. We want news," and "Vice is news, and virtue isn't," as a cynical editor of the new school is said to have told his reporters.

The immediate and great success of the *Daily Mail* soon provoked imitators, of which the most successful was the *Daily Express*. It also induced nearly all the existing daily papers to change their style. The *Times* has continued to maintain the old formula. The *Daily Telegraph* has done so to some extent, but has made many concessions. All the others have followed the *Daily Mail*, or have simply ceased to exist. In one respect, they have gone even farther than the *Daily Mail* in following the American form of presentation. They have all made the front page their principal news page, and have relegated advertisements to the back. The *Times* and the *Daily Mail* are consequently the only London dailies which now have advertisements on their front page—though the *Observer*, among the Sunday papers, also retains the practice. The advertisement value of the *Daily Mail* front page is therefore great. It lets, as a whole, for £1400 a day.

One result of this revolution was to establish still more firmly the freedom of the newspaper proprietors from outside financial or even Government pressure. The astronomic increases in circulation, which were aimed at and achieved, turned what had previously been sound family businesses into great financial trusts, more than ever impervious to the temptation of being bribed, subsidized or bought.

On the other hand, the trend of these trusts to amalgamate would appear to present today the danger of placing the effective control of the Press of the country into fewer and fewer hands, which thus hold a power as irresponsible as it is great.

There are fewer morning and evening papers in London than there were twenty years ago. The morning papers which have disappeared or have been swallowed by others include the hundred-and-seventy-year-old *Morning Post*, doyen of English newspapers, the *Standard*, the *Daily Chronicle*, the *Morning Leader*, the *Tribune*, the *Daily Dispatch* and the *Daily Graphic*. Among the defunct evening papers are the *Globe* (also more than a hundred years old), the *Pall Mall Gazette*, the *Westminster Gazette*, the *Saint James' Gazette*, the *Echo*, which had been the first London halfpenny paper, and the *Sun*.

Today there are six regular morning papers—the *Times,* the *Daily Telegraph,* the *Daily Mail,* the *Daily Express,* the *News Chronicle,* and the *Daily Herald.* In addition, there are two picture papers, consisting mainly of photographs—the *Daily Mirror* and the *Daily Sketch*—there is one sporting paper, two financial papers and one, the *Morning Advertiser,* which is really the organ of the liquor trade; for it has little general sale, and is chiefly distributed to public houses and restaurants which subscribe to it. This makes twelve morning papers in all.

There are three evening papers, the *Evening Standard,* the *Evening News* and the *Star.*

In addition, there are the Sunday papers, the circulation of which is greater than that that of almost any daily paper. These Sunday papers came into existence because old Sabbatarian tradition had long prevented the publication of the daily papers on Sundays. This tradition is of course quite illogical in the sense of expressing disapproval of work on Sundays, as it is the paper of Monday morning and not that of Sunday which involves Sunday work. The result of it, however, has been to create a group of papers which, on Sunday, give the news of the day, as well as the news of the week, together with a mass of reading matter of a general kind, which is distinguished in the case of the two journals—the *Observer* and the *Sunday Times*—and popularly discursive in the others. In one respect the Sunday papers are made up on a principle diametrically opposed to that of the dailies; for whereas the latter aim at conciseness, on the assumption that the reader has very little time, the former are voluminous, because he has the whole unoccupied day before him.

These Sunday papers include, in addition to the two just mentioned, the *News of the World,* *Reynolds' Newspaper,* the *People,* the *Sunday Dispatch,* the *Sunday Graphic,* the *Sunday Chronicle,* and the *Sunday Express.* It is only the last of these which has any connection with the daily paper of similar name; for it is under the same ownership. The *Sunday Chronicle* has nothing to do with the *News Chronicle*, any more than has the *Sunday Times* with the *Times*.

Finally, there are just over a hundred daily papers, which appear in the sixty-five large towns of England, Scotland and Northern Ireland.

Now some of these journals have immense sales. That of the *Daily Express* is 2,400,000, and that of the *Daily Herald* exceeds 2,000,000. That of the Sunday paper the *News of the World* at one time touched 3,000,000, and is not far from this figure today. That of the *Daily Mail* must be at least 1,500,000, and there are several of the other London dailies, which go beyond 500,000. The *Daily Telegraph* sells about 650,000, and the *Times*—of which the price is two-pence, whereas all the other papers cost only a penny—about 200,000.

The fluctuations in the sale of the *Times* at different periods give an interesting glimpse of the history of British daily journalism. In 1815, it stood at 5000, in 1834 at 10,000, in 1844 at 23,000, in 1854 at 51,000, and in 1908 at only 40,000—this was after the *Daily Mail* had successfully established itself. At this date, it was taken over by Lord Northcliffe, who succeeded in increasing the circulation to 165,000—which was then more than that of the *Daily Telegraph*—but only by reducing the price to a penny. When the cost of the superior paper on which the *Times* is printed made it necessary to revert to a price double that of the *Daily Telegraph*, the circulation went down accordingly, but recovered later to its present figure.

It should be noted that the enormous modern circulations of some of the popular dailies are to some extent factitious. They are in part created by spending large sums upon canvassing for insurance schemes, coupon competitions and similar means of inducing the public to buy the paper for other purposes than reading it. Nevertheless, there remains a large part of the increase which is genuine.

Some of the London and provincial dailies and Sunday papers are owned, each by a separate company or individual; but a disquietingly large number of them have been acquired by one of the several important newspaper ownership groups, so that a single company, and even in practice a single person, often controls several journals, and in two cases each of two members of the same family controls a group.

Thus, one member of the Harmsworth family directs what is known as the Northcliffe group, including the *Daily Mail*, the *Evening News*, the *Sunday Dispatch* and ten provincial dailies, while another, Sir Harold Harmsworth, has four provincial dailies. One brother of the Berry family, Lord Camrose, owns the *Daily Telegraph* and the *Financial Times*, while another, Lord Kemsley, owns the *Daily Sketch* and the *Sunday Times*, as well as two other London Sunday papers, three provincial Sunday papers and fourteen provincial morning and evening papers. Lord Beaverbrook is the proprietor of the London *Daily Express*, the *Evening Standard* and the *Sunday Express*. Moreover, all of these groups have bought and sold papers to one another.

Consequently, these five men, belonging to three families, control, between them, two London morning papers with enormous circulations, one of the two morning picture papers, one of the two middle-class morning papers, one of the two financial morning papers, two of the three London evening papers, five of the London Sunday papers and thirty-one morning, evening and Sunday papers in the provinces. In addition, there are two companies, which own, in the one case thirteen and in the other case four, provincial morning, evening and Sunday papers; and there is another company, which is the proprietor of the one Labor daily paper in London and also of one of the biggest Sunday papers.

The concentration of ownerships, with its resulting suppression of certain newspapers—which, however, has not yet reduced London to the two responsible dailies alone surviving in New York—undoubtedly offers dangers to the real freedom of the Press. One of them is that each journal which is suppressed represented a particular section of opinion, which now has no outlet. This was typically true in the case of the *Morning Post,* whose aristocratic Toryism was not the same thing as the Conservatism of the *Daily Telegraph,* which has absorbed it.

These dangers are all the graver because what would appear to be the natural corrective, that is to say, the creation of new papers to replace those which have gone, today involves such an enormous outlay of capital, and is accompanied by such a formidable risk of failure that the existing papers, which are going concerns, with regular subscribers and readers, have acquired what is almost a monopoly.

The conditions which have produced this virtual monopoly are of recent origin. They are largely due, not only to amalgamation, but to the fantastic over-capitalization of newspaper enterprises, whose finances have been built up on selling to the public debentures based on no more than the psychological asset of "good will." They are also due to the practice—referred to above—of artificially increasing circulations.

The circulations exist, however; and they mean that, to enter into competition with them, it would cost certainly over £1,000,000 to found a London morning paper today and to carry it on until it showed a profit—if ever it did show a profit. It has even been estimated that the *Daily Herald* spent over £2,000,000 before turning the corner. And yet Lord Northcliffe certainly spent less than £50,000 to start the *Daily Mail* at the end of the last century, and perhaps—according to one estimate—as little as £15,000; and it made a profit from the first.

Nevertheless, there are certain circumstances which prevent this monopoly from in fact carrying with it the degree of control over public opinion which might be supposed, and might be feared.

The first is that protection is afforded by the very magnitude of the newspapers themselves and the vested business interests involved; for one inevitable effect upon a paper of having, and struggling to keep, an enormous circulation is that its opinion becomes more and more nebulous and colorless. Nothing must be said which might lose any section of readers, and the solution is to give no opinion at all. It may be noticed, for instance, that papers which in the past would have been described either as Conservative or Liberal are now given in the reference books as "Independent," which really means that they are noncommittal.

It is true that this disinclination of the papers with the large circulations to print anything vigorous or disturbing or unconventional prevents the courageous and original and outspoken journalist from reaching any but a limited public; for he is obliged to write for other papers, which have only a limited number of readers. It is also true that this same timorousness operates as a censorship on news, as well as on opinion; for reference to any event or any public speech which might give offense to any one is either suppressed altogether or reduced to a minimum and pushed into a corner.

At the same time, these very conditions tend to discourage the newspaper proprietor himself from using his papers for propaganda. Moreover, it is some consolation to note that, if he does take the risk of adopting an attitude which is at all controversial, he finds, to his surprise, that in spite of the enormous circulation of his paper, his political excursion has little effect. The readers have not been accustomed to looking to his columns for opinion, and when they find it there they hardly take it seriously, especially if they have reason to think that it is lacking in solid foundation and consistency.

Lord Northcliffe realized this with regard to the *Daily Mail*. He discovered that in spite of its immense circulation, it had very little political influence; and when he wanted to exercise such influence through the Press, he had to acquire a controlling interest in a paper of the old-fashioned kind, the *Times*, and he had to conduct the paper in the old-fashioned way. When he showed signs of making changes in the traditional principles of its management, even so firmly established a force as the *Times* began to lose its influence and its prestige.

Another reason for not exaggerating the danger is that fortunately the present owners of certain papers, which have long been recognized as leaders of opinion, have had the public spirit to take precautions against the policy of the paper ever being at the mercy of the judgment—and possibly the caprice—of a single individual.

The *Times* itself is one of these papers. After the death of Lord Northcliffe, the controlling interest in it was acquired by Major the Honorable J. J. Astor. He formed a company with a special charter, under which the *Times* can never be sold except with the assent of a body of trustees composed of the Lord Chief Justice, the Warden of All Souls College, Oxford, the Governor of the Bank of England, the President of the Royal Society and the President of the Institute of Chartered Accountants—that is to say a body representing the Law, Learning, Finance, Science and Accountancy. Without the consent of these trustees, shareholders can sell their shares only to Major Astor, or to Mr. John Walter, the present representative of the family which owned the *Times* throughout the nineteenth century and were mainly responsible for its rise to greatness—notably in the person of John Walter II. In this way the danger of the *Times* falling into undesirable hands is removed.

Much the same sort of thing has happened in connection with another great journal, the *Manchester Guardian*, which is not a London paper, but enjoys a national and international prestige second only to that of the *Times* among British dailies. The *Manchester Guardian* was owned and edited for many years by C. P. Scott; and after his death, it was found that although, under his will, his heirs retained their property in the paper, the control of policy was placed in the hands of those who were editing and managing it, and the profits, beyond a certain amount, were to return to the paper itself, and were to be devoted to its improvement.

The *Economist*, the very influential weekly economic and financial journal, also has its policy and management protected in much the same way as the *Times;* and arrangements with a similar object, but rather different in detail, have been made with regard to Reuter's News Agency, which will eventually pass under the control of the Press Association, an agency which specializes in home news, as Reuter's does in foreign, and is jointly owned by the provincial newspapers of Great Britain.

Precautions of this kind give a certain guarantee against a new proprietor's rushing a paper which has acquired a reputation and is known for following a certain policy into a course which will reverse that policy and ultimately destroy that reputation.

A further guarantee is afforded by the fact that experience has shown that when the policy of a paper is reversed, it rarely happens that the paper itself survives for long.

The most important safeguard of all, however, is provided by the fact that there are considerable sections of the public who are not satisfied with the colorless views of the papers with the enormous circulations. They really want opinion; and although no one of these sections may be big enough always to make a paper into a best seller—though the *Daily Herald*, with its two millions, would appear to be an exception—it can keep one very comfortably alive.

Indeed, the future may show that it will be a paper of

opinion, and serious opinion, which will score the next big journalistic triumph. After all, the superficially educated public, for which Harmsworth cat~ in the *Daily Mail*, is no longer superficially educated. It has made the success of the Everyman Library, and it may make the success of some serious venture and the failure of the present big circulations, unless they adapt themselves to its needs in time.

In the British daily and Sunday Press, the newspapers of opinion are of two kinds. There are those whose political comment clearly appeals to the intelligent readers, though it is never allowed to be long, but whose other columns are frankly popular and sometimes trivial; and there are those which are addressed entirely to the more cultivated public, which are not afraid to develop an argument at length, and make a certain feature of literary and artistic criticism.

To the first category belong the *Daily Herald*, the one London Labor daily, the *News Chronicle*, the one London Liberal morning paper and the *Star*, the one Liberal evening paper (the last two being published from the same office). One might almost say that the *Evening Standard* belongs to this category also, although its Conservative political color is not always very evident.

To the second category belong the *Times*, which is really Conservative, although it calls itself "independent," the *Daily Telegraph*, which is Conservative, the *Sunday Times*, which is Conservative, and the *Observer*—also a Sunday paper—which is called Conservative, but is really independent in the strict sense of the word; for although it is far from being unpolitical, its views are the very personal ones of its editor, J. L. Garvin.

Though Wickham Steed, who has been editor of the *Times*, continues to hold a unique position as an independent journalist, though H. A. Gwynne, of the *Morning Post*, and J. A. Spender, of the magnificently edited *Westminster Gazette*, are alive, Garvin is the last survivor in harness of one of the two kinds of newspaper editor who made the reputation of their papers in the nineteenth century—editors who were left a free hand by the proprietors in regard to policy as long as they maintained the paper's success and prestige, editors whose personality really was an inspiration to every member of their staffs and in every line that was written. C. P. Scott, of the *Manchester Guardian*, was the type of one kind. He never, or hardly ever, wrote anything in the paper. His name never appeared in it. Yet, until he died at over eighty years of age, he was in the office every night, with his small combatant figure and his divided beard which made him look rather like an Afghan chieftain; and nobody who knew anything about the *Manchester Guardian* would deny that he made it. Such legendary mid-nineteenth-century figures as John Delane, editor of the *Times* for thirty-six years until his retirement in 1877, John Robinson, editor of the *Daily News* for thirty-three years until 1901, and Frederick Greenwood, of the *Pall Mall Gazette*, were of this kind.

Of other and rather later kind, belonging to a period when anonymity was no longer a fetish, were the men whose personality radiated, not only indirectly and anonymously in the office, but openly in the column of the paper, who wrote regularly and at length in it over their signatures. Such was Robertson Nicoll, whose paper, the *British Weekly*, died with him. Such is Garvin, of the *Observer*, who, at the New Year of 1941, was awarded the high and well-deserved distinction of being made a Companion of Honor.

If you ask any journalist which he considers to be, from a professional point of view, the best conducted and the best written papers in England, he will almost certainly reply, the *Times*, the *Manchester Guardian* and the *Observer*. I am proud to be able to say that, although I have never worked for the *Times*, I have been closely associated with the last two for more than twenty years.

The *Times* has and has maintained a great tradition. Its authority has long been unrivalled. In the nineteenth century, it used to be described as "the Thunderer." It represents, not so much political Conservatism, as the stability which is a Conservatism more profound and less partisan. It was the first newspaper to establish a service of well-informed, responsible and unbiased special correspondents in every foreign capital, and it maintains that service. It has become an institution. It is also a safety valve; for how many distinguished persons are there, who, dissatisfied with the way things are being done or burning with a suggestion to put forward, find relief for their feelings in writing a letter to the *Times?* These letters, which occupy a considerable space in the paper, have become one of its principal features.

The *Manchester Guardian* is the most important of the three leading provincial dailies which are independent of "Group" ownership, the other two being the Conservative papers, the *Yorkshire Post* and the *Glasgow Herald*. It is the sturdy and impenitent representative of traditional Manchester Liberalism—Free Trade and democratic sympathies, which extend beyond the borders of Great Britain to include the true democrats of every country. It is perhaps the greatest and most intelligent champion of freedom and enemy of injustice to be found among the newspapers of the world.

The foundation of the *Observer* dates back to 1792, and it is therefore only four years younger than the *Times*. However, it has never, in its long life, attained to such prestige as it now enjoys. Mr. Garvin's ingenious formula of making it at once a newspaper, with Sunday morning's news and his own interpretation of the political and international scene, and also a literary review, with signed articles by authoritative writers, has been responsible for much of the success. Indeed, it may be said that the *Observer* and its rival, the *Sunday Times*, have taken to themselves the greater part of the literary and critical public, which used to buy such weekly papers as the *Spectator* and the *Saturday Review*. Price may have had something to do with the victory. The *Observer* and the *Sunday Times* cost twopence—more than most of the daily papers, which are at a penny, but the same as the *Times*—and the buyer gets a newspaper as well as a literary journal. The *Saturday Review* and the *Spectator* cost sixpence, and even the *Times Literary Supplement*, which has a considerable following, is priced at threepence.

It is true that the *Economist*, which is also a weekly review, can sell at as much as a shilling and find buyers; but then the *Economist* must have subscribers among all the bankers of the world, and is in a very special position. It is true that well-printed picture papers, like the veteran *Illustrated London News* or the less serious *Sketch* and *Tatler*, full of photographs of actresses and society women, can sell at a shilling also, as can fashion papers like *Vogue* and the *Queen* and country house papers, like the *Field* and *Country Life*; but all of these depend largely upon clubs and regular subscribers and on the advertisements which make their appeal to these special customers, and are hardly bought at all by the general public.

It is the clubs all over the English-speaking world which really keep alive, not only weekly reviews like the *Spectator*, the *Saturday Review*, the *New Statesman* and *Life and Letters*, which nevertheless still have a public, but also the once famous serious magazines, like *Blackwood's* and the *Cornhill*, the monthly reviews like the *Nineteenth Century*, the *Fortnightly*, the *Contemporary*—all famous also in their day —and more recent ones, like the *Round Table* and the *National*. For their prices range from half a crown to five shillings, and they can no longer be said to have any living contact with general readers.

These general readers want to be catered for at much cheaper prices. For picture papers, they will buy the threepenny weekly, *Picture Post*, with its large-scale photographs, and they will buy one or other of the thirty-seven women's weekly papers, whose prices range from fourpence to sixpence.

If the list of the three hundred or so weekly and monthly publications of general interest, which are issued in London, is examined, it will be found that the prices of most of them are between twopence and sixpence; and it is certainly these which are the most read and the most alive. They include papers which deal with gardening, with fishing, with housekeeping, with art, literature and the theatre, with politics and poetry.

In addition, there are twenty-one papers representing the various religions which, you will remember, the Frenchman said you could find in England, where, however, there was only one sauce. There are also well over two hundred trade and professional journals—for instance, the *Milk Industry,* the *Shoe and Leather News, Engineering*—of which the ordinary reader has never heard, but many of which are valuable properties on account of their specialized advertisements.

It may be a sign of the times that what used to be called the Society papers, such as the *World, Vanity Fair* and others, which were very successful thirty years ago, have ceased publication, while what was once the great daily for social news and announcements, the *Morning Post,* no longer has an individual existence; but any one who thinks that this indicates the end of snobbishness in England will be corrected by looking at the photographs—only in peace time of course—in the *Sketch* or the *Tatler* of titled persons shooting, attending race meetings or bathing.

A curious incident of contemporary English journalism is the disappearance of the comic papers, which many of us can remember as having delighted our youth. Perhaps the reason is that the daily papers have all introduced comic features. Of course there is *Punch;* but I am not quite sure that *Punch* can be described as a comic paper. I remember that W. B. Yeats, the Irish poet, once said to me that it was the uneasy conscience of the English governing class. In any case it is a typically English phenomenon, and must certainly not be missed by any one who wants to try to understand the English genteel mentality, and also something of an English spirit, which is more profound than the genteel. Although *Punch* is sold at sixpence, it has a vast circulation, and its advertisement revenue must be very great.

Another recent development is the creation of several weekly sheets which have taken the old title of "news-letters." They are not newspapers, as they cannot be purchased publicly, but are sent out, to subscribers only, through the post. Their semi-private and personal character is even sometimes accentuated by their being reproduced, not by printing, but by typewriter duplicating. They are not long, and they do not claim to be exhaustive. What they implicitly purport to do is to take their readers behind the scenes of politics and affairs by telling them things which have not appeared in the papers. Their success is certainly the reward of an ingenious catering to natural curiosity, to the desire to be "in the know." Their existence may also represent a reaction against the impediments, already referred to, which stand in the way of an unconventional journalist freely expressing his opinion, and against one other impediment, to which I have not referred.

This is the control which the few large wholesale newsagents exercise over the papers which they distribute to retailers and sell themselves by retail on their many railway bookstalls. Without refusing to take a journal of whose views they may disapprove—and occasionally they may do that—they can restrict its circulation in a number of ways—by not exhibiting it to a reasonable extent on bookstalls, by not distributing a sufficient number, and so forth—and they can drive very hard bargains with papers which are not powerful enough to resist their demands. The "news-letter" is independent of this interference.

It is not, however, independent of the penalties—in origin wholesome, but in practice sometimes very severe—which may be imposed by the law; for the "news-letters," although not publicly on sale, are published in the legal sense.

That these penalties are not, strictly speaking, restrictions is of course true. There is no Press Censorship in England in peace time; and any newspaper, if it is prepared to take the consequences, may publish anything without consulting anybody. Yet the penalties for certain offenses are heavy, and for one class of offense they may be immediate. This is the offense called "contempt of court," and it consists of any comment upon a pending trial or legal action which may be interpreted by the Judge as trying to influence the course of justice by creating prejudice against one of the parties—such as assuming that an accused person is guilty—or trying to create prejudice against the presiding Judge or the fairness of the court proceedings. Although it has been ruled that there is a right of criticism, if it is not malicious or if improper motives are not imputed, the fact that a Judge can immediately commit to prison an editor whom he considers to have offended, and can have him tried for the offense by a panel of Judges, without a jury, produces the result in reality that few newspapers dare to criticize legal proceedings.

The severity of the penalties for libel—which may be treated as a criminal offense—and the extent of the money damages which juries tend to grant against newspapers when it is merely a civil action, also produce the result that many claims—for the most part due to the involuntary errors of the newspapers—are settled by payments out of court without ever being brought to trial. It has even been alleged that no more than 2 per cent of such claims are actually tried. Even supposing the libel to be voluntary on the part of its real author, he usually escapes scot-free; for the editor of the paper, out of professional loyalty, does not disclose his name, and it is the editor and the printer who are prosecuted and held responsible in the first instance.

In the day-to-day conduct of a newspaper there have been many changes in recent years. The regular journalist has much less space and much less time at his disposal than he used to have. One of the reasons why he has less space is that more articles are offered by, and accepted from, well-known persons, who are not regular journalists. Although members of the Government do not write in the Press, the same politicians, when they are not members of the Government, do so in a way which would have been considered unseemly twenty years ago. The working journalist has less space for the further reason that all articles are shorter today, even in those papers which publish what may be called articles at all.

Above all, he has less time. I can myself remember returning to the office of the *Daily News* after the first performance of a new play, and not finishing my criticism of it until half past one in the morning, when the head printer, who was really the ultimate dictator, used to come into my room and snatch the last sheet out of my hand. Even that was then considered unreasonably early by journalists who could—and can—remember being allowed to write up to a quarter to three for a paper which went to Press at five and perhaps later. Today a daily paper goes to Press not later than midnight for what is called the London edition, and earlier still for the editions which have to catch trains to the provinces or be conveyed thither in motor lorries by road. Everything is now feverish and hurried, from the work of the editor, who has to make vital decisions at a moment's notice, to that of the writer, who may have to compose an important article in twenty minutes, and that of the many subeditors, at work at their long table classifying messages, abbreviating or amplifying them according to circumstances and inventing descriptive and striking headlines for them.

It was always rather feverish and hurried. That is one of the conditions of daily journalism and part of its delicious excitement, the excitement which any journalist feels when he walks into a newspaper office, hears the old clang of the machines and smells the old acrid smell of printer's ink. The man who merely writes for the papers cannot have it.

At one time, G. K. Chesterton used to write "middle" articles for the *Daily News*—a "middle" article being a generally discursive treatise on a subject unconnected with the day's news. All daily papers used to—and the *Times* still does—follow the more ponderous "leaders" with "middle" articles. Belloc, whose name naturally occurs to one in connection with that of his great friend Chesterton, once proposed to me, as a typical title and subject of such an article, "Do cats believe in God?" Well, I remember that one day Chesterton came down to the *Daily News* office in the afternoon to write his "middle." He shut himself into a room, and was forgotten by every one except the "printer's devils" —small boys—who used, from time to time, to open the door to ask whether he had any "copy" ready for the Press, only to be angrily sent away. The hours passed. The excitement in the building rose. The center of interest moved upstairs from the editor's room to the composing room, where urgent corrections were hurriedly made in the last two pages of the paper, as they lay in type upon the "stone"—really a metal-topped table—before the "forms" were locked up. Eventually, at one o'clock, these last two pages were sent down to the foundry, and the paper was "put to bed." Those of us who had had last-minute articles came downstairs, lighting our pipes, to fetch our coats and go home. At that moment, Chesterton came out of his room with the pages of his article in his hand. "Will this be in time for tonight's issue?" he asked the editor on the stairs—a great writer, but never really a journalist, and still less a newspaper man, as such specialists as news-getters, reporters and subeditors describe themselves in proud distinction from the journalist himself.

In the office of an evening paper there is another kind of excitement. Work begins in the early morning, for editions follow one another all day. They start with the fourth about 11 o'clock. It is said that there used to be a second, but no one has ever heard of a first or a third. After that, there is the "Special," about midday, and, in the course of the afternoon, the "Extra Special," the "Final," and the "Late Night," with perhaps a "Home Edition," a "City Edition" and a "Late Sporting Edition" coming somewhere in between. These editions are handed out to the little motorcars—they used to be little two-wheeled carts—which "rush" them across London, and deliver them to newsagents and particularly to more humble vendors, each of whom has his or her "pitch" or accustomed place on the pavement at some street corner—for there are no open-air newspaper stalls or kiosks in London. They are also handed out to the newspaper boys, who run crying them through the nearer streets.

Each boy is also given a large printed contents bill, about three feet by two, which he holds before him as he runs. There is great art in the composition of these bills, which are not really contents bills, as they announce only one thing in very large type, and their real purpose is to arouse the curiosity of the reader, without giving him the news unless he buys the paper. "Defeat of England," announced one of them at the beginning of the other war; but the excited buyer found that what was really meant was that a representative cricket team, which was then in Australia, had lost a match. J. M. Barrie, in one of his books of journalistic reminiscences, gives another suggested contents bill—"Burying the hatchet" (in large type), followed by "In the head of the settler" (in small). Morning papers have their contents bills also;

but they are real contents bills; for they are longer and more full, and they do not play such an important part in the sale; and it used to be the tradition of the *Morning Advertiser*, up to the beginning of the century, that each line of its contents bill should consist of words in alliteration.

I am afraid, however, that what—in peace time—appears on most of the evening paper bills is "3.30 winner," indicating that the paper contains the name of the horse that won the race at 3.30, or some other hour, and that what the boys shout, as they run through the streets, is merely the word "Winner." For the evening papers live largely on horse-racing—the earlier editions containing the "selections," by the paper's specialist, of the horses that he considers likely to win, and the later editions, the results, with the "prices," that is to say the betting odds recorded. Cricket and football news also looms large, and it is that which usually occupies the space left blank for the "stop press news," which is added, in a special slot on the cylinders carrying the type, after the printing of the edition has started.

What in newspaper language are called "scoops," exclusive pieces of important news, are much rarer today than they used to be, especially upon political matters. Every Government Department, from the Prime Minister's office downwards, now has its Press attaché; and all important pieces of information are distributed impartially to the newspaper men —though the news agencies are often given a slight preference. It is unlikely, therefore, that any modern correspondent will be able to renew the feat of de Blowitz, the famous Paris correspondent of the *Times*, who, in 1878, enabled his paper to publish the full text of the Treaty of Berlin on the morning on which it was to be signed.

There is another reason why isolated pieces of news of all kinds are assuming less and less journalistic importance; and that is that the public has nearly always learned them already over the wireless before any newspaper can bring them out.

It must not be considered, however, that this means that the wireless is destined to replace the newspaper. The success of a paper called the *Listener,* which reproduces the principal talks given over the B. B. C. service, shows that the public wants to be able to read and think over the printed words, even after it has heard the same words spoken. The memory of the normal person enables him to retain only a bare fact given to him by word of mouth; and even that he prefers to verify it afterwards by reading it. As for detailed news, and, even more, argument and opinion, the newspaper will not only still have the greater prestige and authority—for there is a mysterious authority about print—but will still present the greater interest.

Chapter VII

INDUSTRY, COMMERCE AND FINANCE

WHAT are the foundations of the industrial, commercial and financial greatness of England, and what are the conditions which are essential to its existence?

The foundations are two—first, maritime transport, and then, coal. The essential conditions are also two—first, the freedom of the seas, and then, the maintenance of purchasing power.

Before the industrial age of the nineteenth century had given coal its enormous importance, London had already become the chief trading center between Europe and the other continents, and afterwards, as a natural consequence, the financial center of the world; and London had attained this position owing mainly to the fact that the goods exchanged between Europe and these other continents were carried almost entirely in British ships. There were geographical and historical reasons for this. The British Isles were favorably placed at the door of Europe and in the temperate flow of the Gulf Stream. The British Navy had successively driven other competitors off the seas—first the Spanish, then the Dutch and then the French.

Thus, by the end of the eighteenth century, England had firmly established herself as a great commercial nation.

In the nineteenth century, she became a great industrial nation as well; and she became so largely because she possessed coal in enormous quantities, in excellent quality and in readily accessible places, so that she had, under her hand and cheap, the power for driving the steam engines, which she had herself invented for her factories, her railways and her ships, which, in their turn, provided her with cheap delivery abroad.

The industries were built up in close proximity to, and indeed on the top of, the coal fields; and these coal fields were within easy distance of the seaports—there is no place in England which is not within easy distance of the coast, and the English coast is dotted with good seaports. As sea transport is always much cheaper than land transport, the shortness of the land journey to the factories from the sea for the raw material and from the factories to the sea for the manufactured goods was of great importance in keeping down the selling price of the finished article.

Consequently, by reason of having good coal at hand, and therefore cheap, and by reason of being close to sea transport, English manufacturers commanded two important elements of being able to sell cheaply abroad.

This double advantage was so great that it counterbalanced the fact that all except two of the chief raw materials used for the manufactures, which Great Britain exported overseas, had first to be imported from overseas.

These conditions remain the ones which govern the situation today.

Great Britain still has enormous reserves of good quality coal, which can easily be mined; and this coal is still in close proximity to the factories. No shortage of coal is likely to occur for several hundreds of years, either in bituminous coal, the quality chiefly used in industry, or even in the more expensive anthracite or steam coal, although the available quantities of the latter are smaller. In some places, the need of working at greater depths may increase the mechanical problems of extraction; but the coal is and will be there.

Although the British output of coal is not much more than two thirds of that of the United States, the coal supplies and production of Great Britain are so great that, before the war, coal constituted an important British export to certain European countries which are now enemies, such as Italy, and also to France and even to Brazil. Coal was then fifth in importance among British exports, after cotton goods, machinery, iron and steel manufactures and vehicles (including ships), but before woollen yarns and textiles, chemicals and non-ferrous metal products. This export has naturally come to an end since the war; and the coal fields of South Wales and Durham, which are near the sea, but have no industries attached to them, are now working below capacity. The immediate and local unemployment difficulty has been met by the establishment of a compensation scheme, under which the coal fields in the interior of the country, which are working overtime to keep the adjacent factories supplied, contribute to the support of the workers on the relatively idle coastal coal fields. The very existence of this reduced production is, however, an indication of the reserves which could immediately be brought into play if more coal were required, and is therefore a source of strength.

Coal in general is such an important national asset that, under the Coal Act of 1938, all private ownership of coal fields is to be brought to an end by the year 1942, on payment of compensation to the present owners on a scale which the Act lays down.

With regard to raw materials used in manufacture, it is still the fact that only two of the important ones, iron and wool, are obtained to any considerable extent at home; and even they are not obtained to the full extent that is required.

The great iron industry of Great Britain was built up in the past by using exclusively British ore, and in time of peace

Great Britain does still produce two thirds of the iron ore which she needs; but she imports the remaining third. Fortunately, there are considerable natural reserves, both of Jurassic ironstone in Northamptonshire and Lincolnshire and of hematite in Cumberland; but the Jurassic ironstone, although it is relatively easy to extract, and represents over 90 per cent of the British production, is low in metal content, and the hematite, while consisting more than half of metal, is rather difficult to mine. So that in normal times the resources of Scandinavia, French North Africa and Spain are drawn upon, while, during the war, a part of the difference is being made up by collecting scrap-iron.

As for wool, it used to be one of the most famous products and exports of England, and the best qualities are so still. Yet hardly more than a tenth of the woollen yarns and cloths which come from the mills of Bradford, in Yorkshire, or Paisley, in Scotland, and are exported all over the world, is made from the wool of sheep raised in Great Britain, but from the wool of Australia, and to a less extent from that of New Zealand, Argentina and Uruguay.

Several of the metals other than iron have been mined in Great Britain for hundreds of years—the Cornish tin mines, for instance, date back to the Romans—and important industries owe their foundation to these earlier deposits. However, the production has, in all cases, long been insignificant, principally because the foreign ore could be obtained more cheaply; and it is upon imported ores that the industries originally created to work the metals of Great Britain have grown to rely. Thus the relatively small output of lead and zinc from Derbyshire, Durham and Scotland represents only a fraction of what comes from Australia, India and Canada.

It is from Canada and Northern Rhodesia that copper is obtained, as well as from Spain. Tin comes from British Malaya, Nigeria, Bolivia and Chile; manganese from India and Russia; nickel from Canada; chromium from Southern

Rhodesia. Bauxite, from which aluminum is made, used to be imported into England from France and also to some extent from Hungary, Yugoslavia and Italy. It must now be sought in Guiana, the U. S. A. and Russia. Other non-metallic minerals, such as asbestos, magnesite, potash and phosphates, have equally to be imported, and the first and last of these, which England used to obtain from France and French North Africa, must also be drawn now from the U. S. A.

Finally, all the mineral oil, used to make motor and aviation petrol, as well as for lighting, has to be imported, the U. S. A. being by far the largest producer, but considerable supplies being under British control in Iran and Iraq.

When we pass from the minerals below the soil to what is grown above it—animal as well as vegetable—we find that Great Britain is no less dependent upon imports from abroad.

Virtually the whole of the wood used in the country arrives from overseas, as well as the pulp used in paper making, to say nothing of newsprint paper itself. Canada, Scandinavia and Russia are the sources of supply for soft woods, while hard woods are brought from South America and Asia.

All the cotton, which is spun and woven in the mills of Lancashire, is imported—chiefly from the U. S. A., but also from India and Egypt. Much of the flax which is made into linen in Belfast comes from Russia, though much is also grown in the North of Ireland, and it is being increasingly cultivated in England.

All the tobacco which is smoked in Great Britain is imported—chiefly from the U. S. A., though 24 per cent of it comes from the British Commonwealth.

In the matter of food, the percentage of imports to the whole consumption is no less great—80 per cent of the cereals (mostly from Canada, but also from Australia and Argentina); 78 per cent of the sugar (chiefly from Cuba and Australia); 88 per cent of the butter and other fats (the butter principally from New Zealand, but also, until the war, from Denmark); 50 per cent of the meat (chiefly from Argentina in regard to beef, and New Zealand in regard to mutton, but also from Uruguay and Australia); 33 per cent of the milk (in condensed form, mostly from Holland until the war); 50 per cent of the fresh fruit (oranges from Palestine, Spain and Brazil, apples from Canada, Australia and the U. S. A.).

In addition, Great Britain imports the whole of her enormous consumption of tea (most of it from British India), her small consumption of coffee (mainly from Costa Rica and British East Africa) and her considerable consumption of cocoa (nearly all from British West Africa).

It will have been noticed that, in many cases, the country which is the principal source of supply is itself a member of the British Commonwealth of Nations. This is of considerable importance under war conditions, where finance is concerned, as I shall explain later. At the same time, these imports have to be carried over the ocean no less than if they were purchased from a foreign country, and the necessity of keeping the seas open and the ships of the merchant service constantly travelling over them remains as vital as ever.

British shipping is therefore at the very foundation of the commercial and financial greatness of the country, and it is also the life line of Great Britain.

It is not surprising, therefore, that not only is London the largest town in the world, but the Port of London is the greatest seaport in the world, both for the tonnage which enters and leaves it and for the value of the merchandise which passes through it, in and out, this value, in the year 1937, being over £600,000,000 and representing more than a third of the overseas trade of the country; that, after London, there are ten British seaports doing a trade of over £10,000,000 a year, by far the biggest being Liverpool, with £360,000,000; that the tonnage of seagoing merchant steamers and motor vessels owned by the British Commonwealth of Nations in 1938 was nearly two and a half times as great, and that owned in Great Britain alone was nearly twice as great, as that owned by members of the next maritime nation, the United States (whose merchant navy had nevertheless more than quadrupled since 1914); that the tonnage of merchant vessels, built during the year 1937–1938 in Great Britain, or for Great Britain and the British Commonwealth, was in each case more than seven times as much as that built in or for any other country; and that, of the seventy-six merchant vessels in the world of 20,000 tons or more, forty were British, no other nation being possessed of more than eleven.

England has so long been the acknowledged leader of the world's shipping that it was natural that in London should be found the famous institution which is the center of marine insurance, not only for Great Britain, but for all countries. Lloyd's, known everywhere by that single word, is indeed a center of much insurance which is not marine at all; for although there are many insurance companies all over the world, which take their customers' risks, most of them cover part of their own risk by reinsurance at Lloyd's.

The history of Lloyd's goes back to the latter part of the seventeenth century. It was then merely a London coffee-house, where men interested in ships and in the insurance of them had the habit of meeting. Gradually, these men formed themselves into an association, which took over the premises and the name. Later, this association was housed in the imposing structure called the Royal Exchange, which stands on an admirable site in the heart of the City of London, and is now a sort of national monument, although at the time of its foundation in the sixteenth century and for long afterwards, it used to be the place where the merchants of the City met regularly for business. Lloyd's occupied the greater part of the Royal Exchange for a hundred and fifty years, but now. has its own building in Leadenhall Street. This was opened by King George V in 1928. Today, the Royal Exchange is still given over to insurance; for nearly the whole of it, except the main hall, with its statues and frescoes and its famous chimes—which play British national melodies four times a day—has been taken over by an insurance company called the Royal Exchange Assurance, which was established in part of it even before Lloyd's moved there.

Lloyd's itself is not an insurance company. It is an incorporated society; but it does not do business as such. The business is in the hands of its individual members, each one of whom can become a member only when he has satisfied the committee that he can undertake insurance business, and when he has deposited with it a large sum as a guarantee that he will fulfil his obligations. These members, who are called underwriters, habitually associate themselves in groups to take risks; but the liability of each man is limited to the proportionate share which he subscribes to a particular policy.

The eminence of Lloyd's as an association of marine insurers has led to its acquiring an importance of another kind in relation to ships and seamen. Two obvious interests of the members are, first, to acquire reliable information as to the seagoing qualities of the ships which they are asked to insure, in order to determine the rate, and, second, to support and even organize any efforts to save the insured property from damage and eventually from loss.

In pursuance of the second object, Lloyd's has always been ready to contribute to rewarding gallantry at sea; and, in the present war, it is issuing a special war medal for bravery to merchant seamen. It has always been a strong supporter of such bodies as the Royal National Lifeboat Institution, which organizes the dangerous but virtually unpaid service by fishermen of the life-saving appliances and lifeboats which are now installed all around the coast of Great Britain. Lloyd's used to contribute to the rewards paid for the salvage of property at sea, before maritime law had established that such rewards could legally be claimed against the owners of the property or the insurers representing them.

The same sort of thing used to happen in the early history of the Fire Insurance Companies. At that time, when there were no publicly organized Fire Brigades, each Insurance Company had its staff for putting out fires. Indeed, it used to be said that if such a gang arrived, and discovered that the property was not insured in their Company, they simply went home without taking any further interest in the matter. Naturally, such selective methods, even if they were ever really applied, would have had no sense in the case of Lloyd's and shipping losses, as all maritime insurance has always passed through it.

The desire of the insurers to obtain information about ships to be insured has had the most far-reaching effects. Lloyd's issued a *Register of Shipping* as early as 1760; but it was in 1834 that the famous *Lloyd's Register,* in more or less its present form, first appeared. This was a list of the shipping of the world, scientifically classified by Lloyd's local inspectors and agents according to the seaworthiness of each vessel. There were five groups, indicated by the five vowels of the alphabet, the first of which represented the highest class for the ship; and each vowel was followed by a number, number 1 representing the highest class in equipment. Thus, to be A 1 at Lloyd's meant a first-class ship, equipped in a first-class manner. Today, the method of classification has been slightly altered—all ships being described as A 1, but the second and third class being diffentiated as 90 A 1 and 80 A 1 and the first class standing as A 1 alone.

The result of this classification has been an enormous improvement in the quality of the ships sent to sea, and in the state of their equipment; for shipowners, in order to pay lower premiums, have taken care to conform to the conditions which Lloyd's lay down for marking a ship up to the highest category. They have thus avoided overloading, insufficient repairs, worn-out machinery and all the elements which militate against safety. A cynical shipowner might be indifferent to them, if he could insure his vessel. He pays attention to them if he finds that he cannot insure otherwise.

I have spoken of shipping to begin with, because that is Great Britain's most essential activity in the sense that if it collapsed, Great Britain could not live. There are, however, other occupations which employ far greater numbers of workers. Look first of all at the productive industries, as they stood before war diverted the activities of so many factories from their normal course. Textiles and clothing, taking cotton and wool together, show the largest figures, the number of the women employed being double the number of the men—the totals in 1931, when the last detailed reports were made, were 1,200,000 women and 600,000 men. The industry in which the greatest number of male workers is occupied is that of metal trades and engineering (1,500,000), followed by agriculture (1,200,000), then by coal mining (1,000,000) and then by the building trades (950,000). Transport of all kinds, including ships, railways and road vehicles, accounts for a larger number of workers (1,750,000) than any of the industries just mentioned; and commerce of all kinds is responsible for almost as many (1,600,000); but these last are rather arbitrary groupings, and are of relatively little interest as an indication of the productive efforts of the country.

The enormous number of people who depend upon the textile industries shows what a great factor these industries are in British prosperity. As far as England is concerned, they are concentrated in South Lancashire for cotton and in West Yorkshire for woollens—that is to say, looking northwards at the map, in that part of the country where the island begins to get definitely narrower. The products of these industries are among the most important of British exports; and it is significant that not only has the demand for Yorkshire woollens and Lancashire cotton goods been maintained since the beginning of the war in such important foreign markets as South America, and has even been increased, but that Great Britain has been able to make regular deliveries to meet the demand.

The metal-working industries follow the Yorkshire coal-field southwards from Leeds to Sheffield and then to the neighborhood of Nottingham, and are found again, rather to the southwest, on the Midland coal field—Wolverhampton, Birmingham and Coventry.

Around London and Liverpool are other industrial areas, producing various kinds of goods; but they are to be found there, not because there is coal—for there is none—but because, for various reasons, it is more convenient for them to be immediately in touch with a great seaport, where the raw materials arrive and whence the finished goods are despatched, than to be on a coal field.

The shipbuilding industry is established on the estuaries of the Clyde and the Mersey on the West coast and the Tyne and the Thames on the East.

Among the British industries which manufacture for export, and make the economic greatness of the country, I have spoken of only one or two of the most important; but there are many others. There are ships, locomotives, aircraft and motor cars, the value of whose exports, taken together, was only exceeded, in 1938, by two exports, machinery and cotton, and exceeded that of iron and steel and that of woollens. There are chemicals and dyes, whose normal export is worth more than £22,000,000. There are electrical goods, pottery and cutlery, each of which export far more than £9,000,000. There are high-class paper goods, the value of whose export in 1938 was £7,000,000, manufactured oils £5,000,000, and leather goods, £4,000,000.

As for the foreign buyers of these exports, the largest buying country in 1937 was the United States, closely followed by South Africa, Australia and India. France, Germany, Canada and Eire formed a second group. A third group was composed of New Zealand, Argentina and Russia. In 1938, the United States took less than three quarters of what she had bought in 1937, but otherwise the list was unchanged.

I have mentioned some of the manufactures, whose export in normal times helps to pay for Great Britain's enormous imports of food and raw material. How is the remainder of these imports paid for, and how is the balance created, which enables British foreign exchanges—in normal times, once more—to show a profit instead of a loss?

Of course the transactions take place in terms of money; but nowadays so many people understand the elements of economics that it is hardly necessary to remind them that money only represents something else. In dealings between independent countries, it immediately represents gold; but there is no country whose gold reserve—even when it is very great—would last very long if it had to be drawn upon every year to liquidate even a small adverse trade balance. Besides, drawing upon it at all would mean that the country is trading at a loss.

When a country really is trading at a loss, it in fact pays for the adverse balance only to a very small extent by exporting gold, and chiefly by three methods—first, by exporting materials, which do not represent production, but are a drain upon the country's possessions of capital values, second, by parting with the ownership, at home, of property which represents capital values, and, third, by parting with the ownership of property, which its nationals possess in other countries.

Strictly speaking, any country exporting minerals, which cannot be renewed, or other commodities, such as timber, which it does not in fact take the trouble to renew, is drawing upon its capital values; and, according to this severe standard, Great Britain, even in normal times, is parting with capital when she exports, or even uses up, coal. However, the enormous reserves already mentioned place the day of reckoning in the far-distant future; and in no immediate sense can the export of coal be considered to be an export of capital at all.

In any case, something has to be exported to pay for imports. That something need not necessarily be sent direct to the country from which the imports were acquired, but to another, so that the exchange is not direct; but exchange there must be.

Therefore, in normal times, Great Britain is really exporting something in addition to the visible exports, which only partly balance her imports; for she is not trading at a loss.

These "invisible exports," which more than make up the difference and leave a profit, are of several kinds, among which are the relatively small but not negligible sums which foreign tourists spend in Great Britain, the very large sums which British shipowners receive from foreign customers in payment of the carriage of goods and persons, the banking and other profits, which the City of London, as a great financial and insurance center, makes out of its foreign customers, and, finally, interest paid by foreigners on the capital invested by Great Britain in their countries.

The financial position of Great Britain is made all the stronger from the fact that, as I have already indicated, about half of her imports come from the Dominions, which are members of the British Commonwealth. As the capital of these countries is based upon sterling, payments to them do not represent a net loss of sterling; and if the Dominions accumulate credit balances in London, they can use them simply to cancel some of their debt to the United Kingdom.

The exports of Great Britain, the invisible and the visible, are what, in normal times, are the constant expression of the purchasing power, to which I referred at the beginning of this chapter—the purchasing power whose continued existence in time of peace is one of the two main elements upon which the economic and financial greatness of the country depends.

However, we are not now at peace, but at war, and it is upon her reserves of purchasing power that Great Britain is obliged to draw—temporarily, of course, as she could not draw upon them indefinitely. The first of these reserves consists of the prestige and the credit, which have been built up by the enormous capital wealth of Great Britain, and now enable the British Government to use the security of the national wealth to finance part of the payment of the huge acquisitions from abroad, and especially from the United States, of arms and munitions, and the raw materials for making them, which have become necessary under the exceptional conditions of war time. The second of the reserves is the nation's capital wealth itself, or, rather, that part of it which is lying abroad and can be liquidated, so as to become available to be used in payment of another part of these acquisitions.

For, during the war, British exports, visible and invisible, although maintained to a surprising extent—they even increased by £5,500,000 during the first ten months of 1940 as against the corresponding period in the previous year—are necessarily liable to certain restrictions, due to factories being engaged upon war work and other similar causes; and in any case, they cannot possibly balance the huge imports of war material. Consequently, there is a large adverse balance, which has to be met by drawing upon the credit secured by the country's accumulated riches and upon those riches themselves.

It is to the United States that the bulk of the payments for war material have to be made. According to the estimate of the financial position of Great Britain, which was presented by the American Secretary of the Treasury, Mr. Morgenthau, to the Foreign Affairs Committee of the United States House of Representatives on January 15, 1941, Great Britain would, if the United States had continued to insist upon cash on delivery, have had to pay, during 1941, $1,554,000,000 for purchases ordered before January 1. Other dollar requirements of the British Empire—Canada being left out of account—bring this sum up to $3,019,000,000 for the year. As against this, the dollar receipts of the British Empire will be $1,555,000,000, again excluding Canada, but including South African and Australian gold exports to the United States. There would therefore be a deficit of $1,464,000,000 for the year.

This deficit could have been more than met by the liquidation of $1,775,000,000 of dollar assets estimated to be owned by Great Britain in the United States in the form of American securities held by British subjects, other investments and gold, especially as this total once more does not include Canada, whose holdings in the United States have been estimated at $2,500,000,000, and as it leaves out $305,-000,000, representing cash balances held by British subjects, which are not included, since it is necessary that they should retain them for the conduct of their business. It also leaves out $33,000,000 of gold owned by the British Government in various countries, not easily accessible at present. Above all, it leaves out the British investments elsewhere in the world than in the United States and Great Britain, which amount to the formidable estimated total of $15,500,000,-000—nearly two thirds being in the British Empire and less than one third in Latin America. This total, moreover, while it includes Great Britain's assets in the Dominions, does not include Dominion assets.

These figures show three things. First of all, they are evidence of the enormous drain of war expenditure even on a country so rich as England; for the United States Federal Reserve Board had estimated, just before the outbreak of the war, that the British Empire possessed gold and dollar assets in the United States to the value of $7,115,000,-000, and Great Britain alone possessed $4,500,000,000, which last now becomes $1,775,000,000. Second, an examination of the assets reveals the fact that even although Great Britain would be ready to sell her shirt in order to procure war material, it is not certain that she could have done so, if the United States had maintained the "cash and carry" attitude, for some of the immediately available assets could not easily be liquidated, even at a loss, and the more important assets still less so. Third, however, the figures display the enormous real wealth of Great Britain and the British Empire, and the confidence which is justified by this solid security, as well as by a certain reputation for honest dealing, good quality and efficiency, which is by no means a negligible moral asset.

There is one aspect of the resources of the British Empire to which sufficient attention is not always given. I have pointed out that the capacity of the various Dominions to furnish valuable raw materials to the Mother Country greatly relieves the financial strain upon London, as the transactions are carried out in sterling and do not involve the acquisition of foreign currency. The capacity to furnish these raw materials to Great Britain, however, also carries with it two others—the capacity to furnish them to friendly neutrals and the capacity to refuse them to the enemy in war time. The importance of the former will be realized when it is said that in the figures given by Mr. Morgenthau, the exports from the Dominions (excluding Canada, moreover) to the United States for the year are given as having been worth $560,000,000 while those from Great Britain (naturally reduced by war conditions) stand at only $165,000,000.

As for the power of refusing raw materials to the enemy, the importance of this will be understood when it is remarked how many raw materials there are of which one or other country of the British Empire is the largest producer and exporter in the world. This is the case with British Malaya in regard to rubber, the Dutch East Indies being second and Ceylon a rather unimportant third. It is the case with Australia for wool, British West Africa for cocoa, British India for cane sugar, Jamaica for bananas, Malaya again for tin, Canada for newsprint paper and platinum and nickel and the Transvaal for gold, the British Empire production of gold being three times as much as that of Russia, which comes second. The British Empire (Canada, Australia and India together) heads the world in the export of wheat, and Canada, as a single exporter, is second only to Argentina. British India is the second exporter of cotton, after the United States, the second of tea, after China, the second of manganese, after Russia, and she is the third producer of tobacco, after the United States and China, although only a small proportion of her tobacco is exported.

So much for the international position; but the economic and financial standing of a people in the markets of the world does not represent the whole of its economic and financial strength. The home front also has its importance.

There are at home the industries which produce that still considerable part of the national food supply which is not imported.

I have mentioned that agriculture stands second among the main productive industries of Great Britain with regard to the number of male workers employed. It is only surpassed by the metal and engineering industry, and that by a bare 2 per cent.

This may sound surprising for a country which is without doubt mainly industrial, a country, moreover, which has to import the greater part of its food; but it shows that the industrialization, great as it has been, has nevertheless left agricultural districts, an agricultural class and a considerable degree of agricultural production.

Before the war, this production was to a great extent confined to what may be called quality goods. Southdown mutton, Scotch beef, Yorkshire and Wiltshire ham, Wiltshire bacon, Cheddar cheese, were better than any imported mutton, beef, ham, bacon or cheese, just as home-grown peaches, grapes, apples, pears and cherries were better than any imported fruit.

Today the production has been intensified; and, naturally, what is now in view is, above all, the amount, in order to reduce the tonnage of food which must be brought in from overseas. Two million acres of rich grass land have been ploughed up during 1940 to grow wheat or potatoes, and there will be more ploughing up this year. The advantage of potato flour to replace wheat flour in bread has been urged by experts, who point out the rapidity and facility with which potatoes can be grown. County War Agricultural Committees have been established, not only to control the compulsory ploughing up of land but to give advice as to its cultivation. These committees have also been authorized to offer assistance of certain kinds. For example, they carry out drainage works in water-logged clay soil, and the farmer is allowed three years in which to repay the half-share of the cost which he will bear. As for extra labor, the Women's Land Army, consisting of volunteers between the ages of eighteen and forty, who are given a month's training, is already 9000 strong, and more are being enrolled. The women serve as tractor drivers, wagoners, shepherdesses, milkmaids and general farm hands. With regard to sheep and cattle, the Government policy is that imported fodder is to go first of all to the milk and dairy herds, as it is considered a first essential to keep up the milk supply of the people; and the Ministry of Food is even arranging to sell milk at a reduced price to every householder where there is an expectant or nursing mother. What further fodder is available is to be distributed for beef cattle and sheep; but the quantity of the meat is to be the aim rather than the quality, and such luxury articles as fat lamb and prime beef are no longer to be produced.

Next in importance to agriculture in the home production of food is fishery. The 45,000 men and 10,000 boys engaged in it are a small number as compared with the 1,500,000 metal workers or the 1,200,000 agriculturists; but they are at work along the whole long coast line of Great Britain, and they catch about 850,000 tons a year— more than any country in Europe, except Norway. This catch is of a total value of about £12,000,000, which is brought up to £15,500,000 if shellfish are included. Many of the 13,300 boats, of a total tonnage of 274,000, have now been mobilized for war purposes; but those that are left still contribute manfully and effectively to the national food supply.

It must not be supposed, however, that the necessity of intensifying the home production of food, in consequence of the difficulty of importing as freely as in normal times, means that there is or is likely to be any real want. German submarines would have to torpedo an enormously greater number of ships than they are ever likely to reach if they are seriously to hamper the supply of food or even of raw materials and armament to Great Britain. Up to the present, there have hardly been any food restrictions. There are some now, and there will be more; but they are and will be caused, not by the difficulty of ships reaching Great Britain, but by the fact that so much of the production of Great Britain has been diverted to war purposes, and that so many of the ships reaching Great Britain are carrying war material instead of other goods and food.

Great Britain is in fact now turning her attention to the production and the importation of guns instead of butter. Germany has been doing this for the last six years; and although the fact has certainly given Germany a considerable start in the matter of guns, it has brought her much nearer to the point of exhaustion in two ways—the point when a country can no longer bear the economic burden of full war production, which brings no economic return, and the point when the inhabitants of a country can no longer stand the physical strain of the privation and undernourishment which inevitably follow the severe rationing of nearly everything. During the six years in which Germany has been carrying this double weight, Great Britain was still keeping up the physical condition of her people, on the one hand, and increasing her reserves of real wealth on the other. With regard to the latter, it has been estimated that the total loss during the first year of the war, in ships torpedoed, buildings destroyed and in other ways, is less than the amount by which the national wealth was increased in the last three years before the war.

Now that Great Britain is concentrating upon war production, which, it must be remembered, includes the production of goods for export, so that the sale of them shall keep up British purchasing power of raw materials, she must reduce the consumption by her own people of everything that is not essential, whether it is food or other goods. This is being done in three ways. The first is by a form of food rationing, whose object is not so much to reduce the total quantity of food eaten as to direct the demand for foods towards those, such as potatoes and oatmeal, which can easily be grown in the country, and are in fact very nourishing, and away from those, such as meat, which have generally to be imported. The second is to discourage luxury spending of every kind, so that unnecessary goods will be neither produced, imported nor sold. This is being done by not allowing the importation of what in war time must be considered to be luxury foods or fruits—oranges for marmalade being excepted—or luxury goods of any kind or the raw material necessary for their manufacture. The released shipping space can be used for absolutely essential materials, and the released labor at home can be applied to production for direct or indirect war purposes. The third method is to reduce the amount of ready money which people might spend on luxuries; and this takes the double form of extracting as much as possible of the surplus income of the people by taxation, levied according to capacity to pay and falling upon the prosperous workingman—who is often drawing very high wages under war conditions—as well as upon the upper and middle classes, and then of floating voluntary loans in such a form as not only to attract the investments of the rich, but to tempt the workingman to accumulate his surplus earnings by saving them instead of spending them.

There are two other effects of this policy. The heavy taxation means that the present generation is adopting the courageous and financially sound policy of paying a large part of the cost of the war itself, instead of handing on the whole debt to their descendants. The savings mean not only that many individuals are laying by resources for the future, but that the nation has avoided and is continuing to avoid the inflation of the currency, which would impoverish every man by sending up prices at a rapid and increasing rate, and thus reducing the real value of the money that he has and that he earns.

This inflation would have been the inevitable consequence of indiscriminate spending today, but it has not taken place. Certain wholesale prices have risen—even as much as 35 per cent. or 40 per cent; but almost the whole of this rise occurred in the first month of the war, and represented real increased costs and risks with regard to certain imported goods and reduced supplies of these goods as the result of war conditions. Since then wholesale prices have risen very little. Moreover, the rise in wholesale prices since the beginning has been followed by a rise in retail prices to only half the same extent.

The weight of direct taxation is such as no people, which had not been trained for generations in the duty of openly and consciously paying for the cost of Government, would have been ready to accept. The income tax now stands at 8s. 6d. in the pound on normal incomes, which means that a man is handing to the State 42.5 per cent of what comes in to him during the year. The sliding scale, operating in the super-tax, brings the percentage to 90 on the highest incomes. Indirect taxation has been as sternly increased as direct, and is estimated to bring in £1,500,000,000 this year, and still more next year.

The taxation part of this financial policy is, of course, compulsory; but it has been ungrudgingly, if not cheerfully, accepted by the nation, and the main criticism in Parliament was that it was not severe enough. As for the savings part, Mr. J. M. Keynes, the most brilliant of British economists, had advocated compulsory savings, as he did not believe that the mass of the British people would ever consent voluntarily to put aside the greater part of their surplus earnings. He has now admitted that the voluntary savings movement has achieved more than could ever have been expected.

Of course there has been a movement, and the satisfactory result has not been reached without a vigorous propaganda. The National Savings campaign was started in November, 1939, and it was hoped to reach £475,000,000 in the first year. In fact this total was exceeded by £500,000 in the purchase of War Savings Certificates alone; and if the sale of Government securities to small investors through the Post Offices is included, the total of money lent to the State by the working classes during the year reaches £482,-000,000. Add to this the sums subscribed in larger amounts, and the year's savings of the nation reach £1,140,000,000.

It may be deduced from what I have said about the savings of the working classes that their lot since the beginning of the war has not been such a very unhappy one, and is not today. They have often been in discomfort and in danger; but they have been in work, and their wages have steadily been increasing. The new national minimum wage of £2-8-0 a week for agricultural workers means an average increase of 30 per cent. In the metal, engineering and shipbuilding trades there has been an average increase of 43 per cent. In the textile and clothing trades the average has been 25 per cent. These rises more than compensate for the 20 per cent increase which is believed to have taken place in the cost of living; and although wages have fallen in some cases—especially in the industries which are not essential to war production—the general body of workingmen is undoubtedly in an improved position. So are the majority of those who were previously unemployed; for then they had no position at all, and at one moment there were 2,000,-000 of them. The number of employed receiving assistance had already dropped, in July, 1939, to 462,000, the lowest figure for fifteen years, and now it may almost be said that the only unemployed are the virtually unemployable.

That organized labor should cooperate wholeheartedly in the British industrial war effort was essential to the establishment of this huge machine in so short a time, and to the results, which it is already producing and will produce in increasing proportion; but that Labor has in fact cooperated in this way may surprise any one who knows the history of industrial conflicts in Great Britain during the last thirty years.

In the other war, Labor goodwill was by no means so easily obtained as it has now been. For several years before 1914, the Trades Unions had been trying and asserting their strength, and they continued in the same temper through the war, during which several disastrous strikes were averted only by the persuasive genius of Mr. Lloyd George.

After the war, relations between the employers and their men became still more bitter, and eventually culminated in the prolonged coal strike and the General Strike of 1926. The General Strike collapsed, chiefly because the public opinion of the nation was not with the men, and the mass of people readily responded to the Government appeal for volunteers to keep the essential services at work. The result was that the Trades Unions became discredited, even among their own supporters, many of whom resigned; and their powers were even reduced by legislation.

Fortunately, the majority of the employers did not press their victory home by becoming intractable and domineering, but saw that it was to their interest to avoid the waste and loss which are caused by friction and by strikes, and to settle future differences by consultation. This conciliatory spirit was maintained on both sides up to the present war, and is one of the reasons for the cooperation of Labor in the great armaments drive of today.

There is another reason, however. It is that the working-men of England have realized that this war is not only the Government's war, but their own war. They have realized it partly because they have seen their own houses bombed, and their own wives and children killed before their eyes; but they have realized it also because they have understood that the enemy which Great Britain is fighting is also the enemy of what they themselves hold dear—freedom to speak their minds, freedom to create their own organizations in their own way. They have understood that the pacifism and disarmament which they had supported might be bought at too dear a price, and that the new threat of force must be met by force.

The support which Labor has thus given to the prosecution of the war from the beginning was confirmed when Mr. Churchill had the vision and the good sense to offer to the Labor Party two places in the small War Cabinet of eight, and when the Labor Party, which had previously refused to join the Government, authorized the acceptance of the offer—an acceptance whose spirit was heartily confirmed last autumn at the annual meeting of the Trades Union Congress.

Great Britain can hardly be described as a pioneer in social legislation, and she has not yet advanced as far in it as some other countries; but it may be said that today the wage-earning classes are well protected by the State against the misfortunes arising from sickness, accident, unemployment and old age.

What is called "Poor Relief" has been in existence since the sixteenth century; but for hundreds of years it was very limited, and its administration was harsh and unimaginative right up to our own time—see the early chapters of the *Oliver Twist* of Dickens. Fortunately, it was supplemented by much private generosity, which, however, was not always without condescension and patronage.

The stage has now been reached when the workingman can demand certain compensation and assistance as of right, and is entitled to certain other insurance benefits, which are provided from a fund to which the employer and the State have compulsorily contributed, as well as himself.

The first principle to be established was that an employer must compensate his workman for any accident arising out of or in the course of the employment. This dates back to 1897, and, as the law stands at present, compensation may amount to as much as £600 in the case of a fatal accident or £1-10-0 a week during total incapacity as the result of a non-fatal accident.

The next step was taken in 1908, when was passed the first Old Age Pension Act, under which any person, male or female, who reached the age of seventy, was entitled to a pension of 10/– a week from the State—a married couple, both of whose members were over seventy, being therefore entitled to a joint pension of £1. Certain "means tests," limiting the benefits to those whose income from other sources was below a certain amount, were afterwards introduced, but these have now been abolished.

National Health Insurance, which was first established in 1911, introduced a new principle, that of compulsory weekly contributions by both employers and workmen, which were made by sticking stamps on the insurance cards. The total weekly contribution is 1s. 8d. for men and 1s. 2d. for women (employer and employed each having therefore to pay 10d. and 7d.); but of this total only 9d. for men and 8½d. for women is allocated to Health Insurance, the remainder going towards a contributory pension (independent of the State pension for Old Age described above). The sickness benefits include free medical treatment and drugs, and a temporary sickness allowance for a maximum of 26 weeks of 15s. for men, 12s. for unmarried women and widows and 10s. for married women. If the illness continues for more than 26 weeks, what is called Disablement Benefit, at half the above rates, is payable.

Finally, the workers in certain trades, which have recently been extended to include agriculture, are entitled to unemployment assistance, after having been employed for a certain minimum time and having paid the necessary contributions—for the unemployment scheme is also contributory, although the contribution is divided into three equal parts, employer, workman and the State. The details of the scheme cannot be explained briefly; but it may be said that in 1938 the average weekly allowance was £1-4-3, to which special winter allowances, averaging 2s. 1d. a week, should be added.

In the foregoing pages, I have been giving you a quantity of facts and figures, because to do so is the only way to record the pulse of laboring, trading, manufacturing and seafaring England. I should, however, like to be able also to give you a sense of the living blood that courses through that pulse. I should like to take you to the offices of a great Trades Union, and show you how efficiently Labor manages its wide organization, to a Trades Union Congress, and let you hear what direct and powerful orators the Labor movement throws up from its ranks, and with what sound common sense those ranks react to what is said to them.

I should like to make you feel some of the romance of industry and commerce; for they have their romantic side. There is a fierce beauty in the roaring flames of furnaces, in the white heat of molten metal, and in the tall chimneys and the smoke which blacken the sky for miles and miles across whole areas of Central England, and eat into the rolling silences of the Yorkshire moorland. There are tenderness and passion and sacrifice even in the long, low and unlovely rows of dull gray homes of the factory workers. There is grandeur in the towering sides of ships in the seaports, in the dizzy drop of the quayside walls into the water, in the great piles of merchandise just taken on shore or waiting to be loaded.

There are visions of distant lands to be called up by a walk through the warehouses of a great port like London or Liverpool, warehouses stacked with goods, which are "in bond," that is to say, in transit from one foreign country to another, and therefore have not been made to pay the Customs duties for entrance into England. In one of these warehouses, you will see tusks of ivory, piled up to the roof, and the mind pictures all the elephants from which they were taken. In another you will find cases of exotic fruits, from one of which perhaps a serpent, which had nestled in it when it was packed in a tropic land, now escapes into the damp and smoky English air.

Above all, I should like to help you to feel some of the spirit of the City of London, which is the hub of all this industry, the heart of all this commerce, the great center of distributors and middlemen, of importers and exporters, of bankers and financiers. Factory furnaces and chimneys you can see elsewhere, with the rough little lodgings of those who work in them, and they will not be so very different from those of England, although there are not many countries in which they cover such great areas. Seaports you can see elsewhere too, and one seaport is much like another, if it is big enough. But nowhere will you find anything quite like the City of London.

Remember that the City of London is not London. It was once, but that was more than three hundred years ago, when the whole of London was contained within the City Wall. Today, the City of London still has the same boundaries, though the wall is gone; but London has spread for miles and miles beyond it on every side. Eight million people live in London, but not 11,000 live in the City. To be sure, the comparison is not quite fair, for a great many more than 11,000 people work in the City during the day, though they go home to sleep outside it. Nevertheless, the City is only a small enclosure in London's vastness. Yet in the City are the head offices of all the great banks and financial firms, all the insurance companies, all the mercantile houses, all the shippers, most of the manufacturers, whose works are in various parts of the country, and the innumerable agents, commissioners and speculators, who congregate around these many businesses. The City of London is, in

fact, a hive of offices, and, like a hive, is in a constant state
of activity.

Even so, there are other places of which the same could
be said; but the City of London is an entity. It has a tradition and a personality; and Londoners in general—it may
even be said Englishmen—would be sorry to see that tradition and that personality go. They guard it jealously.

That is why it was decided in 1888, when the London
County Council, as a popularly elected body, was created
to take over London's government, that the City of London should remain, as a small central enclosure, under the
administration of its Lord Mayor and its Aldermen and
Common Council, who are not popularly elected at all, but
are chosen by the very restricted franchise of the ancient
City Companies or Guilds, under a charter which goes back
to the year 1214, and with municipal traditions which are
as old as the Roman occupation. That is why the City of
London still has its own police force—whose helmet is slightly
different from that of the Metropolitan Police—and its own
Courts of Summary Jurisdiction, though in many other
matters it falls into the general London system, and sends
four members to the London County Council.

The men who do business in the City can hardly be said
to look romantic. Bankers and stockbrokers and financial
magnates maintain the tradition of wearing black, and they
have short black coats, striped trousers, stiff white collars
and black hats—but not always the black silk hat which used
to be *sine qua non*—and they carry neatly rolled umbrellas.
Many clerks are in black also, with hard round hats and
umbrellas not so neatly rolled. Other clerks, and most of
the men engaged in general business, permit themselves to
wear colored suits; but they all look prosaic enough.

And yet each one of them, even though it be uncon-
sciously, is touched by the historic spirit of the place. The
institutions where their dealings are conducted or where

their credit is enshrined all have about them something which is not only as traditional, but as little based on logic and legality as the English Constitution.

Lloyd's, which I have already mentioned, is an example of England's traditionalism. The Stock Exchange, which no one who is not a member can enter, so that the real buyer or seller has to apply to a stockbroker, who in turn effects the transaction through a stockjobber, is an example of English individualism.

The most curious institution of all, however, is the Bank of England. It is one more instance of the English dislike of starting anything afresh, and the English preference for grafting the new on to the stock of the old.

When the Bank of England was founded in 1694, it was formed as a private company to make profits for the shareholders, who had subscribed the capital for it; and a private company in theory it remains to this day. It still has shareholders, and they still draw profits; and although these profits are in fact smaller than those of the ordinary Joint Stock Banks, there is no legal obligation upon the Bank of England to place public policy before private interest. Its Governor and Directors are not appointed by the State, and it is not a Department of the Government service. It may lend money to the Government; but what it possesses does not belong to the Government.

Nevertheless it has been from its inception the banker to the Government, and a military guard watches over it at night to this day. It collects the National Revenue and discharges the National obligations—National Debt interest, pay of the Fighting and Civil Services, and so forth—and the gold which it has in its vaults is practically the whole gold reserve of the country. It also issues Bank notes, and it is the only bank in England today which has the right to issue Bank notes. In peace times, these notes have a world-wide acceptance and circulation; and yet they are not, strictly speaking, based upon the credit of the British Government, but upon that of the Bank of England alone.

Although nearly all the business buildings of the City are modern, the romantic haze of history hangs about the place, and the name of every street carries the imagination back to the time, three hundred years ago, when the City was indeed all London.

Even two hundred years ago, a foreign visitor described Kensington as a village, two miles from London, Marylebone as another village a mile away, Chelsea and Hampstead and Hackney as other villages again, and Islington and Lambeth as small market towns. Today all of them are parts of London.

Three hundred years ago, Westminster itself, with the King's Palace and the Abbey and the Abbey lands, was separated from London by open country. On the way to Westminster, at the end of the Strand, then really a riverside walk, as its name implies, had been erected an elaborate Gothic cross, to mark the last of many halts in the journey by which a Queen's body was carried across England to its final resting place in Westminster Abbey. That monument is Charing Cross, which now stands in the yard of a railway station, and is taken as the center of London for calculating mileage distances and the Metropolitan taxicab area; but then it stood in the middle of fields, as indeed the name of the adjoining church, St. Martin's in the Fields, continues to testify today, as does also the name of the Haymarket, a street a few hundred yards away, where certainly it would now be impossible to buy any hay, as it contains two of London's most fashionable theatres and one of her smartest hotels.

The Haymarket and Covent Garden, which is no longer a garden, but London's chief vegetable and flower market, are among the few street names outside the boundaries of the ancient City which breathe history; but the City itself is full of them. Some of these names are of gates in the former City wall—Bishopsgate and Cripplegate (where cripples begged for alms) and Aldgate and Moorgate and Aldersgate and Newgate and Ludgate. One, London Wall, marks the wall itself. All of them are merely crowded streets today, except that Newgate also gives its name to the oldest of London prisons. Other streets suggest forgotten associations of other kinds. In our time there are no more Jews doing business in Old Jewry than in any other part of the City. Nor is Love Lane any longer a resort of lovers. You cannot get bread in Bread Street, puddings in Pudding Lane, milk in Milk Street, the gilt spurs of a Knight in Giltspur Street, hosiery in Hosier Lane, shoes in Shoe Lane, ironmongery in Ironmonger Lane, nor chickens in the Poultry, though no doubt there must have been a time when these were the places for each kind of shopping. There are no longer any farriers in Farringdon Street, nor is there a pit where cock fights can be watched in Cock Lane, or a falconry in Falcon Street. There is no Basing Hall or Leaden Hall or Copt Hall in Basinghall Street or Leadenhall Street or Copthall Avenue. There must be few angels in Angel Court, there is no stream in Wallbrook, and the offices in Maiden Lane are occupied rather by business men than young women. Old Broad Street is far from broad, according to modern standards of traffic; and although there are certainly bankers in Lombard Street, they are not the Italian Lombardy gold merchants, from whom the street took its name. It is difficult to believe that once there were really fields at Moorfields, and that such greenery was within the City boundary.

One is lost in speculation as to what needle was ever threaded in Threadneedle Street, at the corner of which the Bank of England stands, and when and how the threading took place; and the fact that journalists sometimes figuratively refer to the Bank as "the Old Lady of Threadneedle

Street" does not offer much assistance. Probably none of the hurried people who catch trains every day at Blackfriars station stop to think of the monastery that once was there, any more than the journalists who rush to the newspaper offices in Whitefriars Street remember that other monastery which used to occupy the site.

There are no knights on horseback in Knight Rider Street and no carters in Carter Lane. In Cloak Lane cloaks cannot be purchased. Water Lane no longer leads down to the Thames, but stops on the upper level of the wide street, called the Victoria Embankment, which, in the nineteenth century, was made as a wall along the river's edge and involved the suppression of the water gates, from one of which Watergate Street took its name. One ancient water gate indeed survives, outside the boundaries of the City, at Charing Cross. It is that of the garden of what was once the Duke of York's palace at York House; but it now stands high and dry, on the Embankment, and is preserved only as a curiosity.

In the precincts of Saint Paul's cathedral, there is a group of street names—Paternoster Row, Ave Maria Lane and Amen Corner—which have an ecclesiastical appropriateness, but no longer any ecclesiastical connection; for they are now the home of book publishers, while Saint Paul's Churchyard itself is the address of the principal wholesale drapers.

There are other City addresses which call to the imagination visions much more picturesque than the prosaic present reality. Thus Hatton Garden has not been a garden for centuries, but is a street where most of the London diamond merchants are to be found; and Saint Martin's-le-Grand is not today a church, but the General Post Office.

A round Norman church still stands to remind the barristers who have made the Temple their place of business since the fourteenth century, that the Knights Templars created it before them. The very name of London Bridge recalls the fact that, until the middle of the eighteenth century, it was the only bridge over the Thames in the London area, where there are now more than a dozen. The Tower of London, so famous as a State prison in the fifteenth and sixteenth centuries, still rears its massive head between the City's offices and warehouses and the river, as it did when it was a Norman fortress, and London began to nestle under it; and it still makes its guard wear the uniform of the period of the Tudors.

It is only a few years ago that three middle-class schools, the Charterhouse school, Merchant Taylors' School ("Taylors' " with the old-fashioned spelling) and Christ's Hospital—the last with the pupils still in the long gowns, white neckbands and bright yellow stockings which they wore in the time of Queen Elizabeth—moved from the premises which they had occupied for nearly four hundred years in London to the country, and released their fabulously valuable building sites for business offices.

The City churches, nine of which survived the Great Fire of London in 1666, and fifty of which were then rebuilt by Christopher Wren, the architect of Saint Paul's Cathedral, belong to a time when people still lived in what is now nothing but a business quarter; but, although they are nowadays necessarily almost empty of congregation, they have been maintained as part of London's historic tradition, in spite of the fact that covetous eyes have been turned upon the land which they occupy. So have the thirty-six meeting halls of the ancient Livery Companies, or Guilds, of which I shall speak in a moment. It has been left to enemy air incendiarism to burn down or severely damage eight of the churches, including those with such picturesque names as St. Vedast, St. Andrew by the Wardrobe, St. Mary Aldermanbury and St. Lawrence Jewry, and three of the halls, including the Guildhall of the City of London itself.

However, I fancy it will take more than a few bombs to

shake the foundations of City of London tradition. The legend of Dick Whittington, who arrived in London, a penniless lad, on foot with his cat, and was encouraged to go on by the cheering sound of the bells of Bow Church, so that he prospered and three times became Lord Mayor of London, has fixed itself in the imagination of the people for five hundred years; and even though the office of Lord Mayor of London no longer has any political importance, and is merely symbolic, the legend remains as a children's fairy story, on which every one has been brought up.

The conception of the Lord Mayor of London as a very important person is all the more persistent as the decorative side of his functions has been admirably well maintained. The Livery Companies, of one of which he is a member, and who elect him, are all rich; the City of London is itself rich, and is the owner of great properties; and he himself is almost certainly a rich man, who is glad to spend freely during the year of his tenure of office. Consequently, there is always money for entertaining and for pageantry.

The great occasion for the latter is the day after the new Lord Mayor takes up his duties. On November 9, he goes in procession, in his golden coach, through the City, to pay his respects to the Judges at the Law Courts; and the golden coach is only equalled in magnificence by the one in which the King and Queen drive to open Parliament. As for the procession, it is always historical in part—as I know well, for one year I organized it myself. The costumes, as well as the brilliant red uniforms of the military bands, give a gaiety and color, which delight the London crowds, who always turn out to see it, as well as the middle-class children, who are taken to windows along the route. In the evening, a great banquet is given at the Guildhall. The King and Queen attend, the gold plate of the City is displayed and the Prime Minister of the day usually chooses the occasion to make an important statement on foreign policy.

During his year, the Lord Mayor frequently gives a large luncheon party, at his official residence at the Mansion House, in order to offer the Honorary Freedom of the City to any distinguished stranger who may be visiting London, and he is always ready to call a meeting to open a public subscription in aid of the victims of any disaster which may have taken place in any part of the world. The Lord Mayor of London is not only a traditional figure. He has become an almost indispensable national figurehead, and is so regarded in other countries.

The mediæval pomp and scrupulously observed ceremony with which the Lord Mayor is surrounded, his robes, his fur-bordered cocked hat, his gold and jewelled chain, the great gilt mace that is carried before him, his quaintly named officers—the Recorder, the Chamberlain, the Common Serjeant, the Comptroller, the Remembrancer, the Secondary, the Sword Bearer, the Clerk of the Seal, the Common Cryer (note the spelling) and the Marshal—no less than their salaries, which range from £4000 a year downwards, are all survivals from a past when the London Corporation grew rich and powerful in stubbornly defending civic rights against aristocratic domination. They are also survivals from a past when the Lord Mayor conducted the whole administration of his little walled town. It is obvious, for instance, that the Common Cryer, who draws a salary of £500 a year, no longer goes around the streets of the City with a bell to read public notices. For one thing, he would not be heard above the noise of the traffic, if he did.

Just as the Lord Mayor and the Aldermen were once the defenders of civic rights in general, so the separate Livery companies, to one or other of which they belong, were once trade associations, engaged in fighting for separate trade privileges, and, if possible, monopolies. It was in these struggles that they also grew rich, and acquired their prestige. Today, the struggles are things of the past, as are also many of the trades from which the companies take their names; but the wealth and some of the prestige remain. In the nineteenth century, the wealth was used, partly for giving gargantuan feasts—to which male guests only were invited—and partly for maintaining charitable institutions and schools. This continues today, except that the proportion expended in banquets has considerably diminished.

There are seventy-eight of these Livery Companies still in existence, though some are extinct. One of them, the Mercers' Company, has an income from rents and other investments of £111,000 a year, seven others have more than £50,000 each, five others, more than £20,000 and eight others again, more than £7000. The ancient trades which they represent include the Salters, the Skinners and the Vintners among the twelve most important companies, and, among the others, the Armourers and Brasiers, the Bowyers (who date back to the days when English armies fought with bow and arrow), the Barbers (who were Barber-Surgeons in former times—their hall is one of those which have been bombed), the Broiderers (who embroidered), the Coopers (who made barrels), the Cordwainers (or shoemakers), the Curriers (who curried leather), the Fanmakers, the Fletchers (makers of arrows), the Girdlers, the Gold and Silver Wyredrawers, the Horners (who manufactured spoons and cups and other things out of horn), the Patten (or wooden clog) Makers, the Pewterers, the Playing Cards Makers, the Tallow Chandlers, the Wax Chandlers, the Upholders (upholsterers) and even some, whose trades have not only disappeared, but have never been heard of by any one who is not an historian. Such, for instance, are the Loriners, who used to make spurs and horses' bits, and still have a Guild which is one of the largest in the City, as it includes 380 Liverymen, not one of whom, it is certain, practices the trade in question.

Even the Companies, which bear the names of trades still existing and active, no longer compose their membership exclusively of men practising those trades, even if they include any. Lord Bradbury, the Prime Warden of the important Goldsmiths' Company, has had a distinguished career as a Treasury official and a financier; but he has never been a goldsmith; and when one runs down the list of the Peers, military officers, barristers, clergymen and others, who are the Wardens of the other Companies, one cannot imagine that many of them have any particular connection with the trade which their Company is supposed to represent.

It may be supposed that all this picturesque heritage from the past is destined to be swept away, together with the wealth, the property, the privileges and the vested interests which go with it; but that is not what is likely to happen. Already the property has become to be regarded more and more as a public charge, and the income has been spent less and less irresponsibly, and more and more in the public interest. This tendency will certainly continue, and the value of certain sinecures will be diminished; but the offices themselves and the ceremonies connected with them will surely continue. The English hold fast to their history; and, once more, they will preserve the form of the old in order to give prestige to the reality of the new.

Chapter VIII

LITERATURE, THE ARTS AND

THE THEATRE

IN MANY countries, and especially in Latin countries, the Englishman is admitted to have a good business sense, a good political sense and a good sporting sense; but he is not believed to stand very high in matters of the intellect—in literature, in the arts and in science.

It is true that the ordinary Englishman is not an intellectual. Nor will you find literary or artistic subjects often crop up in the conversation of an English family; and although it may be claimed, as I have said elsewhere, that while the English have no artistic sense, they have a natural instinct for poetry, and also for the beauties of nature, few of them realize that they possess this instinct, or are willing to admit it when they do. On the contrary, they tend to be shy about it, as they are about all expressions of feeling or intelligence.

Perhaps it is this habit of being rather ashamed of cleverness and still more of art, which has brought it about that only in our own day has any British Government ever thought it worth while to tell the peoples of other countries anything about British intellectual or artistic achievements—in marked contrast with the admirable cultural propaganda which has long been carried on by certain other governments. Or is it once more that curious mixture of pride and modesty, which makes the English always refuse to cry their virtues, because they were there for any one who cares to look for them?

And yet there is something to cry; for the achievements of this inartistic and unintellectual people in literature, science and the arts are such that the English have produced a very high proportion of the men of genius of the world.

These English men of genius have always had to struggle in an uncongenial, if not hostile atmosphere; but they seem even to have gathered strength from the want of comprehension which met them. Indeed, it may be that, at least in art, philistinism is not such a bad climate for any talent which is vigorous and original. A really fine artist is in much less danger of his individuality being smothered in philistine surroundings, where he has to struggle to impose himself, than he might be in an artistic society, where it would run the risk of simply being diluted by too comprehending and too sympathetic early praise or confused by the influence of other artists.

I have alluded in another chapter to the splendid body of English lyric poetry, which has existed with hardly a break for nearly four hundred years, as being the greatest monument which our race will bequeath to posterity; but the roll of genius has included great Englishmen in every art. As for science, schoolboys all over the world connect the name of Newton with the law of gravity, that of Harvey with the circulation of the blood, that of Faraday with electricity; and that of Darwin with the origin of man; while every science student of today knows the contemporary fame of Rutherford in radio-activity and chemistry in general, Thomason in electricity, magnetism and physics, Oliver Lodge in wireless telegraph and Jeans and Eddington in astronomy.

More than once, and in more than one branch of literature or philosophy or art, has England led the world. At the end of the sixteenth century, the Elizabethan poets, with the mighty Shakespeare at their head, and the Elizabethan translators of the Bible, were not only forging a language which remains today the richest in vocabulary of any in Europe, but they enabled England to be the first modern country to create a great dramatic literature. It sprang, so to speak, fully armed from their imagination, like Pallas Athene from the head of Zeus; for when Shakespeare wrote plays which still hold the stage, the English theatre itself had only been in existence for some twenty years, and was the only theatre in northern Europe.

In the seventeenth century, English music, written for that very difficult instrument, the lute, was more famous than that of any other people.

In the eighteenth century, the political philosophy of Locke was so much studied and admired in France that it has been said that he might almost be described as the grandfather of the French Revolution.

Early in the nineteenth century, English painting, in the landscapes of John Constable, and English poetry and romance, in the works of Byron and Walter Scott, were at the foundations of the Romantic movement in France and Germany. When Constable's picture, "The Hay Cart," was exhibited in the Paris Salon in 1822, Delacroix, who was then quite young, was so impressed—as he relates in his diary—by the English painters' process of giving an impression of green by different touches of many tones of green that he rushed away to make certain last moment alterations in his own first important picture, "The Massacres of Scio," which was already hanging in another room at the same Salon. On the other hand, the indebtedness of both Victor Hugo and Alexandre Dumas to Walter Scott was immense and was freely acknowledged.

Finally, towards the end of the nineteenth century, the

Pre-Raphaelite painters once more carried an English artistic influence to the European continent.

Perhaps the most striking thing in the long list of English men of genius in literature and the arts is the unmistakable Englishness of almost every one of them. The two who are by far the greatest, Shakespeare and Dickens, have conquered the world; but they also strike chords to which only an Englishman can respond; so that it can be said that it takes an Englishman to understand them fully. The same is true of almost all the great figures in our literature—so varied, so individual and so English. The crystal beauty of Milton's verse is classical, but it is solidly English. English to the bone as well as are the piety of Vaughan, the horror of Webster, the grace of Herrick and Waller, the color, the vivacity and the popular sympathy of Defoe, the rugged and simple faith of Bunyan, the self-revealing pettiness of Pepys, the urbanity of Addison, the placid rural tenderness of Gray, the gay hunting "Hallo" of Surtees, the humorous primness of Jane Austen, the gipsy spirit of Borrow and, to rise to a higher plane, the dark passion of Emily Brontë, the soul purity of William Blake, the dying heart-throbs of Keats, the pagan ecstacy of Shelley, the reverent serenity of Wordsworth, and the rich humanity of Fielding—and each one so personal that no one has ever been able to imitate any of them.

Just as it is impossible to imagine any but an English painter giving that particular kind of humor and character to every face in the street scenes and drawing-room satires of Hogarth, just that upstanding distinction to the portraits of Gainsborough, that atmosphere to the clouds and trees of Constable or that brilliantly colored and wild majesty to the sunsets and storms of Turner, so one can hardly conceive the works of any of the authors that I have mentioned being of any but an English writer, in any language but English, and one can hardly conceive any but an English reader really feeling what they mean.

That is perhaps why so few of our masterpieces have been translated into other languages. The translator is always a traitor, as the Italian proverb has it; for every people has its character, which it is hard for a foreigner to understand. In most countries other than England, however, literature expresses an attitude of mind which is at least European, if it does not extend to the whole civilized world. Any cultivated reader can take the meaning, if only he knows the words—or at least he can take part of the meaning. However, I would defy any one who is not English to take as much as half of the real meaning of any of the authors of whom I have spoken; and, as for some of them, whom we English rate among the highest, to see anything in them at all—Bunyan, or Surtees, or Blake, for instance, to mention only three of widely different natures.

What separates English literature from all the rest of the literature of Europe is also what differentiates English humor from wit. The Englishman is interested in character rather than intellectual imagination, in instinct rather than artistry, in unfettered natural inspiration rather than form. He finds unity in diversity; and yet it is not unity that he seeks, but sympathy. This outlook is no doubt illogical, whimsical, sentimental, simple and sometimes rather childish, and may suggest a mind that is immature; but it is English.

Nevertheless, there are exceptions to the specifically English quality of our masterpieces. It will have been noticed that the names which I have given do not include one or two of the greatest. Byron, for instance, is in the very front rank of our poets; but he is not untranslatable—in so far as poetry may be said to be translatable at all. For he speaks the language of Europe. He has, indeed, often been translated, and is highly appreciated in other countries; but he came of stock which was not English, but Scottish; and the mind of Scotland is much nearer to Europe than that of England. So is the mind of Ireland. No one has written English prose more nervous than Swift, spoken English more eloquent than Burke, evoked images more touching than Goldsmith nor composed dramatic dialogue at once more theatrically living and more witty than Sheridan. They all translate easily into other languages; for they are not English, but Irish. The romances of Walter Scott and the *French Revolution* of Thomas Carlyle have been translated again and again. They are at once in tune with the European, and especially the Latin mind; for they are not English, but Scottish. If the lyrics of Robert Burns, so drenched with wistful beauty, have not found translators also, it is perhaps on account of the Lowland Scots dialect in which most of them are written; for there is nothing in their spirit which is not equally translatable.

The names which I have been giving are those of men whose permanent place in our English Pantheon is already assured. When it comes to presenting a picture of literature and the arts over the period which can be covered by the memory of a single lifetime, it is not possible to classify them so easily; for they are still on probation before posterity. However, one can at least record a few contemporary judgments and personal impressions without claiming or attempting to give a complete catalogue, even of the outstanding names, and, far less, to place the names given in any order of merit; and I can add something to the personal side of these impressions, as it has been my fortune to see and talk with, and in many cases to know well, most of the great writers and artists of my time.

My father used to tell me of the enthusiasm which was aroused among the young writers and critics of his generation when the poems, first of Browning and then of Swinburne, originally appeared. In those days, Browning was considered to be such abstruse reading that there were Browning Societies to explain his meaning, which seems clear enough to us. As for Swinburne, there was still a legend, during my time at Oxford, that when he was an undergraduate, and took too much wine—which he was always rather apt to do—he could be heard, alone in his rooms, extemporizing the sort of gorgeous verse which he afterwards put on to paper. Towards the end of his life, I was taken to see him in that retreat on Putney Hill, where he lived under the jealous care of his friend, Watts-Dunton—the setting has, of course, been immortalized by Max Beerbohm.

The third great nineteenth-century poet, Tennyson, looked the part in a way which was far more theatrically effective than either of his two younger contemporaries, Browning and Swinburne. Imposing, long-haired, bearded, deep-voiced, with a great broad-brimmed hat and a flowing cloak, he was a figure who could not be mistaken and could hardly be forgotten. Today, his verse seems to carry something of the same rather flamboyantly romantic impressiveness—great at its best, but apt to betray a certain pretentiousness at its less good.

There is another poet, a friend of Tennyson and born in the same year as he, but not regarded in his lifetime as being in the first rank, whose stature has, however, grown progressively ever since. This is Edward Fitzgerald, the author of "The Rubaiyat of Omar Khayyam," a poem whose cheerful epicurean pessimism and lyric beauty have taken the fancy of successive generations. It is still more read by educated Englishmen today than perhaps any other piece of verse in the language.

I have described Fitzgerald as the author of this poem; for although it professes to be translated from a Persian original, it would hardly be possible to find anything more representative of one side of the English spirit—its serene and "sporting" acceptance of the best and the worst, as they come.

It is on this single poem that the reputation of Fitzgerald

rests; and it is perhaps peculiar to England to have many poets who are remembered by one perfect thing. The past is full of examples; and in our own time it is sufficient to cite W. E. Henley, a vigorous journalist, author of those four magnificent stanzas, beginning "Out of the night that covers me," and W. J. Cory, of whom three poems do indeed appear in the *Golden Treasury*, but who lives by his short lament on Heraclitus. It may even be said that a poet has sometimes been established by a single line, as was Laurence Binyon, a shy and distinguished man of letters and British Museum official, who is an authority on Chinese art, but who is known to millions because a poem of his on the young men who were killed in the last war contains the beautiful line

"They shall grow not old, as we that are left grow old."

Poetry, which has always had its audience, but an audience which, at the close of the nineteenth century, had dwindled to a select few, has been a rising stock among the general public since the end of the last war, and perhaps earlier; for during that war itself the deep feelings which were touched found their expression in verse—first in what has been well described as the cloistral verse of Rupert Brooke and the gallant self-sacrifice of Julian Grenfell, then in the disillusion of Wilfred Owen and finally in the rebellious bitterness of Siegfried Sassoon.

The new vogue for poetry had indeed begun earlier still, and I think it came to England from Ireland. Much of it was centered around that fine poet and vigorous personality W. B. Yeats. He was a lanky, long-haired, apparently absent-minded, but really very alert creature, whose narrow, clean-shaven face always seemed to me to suggest a horse. He provided most of the inspiration, not only for the Irish literary movement, but for the young Irish theatre, which, with its company of Irish actors, made an impression on literary London at the beginning of the century.

After the last war was over, poetry found a public which it had not had for many years. The classics were bought and read, and so were the works of then still living but no longer young poets, such as Rudyard Kipling, Thomas Hardy and Robert Bridges, already of an older generation, and John Masefield—the present poet laureate, or official poet—and Walter de la Mare of a generation rather younger. Above all, new poets found readers with new work in a spirit entirely new. Some of this work retains a little of the old metric fashions—and even rhyme—but much of it breaks away from all past conventions to seek a fresh expression of an age with which it is felt that those conventions are no longer in tune. The younger poets have sought this new expression in various ways. T. S. Eliot, who is now a man of over fifty, but certainly belongs to the young movement, finds it in sudden changes of tone to colloquialism, as in· his play on Becket, "Murder in the Cathedral." Stephen Spender, W. H. Auden and Day Lewis have chosen other means of breaking down the barriers.

However, if poetry readers have been on the increase, the big book public in England remains the public for fiction; and it really is a big public. The English may not be very intellectual, but they are great readers. They read by taking books through innumerable circulating libraries and book clubs, and they read by buying—mostly the many cheap editions which have recently sprung up. With this public, even the new taste for poetry is but a small thing compared with the enormous demand for novels. In 1938, for instance, over five hundred books of poetry were published, and only two hundred of them were reprints. In the same year, however, appeared not far short of five thousand novels, and two thousand of them were new.

There can naturally be no pretense that the great majority of these novels bears much relation to literature. Many of them are of the superficially sentimental kind, and many others are detective stories—for the fashion in England for this kind of escape reading, though its decline is prophesied every year, is still in being. Indeed, there are examples of better and better writing in this sort of tale. A high standard was set, nearly fifty years ago, in the "Sherlock Holmes" stories by Conan Doyle, whom I remember as a great, good-humored colossus, with a joy in playing cricket, a leaning toward spiritualism and a certain pride in the fact that he never erased or re-wrote a line of his work—which makes it all the more surprising that its literary quality is so good. Ever since, there have been occasional writers of detective fiction, such as E. C. Bentley, who have kept up to his level.

The taste for detective stories is, really, one expression of love of novels of adventure, which is by no means peculiarly English—witness Alexandre Dumas in France—but which is typical of what most Englishmen seek when they read a book. They are little interested in analysis of personality or motive, and still less in analysis of the emotions, although they enjoy the presentation of character in the sense of whimsical individualities. They can be captured by the fanciful and the fairylike, especially if the fairies are close to Nature and the animal kingdom. What they enjoy most, however, is incident.

The English novel of adventure may or may not be given an historical background. Walter Scott gave it one, and so did Harrison Ainsworth, a writer of romances very popular in the nineteenth century, but who has never established a real place in literature. So also, in his well-known *Treasure Island* and other books, did Robert Louis Stevenson, a later and far more considerable literary figure. John Buchan, who died as Lord Tweedsmuir and Governor General of Canada, and A. E. W. Mason, who began life as an actor and has something of the aquiline appearance of the great Duke of Wellington, both placed their early adventure stories in historical costume; but both of them afterwards transferred their settings to contemporary life. It was with contemporary figures also, but against the richly romantic background of India, that Rudyard Kipling made his initial successes; for he may be said to have won them as a teller of stories, which, if not exactly adventure stories, were based on the love of adventure and action.

Equally as a writer of novels of adventure did H. G. Wells first secure the attention of the public, although in his case the background was a sort of scientific fairyland. The English Jules Verne, as he has often been described, has long since forsaken his early manner to become the interpreter of the most vigorous and experimental currents of modern social life; and indeed he may be said to have founded in fiction, as has Bernard Shaw in the theatre, a school in which the author is more propagandist and thinker than creative artist. It is a school of which the slim and pale Aldous Huxley has later been one of the most brilliant exponents, although he also belongs to another school, of which I shall speak.

Wells in himself is a far less complicated person than his work might suggest. He is a delightful companion, and his sense of fun is almost that of a schoolboy, which one might say that he still looks, with his rosy cheeks and mischievous laughing eyes, in spite of the furrows of age.

Adventure once more—both in historical costume and modern dress—is what makes the great sales of frankly popular and artistically unambitious novelists like Phillips Oppenheim and Rafael Sabatini; and it is adventure again which is the real inspiration of a work of an immensely higher caliber, the *Seven Pillars of Wisdom* of T. E. Lawrence, that already legendary figure of the last war, who was almost an uncrowned King among the Arabs, but afterwards renounced his rank of colonel to change his name and become a private soldier in the Air Force.

I have said that the Englishman cares little for subtle

analysis of motive or feeling; but that does not mean that we have not had masters in that kind among our novelists. Meredith, whom I can remember in his old age as the most brilliant conversationalist that I ever met, and the one with the widest range of subject, was the greatest of them in our time; and he may even be said to be the first English novelist to penetrate deeply into the feminine character and temperament. In this he was followed by Henry James, also a good conversationalist, but marred a little by his hesitation over the choice of the exactly appropriate word. I am inclined to annex Henry James as an Englishman; for although he was American by birth, and wrote his first novels from the point of view of the American visiting Europe, he passed the whole of his literary life in England.

Rather later, the psychological novel found a notable exponent in George Moore, who had evolved towards it from earlier experiments in realism, and it is well represented today by Charles Morgan, as distinguished and earnest in his writing as he is in his appearance, with his tall figure, his refined, clean-shaven face and his lock of hair constantly falling over his forehead, and as constantly being replaced by a familiar gesture.

However, the group of the psychological novelists tends rather to overlap that of those who are chiefly interesting for their presentation of the middle and upper class society of their day.

Meredith himself has a considerable importance for his picture of the social life of his ladies and gentlemen, although his greater concern is penetration into the subtleties of their characters.

A much more recent example is John Galsworthy, whose *Country House* describes the prosperous and well-brought-up society of our own time in a way which makes it indispensable to any understanding of modern England, and whose many-volumed history of the Forsyte family is an important social document, but who was also dealing with issues of character and passion. He was in himself very like one of his own creations—high-principled, athletic, scrupulously fair, with firmly set jaw and handsome, clean-shaven, ascetic mouth and chin below a prematurely bald crown.

The tradition of presenting a middle-class social picture as something almost as important as a human story dates back to the beginning of the nineteenth century in Jane Austen's and Mrs. Gaskell's mildly ironic outlook upon the genteel country life of their time; and it can be traced through Anthony Trollope and George Eliot, who are now chiefly read, in so far as they still are read, for what they can tell of the society in which they lived. It found an exponent yesterday in Arnold Bennett, although his middle-class society was rather lower than upper, and another very typically in Hugh Walpole.

There is another group of yesterday and today, whose preoccupation is not so much psychological or even sentimental as sexual. As used by them, the very word "sex" has acquired an almost pathological significance, and its symptoms are examined with grave but unrelenting frankness.

D. H. Lawrence, who died in 1930, was perhaps the most typical writer of this group; but Aldous Huxley belongs to it also. So did the Irishman, James Joyce, although his place is principally that of a writer who is interesting chiefly to writers, and as a daring and sometimes bewildering experimenter in the possibilities of language; so that the purists in literature were even more shocked by his invention of new words than were the purists in propriety by his minute descriptions of every human instinct. He was in himself a gentle, kindly and not talkative creature, who went completely blind towards the end of his life, when I knew him in Paris, and seemed in his person to be the last sort of man in the world to create the scandal of which he became the center, when his principal work had to be issued by private subscrip-

tion to save the publisher from being prosecuted for in-
decency. The discussions which he aroused—not least among
his own countrymen—were well summarized in the remark
which the Irish poet George Russell—whose pseudonym was
A. E.—passed on meeting him: "I cannot make up my mind
whether you are a fountain or a cistern."

It need hardly be said that Joyce never touched the big
public, who, as I have remarked already, have little interest
in, or appreciation for, conscious or finished art. For the same
reason, although Max Beerbohm has recently been given the
honor of knighthood, the exquisitely turned prose which
comes—or used to come, for he has long been silent—from
his pen, is as much caviare to the general as are the subtle caricatures from his pencil of personalities, most of whom are
known only to an inner circle. Max Beerbohm is one of the
rare examples of a writer who, in appearance and manner, is
what, from his work, you would expect him to be. When he
and I were both undergraduates at Oxford, and I published
his caricature of one of the "dons" in an ephemeral journal
which I brought out, he was already cherubic in face, precise
in voice, dapper in dress and slightly precious in manner
without ever being in the least affected; and all these things
he has remained. In my Oxford memories, he stands side by
side with a much older man, also an artist in words and a
master of prose, Walter Pater, author of a great subjectively
analytical novel, *Marius the Epicurean*. Pater has a distinguished place in the literary evolution of nineteenth-century
England, alike as novelist, as critic and as social and artistic
philosopher. He also was precise in his manner and his dress,
and, at a time when the older tradition of always wearing a
top hat in Oxford, when not in academic robes, was going
out, he could still be seen with one, as well as with gloves
and a neatly rolled umbrella. He was my tutor, and I remember that he advised me to adopt, for literary composition, the
method of jotting down ideas on little slips of paper and

then arranging the slips on a table in their most appropriate sequence. Sequence, he said, was everything; and he defined prose as "words in their best order"—poetry being "the best words in their best order."

Oscar Wilde, who was Irish, was another conscious artist, who would probably never have been known to any but a limited public if he had not possessed a genius for getting himself talked about, and if he had not developed later an instinct for the theatre and a talent for witty and paradoxical dramatic dialogue.

In the same class must be placed Somerset Maugham. He is the most distinguished English literary artist now living. As a novelist, he modelled himself upon Maupassant. As a dramatist, he has always scored by the careful construction and exactly balanced execution of his work. He is the exception which proves the rule that it is not art of this kind which reaches the British public; for his success has been great. However, it is perhaps true that he has never quite touched the British heart.

It was no doubt Oscar Wilde who brought paradox into fashion; but it was another Irishman, Bernard Shaw, and an Englishman, G. K. Chesterton, who developed it in their different ways, not merely as a form of wit in the manner of Wilde, but as a potent weapon of argument. Shaw did so by means of his plays, Chesterton by means of his essays, which first appeared as newspaper articles. Shaw was, and is into his ripe old age, a Socialist. Chesterton was not, though his democratic sympathies could not be questioned. Both enjoyed talking in public, and they held several public debates; but they were very differently equipped for the task. Shaw had a long experience, in his youth, of addressing hostile street-corner audiences. He not only has a ready wit, but an excellent ringing voice, which his strong Irish "brogue" does not make incomprehensible to Englishmen. Chesterton's wit was ready enough; but the thin voice which proceeded from that elephantine form was almost inaudible; and he made it the more difficult to understand what he said, when it was intended to be amusing, by chuckling so much to himself over the joke that he hardly let it reach his listeners.

The two men were different from each other in most things; but in my long experience of both of them, I found that they had one quality in common, and that was kindliness. Bernard Shaw is so provocative by temperament that it may be surprising to learn that he is tender-hearted. He is so vain —and he makes no secret of it—that it may be surprising to learn that he is generous; but I know him to be both.

Just as thinking of Belloc calls up the image of Chesterton, so one can hardly think of Chesterton without bringing in Belloc—the Chesterbelloc, they used to be called.

The position of Belloc in literature is curious. He is a fine poet. He is a distinguished historian. He is a powerful journalist. He is a great orator. And yet he is conscious himself of being in England, but not quite of it. His father was French, and he did his military service in the French army, after having had an English education. This has given him a sort of double national consciousness. He feels English in France; and although he has been an English Member of Parliament, he still sometimes feels French in England. The cast of his mind is really Latin. This is nowhere better shown than when his irony is directed at something pompous in English institutions. Now the English have no particular objection to their institutions being made to look absurd; for their absurdity, especially when they are obsolete and only serve to cover a newer reality, is considered to be rather an endearing feature. A humorist with an English cast of mind, like W. S. Gilbert, felt this. All sorts of English institutions are made to look absurd in the Gilbert and Sullivan operas; but these institutions did not annoy Gilbert. He rather liked them. They do annoy Belloc.

I think that W. S. Gilbert is one of four humorists whom

future generations will have to study if they want to understand the English character in the later nineteenth and early
twentieth centuries; and especially English middle-class
character in the case of three of the authors concerned.

Gilbert was the very expression of the attitude of mind
of the English professional classes, their conventions and
their prejudices, and, as I have indicated, their willingness to
laugh at them without having the least intention of changing them; and the Savoy operas remain all the more typical
of these things since the tradition of Gilbert's rigid insistence
upon every detail in their interpretation in his own way has
been preserved in their performance.

Lewis Carroll represented another aspect of the spirit of
the same classes. His real name was C. L. Dodgson, and he
was a professor of mathematics at Oxford; but his fame rests
upon two tales, where the matter-of-fact and the sententious
are allied to the fantastic and the absurd with a solemnity
which can probably seem really comic only to an Englishman.
Alice in Wonderland and *Alice through the Looking Glass*
have long been classics in every English middle-class household; but, although they have been translated, they have
never been found amusing in other countries, except as the
mere children's books which their author intended them to
be, whereas in England they are a delight to people of all
ages. Queen Victoria, when she read them, wrote to Mr.
Dodgson and asked him to send her his next book. He did.
It was a mathematical treatise. My sister was more fortunate.
He gave her an autographed copy of *Alice*, which I still
have.

The other two of the four humorists are W. W. Jacobs
and P. G. Wodehouse. From Jacobs, whose humor and observation and sense of character are in direct descent from
Dickens, it is possible to understand something of the inarticulate but lovable foolishness and also the transparent slyness

of the London workingman. Wodehouse gives a picture of the equally simple knowingness, which is to be found among the foolish youth of the idle rich, and also some delightful portraits of the blandly resourceful and always deferential servants who so easily manage their masters. Both Jacobs and Wodehouse have already earned permanent places in English literature. Belloc has indeed described Wodehouse as "the best writer of English now alive."

Ever since the seventeenth century, there have been English authors who have been moved to observe, describe and interpret the changing face of rural nature—sun and cloud, trees and flowers, winds and waters. There have been books which have consisted of little else than records of such observation, and they have become classics, like the seventeenth-century *Compleat Angler* of Izaak Walton and the eighteenth-century diary of a naturalist country clergyman, White, of Selborne. There have been others, where the landscape and the weather almost become actors in a story of human passion. Such was Emily Brontë's *Wuthering Heights* in the middle of the nineteenth century, and such were the novels of Thomas Hardy towards its close. It was only at the end of Hardy's life that he was recognized for the great man that he was; and it was indeed only towards the end of his life that his novels touched tragedy, as in *Tess of the d'Urbervilles*, and that he wrote his great dramatic poem, "The Dynasts."

Sympathy with nature is not far removed from another sympathy, which has inspired many English writers from time to time, and some of them all the time. This is sympathy with children, the most natural kind of human being, with those grown-up creatures who are nearest to children, and with the fancies which haunt the imagination of children —that is to say with fairyland. There is a whole children's literature in English, and it is being added to every year;

and there have been two authors of the last generation, who made successes of many other kinds, but who will perhaps live longest by what they wrote for children.

One of them is Rudyard Kipling. To say this may sound surprising; for Rudyard Kipling is best known as the poet and the story-teller of the adventurous, pioneering colonizing Englishman; and I have already said that it was as a teller of such modern adventure stories that he began his career in India. It was of the sort of Englishman who went out from home to administer India, and of the English common soldier who went out to serve in India, that he first wrote. He wrote about them admirably, for he was a very great journalist, and he studied them as a journalist. He afterwards wrote admirably about many other sorts of Englishmen, whose lives he also studied with the penetrating curiosity of the journalist. Yet what will be remembered longer, I believe, was what he wrote without studying at all, what came up from the memories of his Indian childhood—that is to say, the *Jungle Book,* which is, after all, in the nature of a fairy story. Kipling was a nephew of the painter Burne-Jones, and the poetic imagination which made him conceive Mowgli and his wild-beast friends had perhaps something in common with that of his uncle's Pre-Raphaelite pictures.

The other man who will live by something written for children is J. M. Barrie. He was the author of a number of novels—most of them about his native Scotland—and a number of very successful plays; but, among them all, the one which will be remembered longest, I think, is his children's play, *Peter Pan,* the boy who would not grow up. It is not only an admirably colored picture of a small English middle-class boy's dreams of pirates and adventure. It is the expression of any little boy's spirit. Barrie's best-remembered play for grown-up people—the modern Morality, *Dear Brutus*—is so far from realism as also to be almost a fairy story.

Barrie himself was a delightful creature, but a curious

figure. Small, frail and shy, he had a gentle lilting Lowland Scottish voice, with which he used to say things of an unexpectedly whimsical fancy—it was fancy rather than humor. He had a passion for cricket; and although he could hardly be described himself as being a player at all, he formed a cricket club of literary men and journalists. It was called the Allahakbari Cricket Club, because that word is the Moorish for "God help us"; and it was founded, as Barrie declared, because one day, walking along a country road with a friend, he threw a stone at a bird in a hedge, and the stone hit the hedge, and from that they began to talk of country sports. The club included Conan Doyle, but only for a time; for he eventually left to "go into second class Cricket," as Barrie announced. It also included A. E. W. Mason, the novelist, Owen Seaman, the editor of *Punch*, Bernard Partridge, the black-and-white artist, and others among whom I figured myself. Barrie drew up a special book of rules for us ("When you hit the ball, run: don't stop to cheer"); and, at a dinner after the first match, he announced to us that his principles in selecting the team had been, with regard to the married men, that he liked their wives, and, with regard to the single men, the oddity of their personal appearance.

In English book catalogues there is always an important section, headed "Travel." Many of the books which it includes and are constantly being added to it are more interesting for their content than for any claim to rank as literature; but there are occasional exceptions. Three authors of travel books in our own time have already become classic. I have mentioned one, T. E. Lawrence "of Arabia." The other two might both be described as "of South America."

W. H. Hudson's book about Uruguay, *The Purple Land*, was first published in 1885. It is not exactly a travel book, for it is clothed in the form of a series of sentimental adventures; but its real interest lies in the way the author makes the country and the people belonging to it come to life in his pages. His *Green Mansions*, whose scene is laid in the forests of Venezuela, is almost equally vivid.

As for R. B. Cunninghame-Graham, his mastery of the English language, his sense of landscape and his great love for the land and the people and the horses, of which he writes, have made him the finest possible interpreter to English readers of the romance of the Argentine and Uruguayan "camp," or "pampa" or pasture country. He was a romantic figure in himself, with his thin, distinguished face, his short beard and his hair brushed back from his forehead. His appearance made one think of Don Quixote, though he was not tall; and his character was certainly what has come to be known as quixotic. I can remember his frequent visits to a house which my godmother had in the country in England. He went there not only to see her, but also to visit his superannuated horses, whom he had sent to pass their declining years in the fields on her property. He would never part with them nor allow them to be destroyed.

The successful English novelists of today include a far larger proportion of women than of men. Robert Graves and Gilbert Frankau stand out amongst those men who are not veterans; but most of the other names are those of women. Virginia Woolf and Storm Jameson are perhaps the most distinguished; but the list also includes Clemence Dane, Daphne du Maurier, Rosamund Lehmann, G. Stern, Angela Thirkell (a granddaughter of Burne-Jones) and Dorothy Richardson.

Since Shakespeare and his contemporaries gave the English theatre its glorious beginnings, it has had many ups and downs. It was suppressed altogether during the Puritan Revolution in the middle of the seventeenth century. It was restored at the end of that century with a number of artificial comedies, of which the most famous, those of Congreve, have their place in literature, but are hardly ever seen upon the stage. Indeed, when I very successfully produced one of them, "The Way of the World," at the time when I had a theatre in London, it had not been acted for more than a hundred years. The eighteenth and early nineteenth centuries showed some great actors—Garrick, Kean, Kemble and his sister, Mrs. Siddons—but no great dramatist except Sheridan; and it was not until the end of the nineteenth that there was a serious revival of English playwriting.

This revival was led by A. W. Pinero, a Jew of Portuguese origin, who had begun as an actor, and gradually evolved as a dramatist from plays which were merely theatrically effective, to others which combined serious artistic conception and purpose with a more complete mastery of the instrument of the stage than any other English author of our time. His first important serious play, "The Second Mrs. Tanqueray," produced in the last decade of the nineteenth century, is perhaps his best-known work. The theatre was thus recovered for literature by a man of the theatre, just as it was given its place in literature by men of the theatre—Shakespeare and Molière were both actors—and not by men of letters writing for the theatre. The men of letters came in afterwards. I have already mentioned some of them—Oscar Wilde, who could not only be polished and witty, but had a natural sense of dramatic construction, and Bernard Shaw, whose capacity for making theatrical dialogue entertaining enabled him to persuade his audience to listen to his views on all sorts of subjects.

J. M. Barrie was perhaps the first successful novelist to become a playwright, but his skill in the latter art was such that he made it a complete expression of his quaint and fancifully sentimental personality. Somerset Maugham is another novelist who has perfected his art in becoming a playwright. J. B. Priestley, who has been very successful in the theatre, also began by writing novels; and A. A. Milne is in the same position. Charles Morgan, who has been a leading dramatic critic, has recently turned his attention from the writing of novels to that of plays; but it can hardly be said that he yet possesses the latter medium as fully as the former.

The transition from dramatic critic to playwright is a natural one; and two other living writers who have successfully taken it are St. John Ervine and Ashley Dukes, the latter of whom has also distinguished himself as an advanced theatrical manager.

This transition is not so natural, however, as that from play acting to playwriting. The best-known living example in England is Noel Coward, who may, I think, be said to be able to express more completely and spontaneously in dramatic form what he sets out to express than any one else now writing, with the possible exception of Somerset Maugham. What he wants to express is generally on the light and often on the cynical side, but the entire familiarity with the form of expression is there. A younger, but already successful and very promising example of the actor turned playwright is the Welshman, Emelyn Williams, who has a powerful sense of dramatic tension and emotion.

The drama at its best and greatest is, first of all, a popular art. It was so in England in the time of Shakespeare, and the instinct which made it so then has remained in the people ever since, although the theatre has sometimes either been suppressed altogether or has become merely the plaything of the rich. During most of the nineteenth century this popular dramatic instinct found one outlet in what was called the music hall. The music hall has little to do with music, but is an entertainment which consists of individual numbers by dancers, acrobats, performing animals, sentimental singers and, especially, grotesque comedians. These last—sometimes of great talent and even of genius, as in the case of Dan Leno—give humorous monologues, of which a song is merely the excuse and the introduction, and a dance merely the finish. Their direct and almost confidential contact with their audience goes back to the spirit of the Elizabethan comic theatre; and their quaint sense of character, their pronounced individualism and their homely humor are all very typically English. It is to be regretted that the economic pressure of the cinema is gradually crowding the music hall out of existence.

The English audience seeks character and incident in the theatre, as in the novel, and this determines the nature of English plays, which must eschew the wordiness and subtle emotional introspection of the drama of many other countries, especially Latin countries. The English audience is also a little slow in its reactions, and it is apt to be bewildered by the "touch and go" effects of comedy, in which, for instance, an American audience delights. Again, the lack of interest in conscious art, to which I have already referred, makes it always seek for illusion. It does not enjoy anything in the nature of a critically detached attitude. It wants to be carried along by the story, to be taken in.

There is something else which the English spectator wants to find at the play, and that is pleasure for the eye. He wants the effect to be pictorial. Great attention was paid to scenery and costume in London long before any importance was attached to them in the theatre of the continent of Europe. No doubt the thirst for illusion has something to do with this popularity of scenery, and especially of realistic scenery; and it has been difficult to educate the English public to be really satisfied with unobtrusive conventional backgrounds, although the process has recently been accelerated by the competition of the cinema, which gives more realism than the theatre can ever hope to emulate, and inclines the public to seek in the theatre the human drama which the theatre alone can fully give.

Apart from its desire for illusion, however, the English public has an instinctive taste for color and show. Official pageantry is always well done in London. The sense of order, which all Englishmen possess, contributes to its efficient regulation; the sense of tradition enables picturesque uniforms, liveries, costumes and customs to be preserved; and the sense of brilliance gives the pictorial quality, in which the English people delight—is any military uniform in the world so vivid as the full-dress English scarlet? The Lord Mayor's show, of which I have already spoken, the ceremonial opening of Parliament by the King and Queen and the military "tattoos" or displays, which are so successful in peace time, are all expressions of the national delight in brilliant cavalcade.

A few years ago, this instinct found an outlet in a number of historical "pageants," or large-scale, open-air theatrical performances, organized by various towns to illustrate episodes in their history. These performances also exploited another English instinct, that of not only looking at the theatre, but taking part in it. In no country, I think, can there exist so many and so active amateur dramatic societies. In these historical pageants, all the performers were amateurs, who spent months during the winter making their own costumes and preparing for the performances in the summer. I know well with what enthusiasm all this work was done; for I myself directed the pageant of the town of St. Albans, in which twelve hundred persons took part.

An expression of the popular dramatic instinct which combines the love of pageantry, the individualism of the music-hall comedian and the sense of tradition is what is called the Christmas Pantomime. It is a form of entertainment which is very typically English. Like the music hall, it is in danger of extinction, but less immediate danger, for it is still pretty vigorous. As Christmas approaches, the theatre in every English town of any size will suspend the visits of touring dramatic companies, which occupy it for the rest of the year, and will devote itself to the preparation of what is usually its one local dramatic effort, its great spectacular and comic festival.

In the form into which it has evolved since its creation

in the eighteenth century, the Christmas Pantomime is not pantomime in the strict sense of the word; for the historic characters of pantomime have gradually been relegated to the epilogue, and there is no dumb-show until then. Nor is it very typically an entertainment for children, although it is traditionally supposed to be so, and although its title and its very thin thread of story are always those of a nursery tale. Indeed, of recent years, there has grown up, independently of the pantomime, a new form of simple children's play, which is not called a pantomime at all, but is exclusively addressed to a childish public.

The Christmas Pantomime is really a rather confused but elaborate entertainment, largely consisting of music-hall "turns," for which the story chosen is merely a peg. There are about a dozen tales which tradition has conse-crated for the purpose—"Cinderella," "Jack and the Bean-stalk," "Robin Hood," "Little Red Riding Hood," "The Forty Thieves," "Dick Whittington and His Cat," "The Babes in the Wood," "The Sleeping Beauty," and "Beauty and the Beast." The story matters little, however; for there is not room for much of it between the comic men, with their topical songs and allusions to national and local politics, the animal impersonators, the acrobats, the sentimental ditties and the spectacular displays; and what there is of it is always much the same. There is always a Prince Charming, played by a handsome woman in tights, who sings a sentimental or patriotic ballad, always two ugly sisters, played by men— even when the story is not supposed to be "Cinderella"— always two bold bad robbers—even when the story is not "The Babes in the Wood"—always a faithful cat—even when the story is not "Dick Whittington"—and always an impecunious baron with a red nose, who has a scene of domestic quarrel in his dilapidated kitchen with his wife, also a male comedian with another red nose.

The spectacular effects, which alternate with the comic

business, work up to a grand climax in what used to be called the Transformation Scene, in which immense cardboard flowers open jerkily to reveal beautiful, artistically posed and scantily clad maidens, while colored Bengal flares smokily illuminate the effect.

And then, immediately upon this climax, is lowered a painted cloth representing a London street of humble houses and shops, and in dance the traditional characters of the real old pantomime in their traditional costumes—Harlequin, with his tight-fitting suit of variegated squares, his black half-mask, which makes him visible or invisible, according to whether he wears it up or down, and his wand or slapstick; Columbine, in her white ballet skirt; doddering Pantaloon, in his loose red tunic, trimmed with yellow and his white face and wig and little nodding plume; and, finally—not Pierrot, but the English Clown, in a white frilled costume, picked out with red, and with a white face and the traditional brilliant vermilion markings. These characters—in dumb show in the case of Harlequin and Columbine only—then proceed to play a number of practical jokes upon the inoffensive citizens and tradespeople represented as living in or passing up and down the street. Two invariable instruments of these practical jokes are a string of sausages, which the Clown steals from a tray carried by a butcher boy on his head, and an enormous red-hot poker, which the Clown uses to save himself from arrest by the Policeman, who is always the eventual butt and victim, just as he is in "Punch and Judy," the ancient English puppet show.

"Punch and Judy" is an even older tradition than the Christmas Pantomime; but I am sorry to say that it may almost be said to have disappeared already; and only rarely can its tall portable theatre, just big enough to hide one man in the lower part of it, and small enough to be carried completely open upon a barrow, be seen giving a performance at London street corners, as it could when I was a boy. The little theatre is tall, because the puppets are worked, not from above by wires, but from below, by the hands of the artist, which the lower part of them fits like a glove. The floor of the little stage—which is about three feet wide—could not be seen by the spectators on the ground level, if there was a floor; but there is not. What there is, in front of the emptiness in which the showman operates, is a little shelf, projecting from where the footlights might be; and, at the end of this shelf and against the little proscenium, sits the one visible living performer in the show, Mr. Punch's dog, Toby, with a Clown's frill around its neck. Toby does not do anything, but he is spoken to by all the characters in the story, which is one of violent action. For this action the shelf is very useful; for, as it is of wood, and the heads of all the dolls are of wood, they can be banged cruelly down upon it with a crack which excites the childish audience to shouts of enthusiastic glee. The policeman can whack his truncheon, which he holds in his crossed arms, down upon the shelf, before trying to whack Punch with it. The coffin and the gallows—which are indispensable to the lurid tale—can be laid upon the little shelf or set up upon it. Judy, who is the wife of Punch, and is almost as much his butt and victim as is the policeman, except when she herself takes the upper hand, and bullies Punch, can be made to sit on the little shelf with her legs dangling over the edge.

The characters in the Punch and Judy drama by no means act in dumb show. On the contrary, they are screaming all the time through the traditional rasping falsetto voice of their master and animator, who not only makes them speak, but hurl themselves at one another in quarrel or intelligently lean towards one another in conversation.

Punch is, of course, the lineal descendant of Punchinello; but his personality has been English for two hundred years, and it would be sad to see him go. His name will, in any case, be preserved as the title of our oldest comic paper; and his portrait, as well as that of Toby, his dog, has fortunately been handed down to posterity on the cover of that paper. There you will see Mr. Punch in his traditional Punchinello costume and pointed cap, with his sharp bump on his back, with his curved nose and chin so long that they almost meet one another, and with his quizzical smile. There you will also see his dog, Toby, complete with frill, and with a feathered cap. You will even occasionally see Mr. Punch in the political cartoons of the paper itself, where he is represented, dressed in a frock coat, as giving advice to one or other of the political leaders or congratulating a naval or military hero.

The British genius for music is perhaps neither so deep nor so widely spread as the genius for drama, and, since the great period of English music in the seventeenth century, the contribution of British composers to the world has been rather limited, although many English and Scottish folk songs have a very individual musical quality. In interpretation, however, there is a long and vigorous tradition of choral singing, especially in Wales and the North of England, and there is a large enough musical public to support several orchestras in peace time in London, Manchester and Bournemouth. A musical revival is perhaps indicated in the relatively recent, but very enthusiastic interest which has been taken in the art of ballet and the formation of professional ballet companies, and also in the performance of old English folk dances by amateurs.

English painting can hardly be said to have had any influence upon the art of Europe since the Pre-Raphaelite school in penultimate decade of the last century, and then it was chiefly upon black and white drawing through the decorative genius of Aubrey Beardsley; but ever since the enthusiasms of that time, the artistic life of the country has been active, and the general interest in art has been a very different thing from the philistinism of Mid-Victorian days.

It is to the Pre-Raphaelites that my own earliest artistic

recollections go back, and especially to Burne-Jones who was the most famous of the Pre-Raphaelite group. He joined it, however, too late to be a member of the original "brotherhood," who, under the inspiration of the painter-poet, Dante Gabriel Rossetti, set out to purge English painting of what they considered to be its sentimental presentation of the commonplace by going back to the severe conventions, the meticulous detail and the truer because more spiritual realism of the Italian painters who preceded Raphael.

What most people understand by realism—that is to say the vivid illusion of the actual thing seen—was magnificently represented by John Sargent. He certainly enjoyed a world-wide reputation; but he can hardly be described as having carried any English art influence abroad, or even as having expressed one at home. This is not so much because he was of American nationality, for he did nearly all his work in England and was a member of the English Royal Academy, but because the inspiration of his art came directly from Paris, and from his master, Carolus-Duran.

Burne-Jones and Sargent were both shy and kindly men, but not in the same way; for they were otherwise as different from one another in themselves as they were in their art. Burne-Jones was small, insignificant-looking and badly dressed, with plaintive, rabbit-like eyes and a thin wisp of beard. He was gentle, soft-voiced and retiring. He never went out into society, and his little jokes—for he was not without humor—were made for intimate friends. I still have certain caricatures from his hand—"Susannah and the Elders after the style of Rubens," a painter whose fleshly manner he detested; "The Homes of England," representing an overfed and overdressed man snoring grossly on a very Victorian sofa; and three lessons in anatomy, "The Good Man," "The Good Woman," and "The Bad Man," drawn for the edification of myself when I was seven, and he was painting my portrait. They reveal the good woman to contain nothing but an enormous and flaming heart, the good man nothing but a heart with wings and the bad man nothing at all.

Sargent, on the other hand, was large and rubicund, with a short and neat beard. He was well turned out, he enjoyed society, in spite of his shyness, and he gave to dinner parties whatever time he would consent to spare from painting; for he painted almost continuously, by night as well as by day—he did my mother's portrait by lamplight. He also painted all day during his holidays; and the only difference was that then the pictures were landscapes instead of being portraits.

An earlier American painter who had also studied in Paris and made London his home was Whistler. Like Sargent, he could be described as an impressionist; but he was not, like Sargent, a realist. He was much more of a poet, and he was the first painter to see the mystery and beauty of urban landscape, especially that of London, especially by the riverside and especially in half lights, and even in fog. His art was essentially decorative, and he owed much to the inspiration of the Japanese woodcuts, not only in composition, but in the use of masses of color—especially yellow and white, of both of which he was very fond. Though his art was in no way English, he can fairly be claimed as an English painter, because he interpreted London as well as lived in it. He even joined the Society of British Artists, as is placed on record by one of his many quips. When he and some of his friends resigned from it after a quarrel, he fired as a parting shot: "The artists go. The British remain."

An entirely native genius, on the other hand, was Phil May, who, with a few strokes of the pen, could not only hit off physical peculiarities and absurdities of all classes of people, but could illustrate far deeper traits of individual and national character. His magnificent draughtsmanship and his humor had the whole country for its public, for his sketches appeared in the Press. He was perhaps the most popularly

English thing in pictorial art since Hogarth. He died, at the age of forty, in 1903.

In recent years, there have been few British artists whose fame has crossed the English Channel. Alfred Gilbert, the sculptor, in one generation, and Frank Brangwyn the painter of heroic compositions, and A. J. Munnings, the painter of horses in another, have perhaps been the only ones. This does not mean that they have been the only ones to deserve an international reputation. Besides, there have been and are others, who are certainly known in America, if not in Europe. Augustus John, probably the greatest draughtsman of the human form now living, John Lavery, the brilliant portrait painter, who died recently, Eric Gill, the mediæval-minded sculptor in stone and wood, also recently dead, Epstein, a great sculptor, who is not an Englishman, but lives and works in England, Wilson Steer, who, before his eyesight failed him, could get more sunlight into a picture of shimmering blossom than any other painter, Muirhead Bone, who can give such an uncanny impressiveness to his towering perspectives of complicated scaffolding or Gothic interiors, William Nicholson, with his significant and economically used line, which survives from his beginnings as a pioneer of modern poster design, Richard Sickert, master of light and shadow— these are a few among what are now the distinguished veterans. C. R. W. Nevinson, Laura Knight, Lucy Kemp-Welch stand out in a rather younger generation, and there are many admirable artists in a generation younger still.

Even under war conditions and bombardment, the literary and artistic life of London goes on. The creation of original work is to a great extent suspended; for it is not during times of great stress, but after them that the emotions which they provoke normally find their expression in art. It is not surprising therefore that such production as there is comes mostly from established writers and artists, and that no new veins of talent have made their appearance. There has, however, been a certain activity in the writing of poetry, as there was during the other war.

Interpretative art, on the other hand, has been bravely maintained, and pictorial art too, in the sense that there have been distinguished picture exhibitions. At the beginning of 1941, drawings by Augustus John were being shown at the National Gallery, and there was an interesting exhibition of contemporary paintings at the same time at the Leicester Galleries. There were no concerts, cinemas or theatrical performances after nightfall; but nine theatres—to say nothing of a large number of cinema houses—were open in the afternoon, one with Shakespeare, two with revivals of serious modern plays (*Berkeley Square*, and J. M. Barrie's *Dear Brutus*), one with a Christmas Pantomime, two with revues and three with ballet, whose vogue remained as great as ever. In addition, two small artistic theatres, Norman Marshall's Gate Theatre and Ashley Dukes' Mercury Theatre, giving nominally private performances before audiences of about a hundred and fifty subscribers, continued to operate in West London, away from the theatrical center, and to produce plays of high literary and dramatic value. Moreover, for those who were prepared to face the "blackout," there was a cabaret performance at night—also to subscribers—in a cellar theatre by that spirited, intelligent and very amusing company, "Ridgeway's Late Joys," whose very individual numbers keep the spirit of the old music hall alive.

Many of the theatrical performances in the ordinary theatres were given, not only in the afternoon, but specifically in the business luncheon hour. This fashion was no doubt set by the great success of the series of luncheon-hour concerts of classical music, vocal and instrumental, which were organized in the Dome-room of the National Gallery at the uniform entrance price of a shilling, and were largely patronized by the many members of the staffs of the adjacent Government offices. Other concerts, of a more ambitious character, were given on Sunday afternoons, notably those of the London Philharmonic Orchestra.

Naturally enough, orchestral performances in London, as well as those of opera, have been much restricted by war conditions, but they have not been entirely abandoned. The Opera at Covent Garden has been closed since the beginning of the war; but popular opera was continued at Sadler's Wells Theatre until the severe air raids of September, 1940, drove the company into the provinces; and the Promenade Concerts at Queen's Hall, with the London Symphony Orchestra, were also resumed in August of the same year, but had to be discontinued for the same reason.

However, if certain musical and theatrical activities have been suspended in London, many of them have put up their heads again bravely after migrating to the country. This is the case with the famous orchestra of the British Broadcasting Corporation. Other musical and dramatic companies, which do not have so powerful a backing, have found some difficulty in keeping together; but they have been assisted in some cases by the semi-official Council for the Encouragement of Music and the Arts, which was formed at the beginning of 1940 with a subsidy from the Anglo-American body, the Pilgrim Trust, to the amount of £25,000, which was made into £50,000 by the Treasury providing a similar sum.

Support from the Council enabled the Hallé Orchestra to give fifteen full concerts in the North of England, and a tour of Concerts by the London Philharmonic Orchestra was sponsored by a fund raised in consequence of a public appeal.

By giving a guarantee to the "Old Vic" Shakespearean company, the Council made it possible for Sybil Thorndike, our greatest living tragic actress, and her husband, Lewis Casson, to arrange a tour of Shakespeare's plays throughout the industrial and mining districts.

Perhaps the most important work of the Council has, however, been the fostering of local manifestations in all the arts. Popular loan exhibitions of pictures have been arranged. Amateur dramatic societies have been assisted with equipment and with professional organizers and stage managers. Musical "travellers" have arranged concerts all over the country, as well as in air-raid shelters and rest centers in London.

For an inartistic people, all this is not so bad.

Chapter IX

SPORT

SPORT, in the several senses in which it can be understood, is so woven into the texture of Britain that one can hardly write about anything British without bringing it in; and I have already touched upon several aspects of it in the chapters on the English character, on social life and on education.

In those countries which have adopted the word from England, it is taken to stand exclusively for games; but that is not the first meaning or the only meaning which an Englishman attaches to it. Indeed, it may be said that, for an Englishman, sport does not mean games. Games can be, and should be, played in a sporting spirit. Games may be sport; but games are not synonymous with sport, and still less are games the whole of sport.

What, then, is sport?

A glance at the history of the word may give a hint of the answer. In Shakespeare's day, in the early seventeenth century, it was sometimes taken to mean love-making. Then it meant jesting—"in sport" being in jest or in fun, and making sport of some one being making fun of him. It might even mean no more than entertainment or diversion—Milton's "sport that wrinkled care derides, and laughter holding both his sides." Then there came to be a slight accent on the kind of entertainment afforded by watching other creatures engaged in a struggle, sometimes a life-and-death struggle—the Elizabethan poet, for instance, conceived the gods as setting human beings to quarrel with one another "for their sport," the sport being, of course, that of the gods. In those days, it was sport to look on at the fighting of cocks and the "baiting," or worrying, of bears by dogs; and although bear-baiting was suppressed by the Puritans, "less," as Macaulay writes, "because it gave pain to the bear than because it gave pleasure to the spectators," it was afterwards revived, and both it and cockfighting continued until the beginning of the nineteenth century. This last period was also the great day of prize-fighting with the bare fists.

During the nineteenth century these "cruel sports," as they were called, were abolished, and even prize-fighting, in which, at least, the participants engaged of their own free will, was replaced by boxing-glove contests, which allowed for the natural human interest in a battle, but prevented the vanquished being more than stunned.

The humanitarian considerations which put an end to prize-fighting were even more severe where the suffering of animals was involved; and thus the bull-ring was condemned, as well as the bear and cock-pits. Indeed, the solicitude for animals, which has become part of the English nature, is such that there is a story of a child, who was shown a picture of Christians tied to posts in the Roman arena and being approached by the lions destined to devour them, but who failed entirely to display the expected sympathy for the human victims, and exclaimed instead, "Oh! There is a poor lion who has not got any Christian."

Today, looking on at a contest, a competition or a struggle is one of the meanings of the word "sport"; for it means different things to different people. Most of those who attach this meaning to it think of horse-racing. An "important sporting event" is a race meeting, and a "sporting man" is a racing man—that is to say, not a man who himself runs, but a man who frequents horse races, and, more especially, bets upon them—a "sporting chance" being a gambling chance. He may also be a man who frequents and bets upon boxing contests. There are other kinds of races, and even games, upon which there is a great deal of betting—for instance greyhound races after a mechanically propelled tin hare, which the greyhounds are never allowed to catch. It has been invented in recent years for no other real purpose than to be an excuse for betting. There is also much betting on football matches, as well as elaborate sweepstakes, called football pools. However, although these would be called sports, the spectators at them would hardly be described as sporting men. Even on the racecourse, every one cannot be described as a sporting man. The jockey, for instance, cannot; but the bookmaker can.

Thus, betting has evidently something to do with this side of the interpretation of sport; and, for a very large number of Englishmen, sport means what is called "the turf"— that is to say, going to horse races if you can go, and in any case betting on them, even if you cannot. There are millions of men, most of whom have probably never seen a thoroughbred, or racing horse, but who bet every day on horse races; for betting and beer are the average working-man's only escapes from the dull monotony of his daily life —or rather, they were until recently; for clubs and other organizations, as well as taking part in games, have furnished the workman with a growing competition of other distractions, although the importance which "tips"—that is to say, prophecies—on the races and the results of races assume in the evening papers all over the country shows how great the interest in betting still is.

One of the conditions which make it difficult for the workingman to frequent racecourses is that in Great Britain racing does not take place on Sundays, and that therefore his only chance is to go on Saturday afternoons, if he can get away from his work on Saturday afternoons. Another is that the racecourses themselves are not in the towns or on the immediate outskirts of them, as they are in so many European and American countries. They all involve a journey by train or by car.

Nevertheless, many thousands of working-class people manage to go to the races, and the attendance at what are called the great "classic" races is enormous. These include the Gold Cup at Ascot, in the middle of June, the great fashionable event, attended in semi-state by the King and Queen, who drive over from Windsor; the four-and-a-half-mile Grand National at Aintree near Liverpool, in March, the great steeplechase; the Goodwood Cup, at Goodwood, in July; and the Saint Leger, at Doncaster, in September —to mention only a few.

By far the most important of them, however, is the Derby, which is run over a course of a mile and a half at Epsom, in Surrey, towards the end of May. The huge Derby crowd, from its gipsies and ragamuffins on the outskirts to its well-dressed upper classes on the Grand Stand, is a sight not to be forgotten. It may almost be described as an epitome of England; for there are many people who go to the Derby every year, but never to any other race meeting, just as there are many men who have a bet on the Derby every year, but never on any other race. At the same time, if the Derby crowd is an epitome of England, of the good humor, the friendly jostling, the class comradeship as well as the class distinctions of the English people, and, particularly, of its instinct for gambling, it must be said that it is far from representing all that is most admirable in the English people, and there are many excellent Englishmen—and sporting Englishmen too, in the wider sense—who refuse to be associated with racing at all.

Nevertheless, when one comes to analyze the various meanings which the Englishman attaches to the word "sport," the notion of chance can hardly be separated from any one of them. At its best, it is generous chance. "Be a sport," says one schoolboy to another—that is, "give me a piece of your cake, because you know you will then stand a good chance of getting a piece of mine, when I have any."

A sportsman, which is quite a different thing from a sporting man, means to most Englishmen a man who goes hunting, shooting or fishing, which again to most Englishmen is what sport stands for much more than it stands for games; but, figuratively, a sportsman is a man who gallantly takes his chance to lose or win in any sort of struggle whatever. He will "play a sporting game"—that is to say, generously, good-humoredly and fairly. He will give his victim "a sporting chance," especially when that victim—and not least if it is an animal that he has been pursuing—has given him "good sport"—that is to say, has made a "game" fight. There is even something of gallantry implied in the word, when one finds it used as a verb in a sense which has no real connection with sport at all—"he sported a flower in his buttonhole," he was wearing a flower. There is something of hazard implied in the use of the substantive in connection with heredity, a "sport" being an unexpected or abnormal example of the species.

In the most usual acceptance of the word in England, sport is, first of all, the chase, and its origins go far back into antiquity. All the ancient arts, from the Egyptian to the Persian, show representations of hunters on horseback, and, to confine oneself to England alone, there was the New Forest in Hampshire, which William the Conqueror's first successor enclosed for his hunting ground, and where he was killed at the sport. The chase, with hounds, is mentioned with knowledge and enthusiasm more than once by Shakespeare, notably in "A Midsummer Night's Dream," though it is not clear whether he was thinking of the chase with horses. For those Englishmen who are rich enough to indulge in the chase at all today, it means fox hunting, although there is a little stag hunting also, and hares are hunted, on foot, with hounds called beagles.

Riding to hounds is part of the rural English aristocratic tradition. To be an "M. F. H."—Master of Fox-Hounds— a man must not only be rich, although he must certainly be that; for keeping up the pack will cost him more money than will be furnished by the subscriptions of the members of the Hunt and by "capping," or collecting occasional contributions at the "Meet" from visitors who are not members. He must also have a certain social position. The district over which he and his pack hunt is spoken of as his "country." A lady of artistic tastes once asked the man next to her at a country-house dinner party in Suffolk whether it was not very interesting to be living in the middle of Constable's country. "Constable? Who's he?" was the reply. "I have hunted these hounds for a number of years, and I always imagined it was *my* country."

The "meet," if it is held on the village green, as it usually is nowadays, and not in the park of a private house, as it used to be, is a great occasion for the whole district. The hounds, surrounded by the whippers in and the huntsmen, all in "pink" coats and white breeches, with hard, round, black velvet caps, and all, of course, well mounted; the Master and the members of the Hunt, in pink also, but wearing glistening black top hats; the grooms, with the spare horses which they will lead off later to wait at appropriate places; the ladies, many of whom are keen followers of hounds, but most of whom no longer ride side-saddle, as they still did only a few years ago; a few farmers, who may not be as smartly dressed or mounted as the rest, but are no less keen; friends and relatives, who are either too old or too young to hunt, but who would not miss the meet for anything, and who, on this winter's morning—for fox-hunting takes place only in winter—have driven up in all sorts of vehicles; and finally the villagers, as proud as any one of "our" Hunt, who have most of them turned out on foot to add to the gay throng. The excitement and enthusiasm have infected every one, down to the farm laborers, who, later, when the fox has been started—or "found"—to use the correct term—will pause in their work in the fields to shout a "gone away," in order to indicate the direction in which "he" has passed. So sacred is the tradition of fox hunting that to shoot a fox instead of hunting him is worse than a crime—though I am not sure that the gamekeepers on large shooting estates do not occasionally do so in secret, for foxes have a way of eating young pheasants. The fox-hunting tradition is even strong enough for farmers to consent to their land being ridden over and their fences and hedges being jumped over—or through—for the very small compensation which most Hunts are able to pay. The Hunt is a social unit. The Hunt Ball, at the end of the season, when the members wear pink tail coats to dance in, instead of pink square coats to ride in, is one of the great events of the society of the County, and the Point to Point races of the Hunt, also at the end of the season, are the most wholesome and typical expressions of English amateur racing. A number of fox-hunting expressions— or at least expressions derived from the knowledge and love of horses—have passed into the language. "Horse sense," to indicate the sort of instinct which most Englishmen would like to possess far more than brains, is merely one of many.

"It's a fine day. Let's go out and kill something," as a humanitarian bitterly remarked to describe the English sporting instinct; and shooting is another form of sport—a less democratic form in England than it is in most other European countries; for nearly all English farmers are tenants, and the landlords, who are usually large landlords, strictly reserve the shooting rights, and strictly preserve the shooting against poachers, towards whom the administration of the law by the country magistrates was, until recent years, pitilessly severe. Shooting in England is consequently nearly always on a larger scale, the birds being driven by parties of "beaters" towards the "guns," who are hidden in "butts" or behind hurdles, each with his two double-barrelled shotguns and his "loader," to take from his hand the weapon which he has just fired, and pass him the one which is newly charged. Walking across the country and shooting over dogs, which used to be the only form of shooting in Great Britain, has almost disappeared.

In the greater part of England, the shooting is not very varied. Grouse exist in large quantities on the moors of Yorkshire, but hardly anywhere else; and it is generally for Scotland that are bound the crowded trains, which leave London on the days preceding the Twelfth—twelfth of August, of course—when grouse shooting opens.

The partridge, whose shooting begins on the first of September, is a native of British corn and turnip fields, and is the most plentiful natural game; for pheasants, though they are also shot in most parts of the country, are not a native bird and have to be reared and fed and tended before they can be chased over the guns on the first of October. There is other game, of course—a few hares everywhere, and wild duck, snipe, woodcock, quail and landrail in certain places; but there is not much of anything except partridges. Rabbits, of course, there are in plenty; but rabbits are not game. They are vermin, and may be destroyed at all times.

Many Englishmen are also fond of fishing. Some of them are prepared to sit for hours behind a rod and a line, watching the float until a fish bites; but most people will hardly admit that this can be described as sport; for it lacks two of the elements which may be regarded as indispensable to sport—energy and difficulty. Fly-fishing for salmon or trout is sport; and there is a good deal of it left in England, Scotland and Ireland, in spite of urban encroachments and the pollution of streams, but even in consequence of the urban requirements that certain streams must remain unpolluted in order to supply drinking water. It is sport, because throwing the fly is not an easy thing to do (especially in the case of the dry fly, which must be made to float on the top of the water, over the trout), because landing a fish which resists so "gamely" as a trout or a salmon is by no means easy, even when he has been hooked, and because the whole thing requires a good deal of energy and involves a good deal of fatigue. Nothing is sport which is too easy; and a true sportsman will refuse to take the opportunity of achieving an easy success. He will not shoot a "sitting" bird or a sleeping animal.

There is another element, which is not indispensable to sport, but certainly adds to its sporting character, and that is danger. Big-game shooting—which few men are rich enough to afford, for it cannot be found in England—has this element. Indeed, it may be described as, strictly speaking, the most sporting kind of shooting; for the tiger or other wild animal not only stands a fair chance of not being killed, but a fair if not an even chance of killing his pursuer.

Difficulty, fatigue, hardship, danger—these are what make the greatest sport; and such magnets are they that men will deliberately seek them, sometimes all of them, but always some. You know the story of the lonely shepherd, who pricked himself all over with pins, because it was so jolly when he stopped. It is in something of that spirit that many men go in for sport. They court the fatigue and the hardship for the sake of the relief and the satisfaction afterwards. Why otherwise do men go on walking tours, or "hiking," as it is the fashion to call it today—and carry heavy knapsacks when no military order obliges them to do so? Why do they go into camps, and eat and sleep uncomfortably, when they might be in houses?

They want the physical satisfaction of having done it, and they want the moral satisfaction of proving to themselves that they could do it.

This is particularly the case where danger is added; but danger brings in another very important element in sport, and that is its own excitement.

There are other kinds of excitement which men get in sport without danger. There is the excitement of effort. There is the excitement of emulation. There is the excitement of conflict. But the excitement of danger is the greatest.

Moreover, those who have humanitarian feelings can get it without killing or trying to kill anything. That is perhaps why there are so many clergymen who take up mountain climbing, or tobogganing or skiing or sailing, and even go on expensive journeys to find them—for although there is plenty of sea to sail in around England, there are no high mountains and hardly ever enough snow for what are called winter sports.

This expression brings me to a category in which nothing is a sport in the sense of what I have been describing, and yet nothing is a game; for they are "sports," in the plural only. When an Englishman talks of athletic "sports" or a "sports ground," the things that he is thinking of are not games, but competitions. To him games and athletics are two separate things. Running, swimming and jumping are not games. They are athletics. Rowing stands by itself. It is not a game; but there is a corporate unity in an eight-oared boat, which gives every member of its crew a quality quite different from, and to an Englishman more admirable than, the finest runner of a mile; and a rowing crew has the team spirit, which the Englishman considers to be the most admirable thing in a game; but all other athletic sports are, subconsciously and definitely, considered to be on a lower plane than games.

This does not mean that little interest is taken in them. Indeed, during recent years, the crowds which they attract

and the enthusiasm which they arouse in England have constantly been growing, after having previously been for some
time on the decrease. The new prominence which is thus
given to athletics is no doubt largely due to the importance
which is attached by all countries to success in the international Olympic Games—which are really not games in the
English sense—and to the renewed efforts which British competitors discovered that they would have to make in order to
keep up to the standard reached by other teams; but the result has certainly been that "sports," and especially running,
appeal to a much larger public than they did. Even such an
eclectic sport as archery, which is interesting today chiefly
for its glorious historical associations with English military
defense, and figures in no international contest, has found a
certain renewal of favor in a limited class.

Nevertheless, games continue to take a prior place in the
Englishman's table of values. It must not be supposed, however, that he is ready to include them all in sport.

There are some that he would instinctively rule out. It is
difficult to define the criterion. One might say that the game
must be played in the open air. Neither billiards nor table
tennis, for all the skill which they can call forth, could, by
any stretch of an Englishman's imagination, be described
as sport. Yet boxing and fencing, which usually take place
indoors, are undoubtedly sports; but then, they are not
games. Indeed, the open-air test is not final either way. Not
every game which is played out of doors can be called a
sporting game. Bowls just slips in for the sake of its ancient
associations, but croquet, even when it is played extremely
well, as it can be, does not.

It is interesting to remark that the general practice of
games, and indeed the passion for them, which exists in England today, and has spread from England to the whole civilized world, is of relatively quite recent date.

It is true that the beginnings of football go a long way

back. The game is believed originally to have been the struggle for the head of the victim at a sacrifice, so that the player,
when he kicks a goal, is really bringing the trophy home. For
centuries, however, and even until the nineteenth century,
football was played only at certain places and on certain an-
niversaries. Bowls is also a game which has a long history, at
least as old as Elizabethan times—witness the historic contest
at Plymouth Hoe, when Drake insisted on finishing his game
before he went out to sea to fight the Spanish Armada. An
even longer history has tennis—not lawn tennis, but the older
tennis, which is played under cover, with penthouses and
"chases" to complicate the game; for King Henry VIII is
supposed to have excelled at it.

These, it will be noticed, are all ball games; and, with
golf in Scotland—which also has its origins in antiquity, as
evidence the Royal and Ancient Golf Club of the town of
Saint Andrews, the premier Golf Club in the world to this
day—they are the oldest in the British Isles. In comparison
with them, cricket, which cannot go back two hundred years,
is a mere upstart.

However, until less than a century ago, these games were
played merely as occasional amusements; and there was no
trace, in the pursuit of them, of what is today their perhaps
secondary but nevertheless very important function, that of
keeping the player in good physical condition—keeping him
"fit," as the modern saying goes. There is no evidence of
their having been taken very seriously or played very regularly, either for the hygienic purpose above mentioned or for
that of excelling in them. The temper which long governed
cricket at least may be judged from the still extant portraits
of cricketers, who played the game in tall hats, dating no
farther back than the beginning of the reign of Queen Victoria.

An indication of the relative shortness of the history of
most games can be found in the records of the contests be-

tween the Universities of Oxford and Cambridge. The eight-oared Boat Race, to whose importance as a national festival today I have alluded in another chapter, began as an annual event in 1838, though the first contest took place nine years earlier. The first Cricket match was in 1827, but also became an annual fixture in 1838. For many years afterwards these were the only sporting encounters between the two Universities. Matches at Rackets and Real Tennis, which are indoor games, and at Billiards and Shooting, which are not sporting games at all, started round about 1860, and the first Inter-University Athletic meeting was in 1864; but it was not until 1871 that was played the first match at Rugby Football, while the first Association Football match was two years later. The first Golf and Polo matches were in 1878, and the first Lawn Tennis match in 1881.

Moreover, until long after the latest of these dates, the only contests to which any real importance was attached were the Boat Race and the Cricket match; for these were the only ones in which the members of the teams were entitled to the honor of what was called the "full blue"—that is to say, the right to wear the plain blue (dark for Oxford and light for Cambridge), tight-fitting, flannel skull cap with a little peak and the intials "O.U.C.C." or "B.C." (Oxford University—or Cambridge University—Cricket Club or Boat Club) embroidered on the cap above it. Even the football players did not have that honor for some time.

Association Football, Lawn Tennis and Golf are the three British games which have been the most widely adopted the world over—for Cricket has never been what the French call an "article d'exportation": it is too fundamentally native to the slow-moving British temperament.

Association Football did not come into existence at all before 1870. To be sure, football of a kind goes right back to tribal traditions, as I have already indicated; and different varieties of the game of football were played in the big public schools long before 1870. There was, and still is, a Winchester variety, with rows of posts and ropes and barriers of cord netting on the right and left of the players; and there was, and still is, an Eton variety, which takes place alongside of a wall. The Rugby variety no doubt spread from that school to the Universities largely because it required no special conditions, and could be played on an open field; but its rules, which permit of the ball, which is of oval shape, being handled and carried, are less direct and simple than those of Association. Moreover, although Rugby has been exported to a certain extent, it was not until Association came into existence that football began to be played to any extent in other countries, and it is Association alone to which, in other countries, the name of football is given.

Lawn Tennis was still generally considered to be a garden-party game in England for a good many years after the earliest University tournament and the earliest Wimbledon championship meeting at about the same date of 1870; and Golf, although its history in Scotland is an old one, was not generally played, even in that country, until the last twenty years of the nineteenth century, when it also began slowly to be known in England.

There are many other games which are played in England; and some of them have gone out to the world. There is bowls, to which I have already referred. It must not be confused with "boules," which arouses such enthusiasm in the South of France, and is played over uneven ground; for it demands a smooth and truly level grass lawn, over which the heavy bowls roll evenly, deflected from their course only by the "bias," or leaden weight, introduced into one side of them and deliberately allowed for by the player. Still less must it be confused with the various forms of the game of skittles. There is curling, which is a Scottish variant of bowls, played upon ice in the winter, with stones which do not roll, but glide. There are lacrosse and basketball, which are now played in every middle-class girls' school in England, and have migrated to other countries—although lacrosse itself was an immigrant into England from Canada. There is hockey, as well as its very popular variant, ice-hockey. There are rackets, squash rackets and fives—all played with a ball against a wall, in a court of four walls, the ball in the first and last games being hard, and the instrument in the first two being a racket and in the last the hand, usually covered with a glove. There is Polo, which came to England from the East, and Water-Polo, which has really no title to the name of Polo; for it is a sort of swimming handball. There is Baseball, the national summer game of the United States, which is, nevertheless, also played a little in England.

These are all ball games, and most games are ball games; but not quite all. Darts, throwing darts at a target on the wall, which is now played keenly in every public house in England, cannot perhaps be said to partake of the nature of sport, for it involves neither fatigue nor danger; but it has certainly the quality of being exciting, and it is certainly a game.

Sporting games may be divided into various categories; but they easily fall into two—the games that only rich men can play and those which are open to every one. Polo very definitely belongs to the first category. Golf almost does so also; for the upkeep of a golf course is expensive, and the clubs and the balls themselves cost money. However, it has been possible in England to organize artisans' golf clubs, which have obtained permission to use the courses of richer clubs on certain days and at certain hours, such as early on Sunday mornings; and this amicable arrangement has been found to work very well. Lawn tennis is also mainly a rich man's game, though the expense in connection with it is not so great as to put it out of the reach of, say, the lower middle

class; and suburban lawn-tennis clubs, whose members belong to this class, abound in the neighborhood of all the big
towns.

However, the only two games which are really democratic both in their own constitution and in their traditional
associations are cricket and football. The latter requires only
a fairly level field, the goal posts and the leather ball. For
the former it is certainly desirable that a small central strip
in the field shall be quite even and closely mown and rolled;
but this is not absolutely essential, and the absence of it adds
only a little to the hazards of the game.

Cricket and football are the only two games which are
compulsory in every middle-class boys' school, and they are
played in all the Universities and in every village in the
country, cricket in summer and football in winter. They may
be said, therefore, to be played by all classes, and in cricket at
least teams are frequently composed of members of different
classes. The players may all be amateurs, as they are in the
village cricket match, to which I have referred elsewhere.
They may in part be amateurs and in part professionals, as
they are in the most important matches.

The entry of professionalism into cricket and football has
been the almost inevitable consequence of the games being
taken more and more seriously, both by those who play in
them and by those who watch them. The players tend to become specialists, even when they are amateurs. The day is
long past, for instance—though it did exist within living
memory—when an Etonian could be, and in one case was, a
member, both of the cricket eleven and the rowing eight.
Nowadays, when a boy arrives at Eton, he must make up his
mind whether he will be a "wet bob"—give his leisure to
rowing—or a "dry bob"—devote it to cricket and football.

As for the onlookers, they can be counted by dozens on
the village green; but they run into thousands at a big match
between well-known clubs. The public is not quite the same,

however, for the two games. For cricket, it is mainly middle class, although the fact that the most famous cricket ground in London is called Lords must not be taken to imply any aristocratic connection. The reason is merely that a man whose surname was Lord was once its owner. There are indeed many working-class cricket enthusiasts, although there are obvious reasons why they cannot be regular cricket spectators. Cricket is a leisurely game, and there are few workingmen who can afford to give the three full days, which are allowed for a big match, in order to watch it; whereas, to watch a football match he need give up only part of one afternoon.

There are more amateur players of cricket than football, and one reason is that it does not demand such concentrated or violent effort, so that a man need not go into such severe training for it, and he can continue playing it to a later age—the great W. G. Grace had one of his most successful seasons when he was forty-seven, and there are many amateurs who still play it long after the school and university age is passed, which cannot be said for football. Professionals have, however, for many years been included in all the big cricket club teams, and for several reasons. The clubs of the various Counties, which are the backbone of spectacular cricket, are in keen competition with each other to win the county championship, or to stand high in it; and money to engage good professionals is forthcoming, not only for the sake of local prestige, but because good players will mean more gate money to pay the general expenses of the club, as well as the salaries of the players themselves. Besides, professionals can be counted upon always to be present, always to be able to go on "bowling" all day, and so forth.

However, in every county cricket team there are always at least one or two amateurs, and generally more; and the Captain of a County eleven is always an amateur, as is also the Captain of the All England eleven in what is called a Test

Match. These Test Matches are played every two or three years against Australia. There are five of them during the season, and they take place in England, when an Australian eleven is on a visit, and in Australia when it is the English who are on tour. They arouse an enormous amount of public interest, and draw large crowds. In the Test Matches, the Australian side is composed entirely of professionals; but the only other occasion on which an exclusively professional eleven appears in England is that of the annual match between professional and amateurs, still called, by a rather snobbish tradition, "Gentlemen versus Players."

Professionalism in Association football is, however, quite another matter. The public is enormously larger, and it is mainly a working-class public. The matches between the clubs composing the Football League are the subject of a great deal of betting, and also of sweepstakes called football pools, whereas there is hardly any betting connected with cricket. The sporting patriotism excited by the Association football matches between England, Scotland, Wales and Ireland, and by matches between these teams and visitors from such Dominions as New Zealand, rises to a fever heat, and the matches are accompanied by a continuous roar of encouragement and denunciation, which any one who knows how friendly all these peoples really are to one another would hardly credit until he has been present.

Association football has therefore become an important business, in which a great deal of capital is invested. Clubs bid against one another for players. Large sums are spent on grounds and grandstands. The railway companies run special trains to the matches and particularly to the "Cup Final," which can take a "gate" of as much as £7000, with an attendance of 120,000. It is played on the outskirts of London, often between two Northern clubs, with the consequence that, for a day and a night, the Capital is almost submerged by unfamiliar visitors, in rough cloth suits and caps, with large partisan rosettes, carrying rattles, buzzers and other noisy machines and speaking in strange Yorkshire or Lancashire accents.

In these clubs all the players are professionals; and all the players in the bigger international Association matches are professionals.

This does not mean that there are not many excellent amateur footballers. Other international matches between the four British countries are played by Association football elevens composed exclusively of amateurs, and there are great amateur Association football matches between the Navy and various clubs in the contest for the Amateur Cup; but professionals and amateurs do not play together.

Rugby Union football, on the other hand, is entirely amateur, except for certain professional matches which are played in the North of England between sides of thirty, instead of the fifteen which is the usual rule in Rugby. There are amateur international matches, and there is an amateur County Championship; but perhaps the contests which attract the most attention are those between Oxford and Cambridge, between the London Hospitals and between the Army, the Navy and the R. A. F.

Association football is already so well known all over the world that it is unnecessary to describe it. Besides, it almost explains itself. One side is trying to kick the ball into a goal at one end of the field, and the opposing side is trying to kick it back into the goal at the other end. Rugby football is not so simple; for the first question which an uninformed spectator is inclined to ask is why the name of football is given to it at all—first because the two sides of players seem to spend so large a part of their time pushing against one another with their shoulders in the heavy and tangled mass called the "scrum," and not doing anything in particular with their feet; second, because they spend the rest of the time, not in kicking the ball, but in running with it in their hands or throwing it to one another, or grasping the man who has it by the legs, so that he falls down; and third, because the egg-shaped object which they carry or throw has no right, strictly speaking, to be named a ball, which is by definition, a round thing. However, I shall not attempt to explain the breathless and highly exciting intricacies of the Rugby game; for it would be impossible to make them clear to the uninitiated. It must be enough to say that its lightning changes of fortune, when the solid "scrum" does suddenly break up, are perhaps more thrilling and exhilarating to watch than the more precise and kaleidoscopic Association game, and that the violence which is tolerated in it is such that it is quite comprehensible that the playing of it should be confined to men who are good enough friends not to be vindictive, and have enough self-control not to be brutal.

An attempt must, however, be made to describe the game of cricket, because it has so many features which make the English character itself more comprehensible.

It is played on a large, open and level grass field, in the center of which may be seen, stuck into the ground, two sets of three sticks—or "stumps"—27 inches, or 69 centimeters high, each set of three stumps in line being 8 inches or 20 centimeters wide, and each line facing the other at a distance of 66 feet, or 20 meters.

Near each of these sets of stumps you will see a man, in white flannel trousers and white flannel shirt—it is the tradition that cricket should always be played in white flannels. Each of these men holds in his hand a wooden "bat," for striking the ball, and he wears on his legs a pair of white leather "pads," to protect him from the ball when it is bowled towards him.

These two men are the only two members for the moment "in play" of one of the two opposing elevens. Their nine colleagues are waiting at the edge of the ground for their turn to take their place at the "wicket"—that is to say, to be "bats-men," as those two men now are.

All the members of the other eleven are to be seen dotted about in various parts of the field. Finally, in the neighbor-hood of each "batsman" is to be seen a man in a long white cotton overcoat, beneath which appear the ends of dark trou-sers. These two men are the umpires, and take no part in the game.

One of the members of the eleven who are in the field then takes the hard leather ball—of about 3 inches or 7.6 centi-meters in diameter—approaches one of the two "wickets," or sets of stumps, and hurls—or "bowls"—the ball towards the other "wicket," where the batsman is waiting to receive it. The object of the batsman is to hit the ball, and send it far enough to enable him to change places with his partner at the opposite wicket before one of the men in the field stops it and sends it back so as to enable one or other wicket to be knocked down with it before the batsman or his partner gets there. If the batsman succeeds in doing this, one "run" is marked to him individually and also to his "side"—or two runs or more if the ball goes far enough to enable the bats-men to change places several times. The total number of runs scored by each side determines the result of the match.

Supposing one of the batsmen fails to get to the other wicket before it is knocked down, he is "out," and must be succeeded by one of the waiting members of his side, until the last partnership is dissolved, when the "innings" of the side is at an end, and the other side takes its turn at the wicket.

There are, however, other ways of getting "out" than fail-ing to reach the opposite wicket during an attempted "run." The striker may fail to hit the ball bowled at him, and it may hit his wicket. He is out. He may hit the ball into the air, and it may be caught by one of the men in the field before it touches the ground. He is out. He may get his leg into the way of a ball which would otherwise have knocked down the wicket. He is out.

If the batsman does not hit any runs, and consequently does not change places with his partner, he receives five successive balls from the opposing bowler. These five balls constitute what is called an "over," at the end of which another "bowler" sends down balls from the other end to the other batsman.

These are the very elementary features of the game; but they express little of its spirit. Much of this spirit is connected with the time limit. An important match will last three days, a less important match, two days, and a less important match still, one day only. In each case, there is a fixed time, at which the umpires must declare the match at an end; and there is not infrequently a great deal of excitement over the chances of either side just scoring a sufficient number of runs to win before "time" is called and the match remains undecided—becomes a "draw," as the saying is—or else of managing just to hold on long enough for the last man not to be "out," and thus to obtain a "draw" instead of a defeat.

The batsmen may consequently be either on the defensive or the offensive. They may be taking risks in order to make the runs quickly, or they may be cautiously and stolidly defending their wickets in order to play out time.

In any case, the issue is not decided rapidly. To any non-English onlooker, the first impression of cricket is that it is almost intolerably slow. And yet it has sudden moments of rapid action. A man "in the field" may stand about for hours without a ball ever coming his way; and then, all at once, he may have to run furiously in order to bring off a great "catch." Men on the batting side may wait their turn for hours while a happy partnership is piling up runs, and then they may have to go to the wicket, one after the other, when a turn in the tide sets in, and they have to try to recover the initiative. It is a game which requires patience, calculation and promptness of execution in the individual, immediate and loyal response between a pair of batsmen and corporate unity on the part of the side in the field. It is indeed, in every way, the typical English game. It is played in every British Dominion and Colony—some of its finest players have been natives of India—but it is the one English game which has never been assimilated by any other country, or played in any country by any but British subjects, the long-established cricket club in Philadelphia, in the United States, being the unique exception which proves the rule.

The very word "cricket" has come, in ordinary life, to mean reasonably fair and honorable dealing and the avoidance of sharp practice, which are part of the tradition of the game; and every Englishman understands the sort of condemnation which is implied in describing any practice or transaction as "not cricket."

What has been described as the game's fetish in England has frequently been denounced, and with some reason. There is no doubt that too much time is devoted to playing games, to thinking and talking about games and to looking on at games. There is too much specialization, too much professionalism and too much of the sort of amateurism which is only professionalism disguised. There is also undoubtedly too much of the hero-worship of the successful player of games—and the hero-worship is not confined to the comprehensible enthusiasm of small schoolboys.

All of this is certainly true; but the average Englishman, even if he can be persuaded of this truth, will remain convinced that it merely represents the excess of something which is sound at the base. He will continue to have more confidence in a man who has had a good athletic record at school and university than in a man who has had merely a scholastic record, even though he will prefer the man who has had both—and they are commoner than may be supposed. He will continue to try and take a house as near a golf course as possible; and he will remark that the English cannot have been so far wrong about games, because the whole world is now following them, both in compulsory games for schools and in voluntary games for grown-up people. Moreover, he will feel some pride in the fact that England remains the international metropolis in all games, and that a lawn-tennis player from anywhere in the world will prefer to win the open championship at Wimbledon, a golfer the championship at St. Andrews, in Scotland, a rowing club the Grand Challenge Cup at Henley Regatta, on the Thames, and an athlete one of the Amateur Athletic Championships in London, to any distinction which they can obtain elsewhere.

The average Englishman's attitude in the matter is supported by the fact that since the playing of games has become general, the physical condition of the English people has certainly improved. Moreover, since the gradual breakdown of the severe sabbatarian tradition has made the playing of games on Sunday possible, not only has this physical improvement been assisted, especially in the classes whose only real leisure is on Sundays; but the moral condition of the workingman has been much healthier since he has had something else to do on his one free day than to lounge about the streets waiting for the public houses to open; and there is certainly far less drunkenness.

It may even be argued that watching games is not so entirely demoralizing as might be supposed, and it has been so argued by Robert Lynd, who calls it "one of the finest moral influences of our time," and points out the "terrific self-control" by which "we gradually subdue the wild animal in our breasts, that clamors for victory at all costs, and train ourselves to applaud—however reluctantly, however tepidly—even the good play of an opponent whose skill has cost our side the game." I fancy that perhaps Lynd may have had his tongue in his cheek, but I have heard the same argument advanced with the utmost seriousness.

I have not been able to speak here of all, by any means, of the sports practised in England. I have said nothing of such vigorously disputed contests in crowded local "games" festivals as scree-running on the steep, crumbling slopes of the Cumberland fells, or tossing the caber—the tree trunk—in the Highlands of Scotland. I have said nothing of wrestling or yachting or skating, or the coursing of hares with greyhounds, which is different from the hunting of hares with beagles— or the coursing of rabbits with whippets—a favorite sport with the Welsh miners. I have not touched upon the extensively practised sport of pigeon training and flying. I have not drawn attention to the remarkable revival of amateur boxing in recent years, especially in the Universities.

I will simply conclude with a glimpse of how sport in England is being maintained in war time. The whole of this glimpse is afforded by a single issue of the London *Times* early in the year. There it was announced that on that day, at Cambridge, a team representing Middlesex Hospital would play against the University at Rugby Football. In Association Football, Oxford would meet Cambridge in a return match for the one which had been played in the autumn, and there would be Public School matches between Winchester, Bradfield, Eton and Charterhouse. Oxford and Cambridge Universities were to have a boxing tournament. At the same time it was stated that the Racing Committee of Lincoln had applied to the authorities for permission to hold their usual race meeting near that town on March 24 and thus to inaugurate the flat racing season.

Looking forward to the summer and to cricket, the Surrey, Essex, London Counties and British Empire elevens were already arranging dates for matches. The County of Nottingham had made fixtures to meet teams from Derbyshire, Leicestershire and the Royal Air Force.

The sporting spirit has not abdicated.

Chapter X

NATIONAL DEFENCE, THE BRITISH EMPIRE

AND SEA POWER

A QUARTER of the land area of the world and more than a
quarter of the populations of the world are included in what
many people still loosely call the British Empire.

This is a remarkable fact; but merely stated in this way, it
is almost as misleading as it is remarkable.

The British Commonwealth of Nations, as it is now officially called, is not an Empire in the sense of consisting of
conquered peoples, ruled by the conqueror, exploited for the
benefit of the conqueror and paying tribute to the conqueror.
Not one of these four conditions applies to the nations which
compose the British Commonwealth.

They did apply to the Roman Empire in the past, and
they have, do and would apply to all countries controlled by
Germany and Italy; but not to the countries which, independently of each other, owe allegiance to his Majesty the
King.

Germans and Italians make no secret of their belief that
colonies should never be allowed to forget that they exist
only to serve and enrich the mother country. They make no
secret of their conviction that Great Britain has committed a
signal error in granting and promoting the complete inde-

pendence of the Overseas Dominions. The spontaneous assistance in money, men and material, which is freely being given to Great Britain today by every part of the Commonwealth, gives that conviction the lie.

There are many people, all over the world and some even in England itself, who vaguely imagine that the British Empire consists of outlying territories which the Government and the inhabitants of Great Britain not only own, but exploit to their exclusive benefit and profit. It is upon this belief that is founded the German propaganda about the supposed injustice of the British ownership of a quarter of the earth's surface, while other peoples lack living space. The whole thing is founded upon a misapprehension which is really quite ludicrous.

The territories in question are not owned, either by the inhabitants of Great Britain or by its Government, which has consequently no power to give away, sell or surrender them, in the way in which a private landowner might give up a part of his estate. They are owned by the people who live there. It is possible that certain individuals in Great Britain may possess property in these territories, if they have bought and paid for it, or may hold shares in commercial or industrial enterprises in these territories, if they have invested their capital in them; but individuals who are not British may be and are in the same position, while, on the other hand, there are British shareholders in all sorts of enterprises in countries which are not British at all. For instance, there is nearly twice as much British capital invested in the Argentine Republic as in all the British Colonies together. These holdings may indirectly carry with them a certain political influence for the individuals concerned, as all ownership of property does; but it is manifestly absurd to pretend that any Englishman possesses, from the mere fact of being an Englishman, any influence in a country other than England itself, even when it is a British Dominion or possession, and equally absurd to pretend that he draws any profit from those countries by reason of the fact that he is English. The British Empire is not the estate or property of the people of Great Britain, and the people of Great Britain, as such, draws no revenues from the British Empire, and is, therefore, in no sense the fat, plutocratic absent landowner which German propaganda represents it as being.

Nor does the British Government, as apart from the British people, draw such revenues. It neither exacts nor obtains any tribute from any part of the British possessions. On the contrary, it has spent money on various British colonies and lent money to them—loans of this kind, making a total of £11 millions, were converted into a free gift by the British Parliament in 1940. Moreover, the British Government has long assumed obligations for the naval and military defence of the whole extent of the Empire, which, in peace time, have sometimes been only in part reimbursed by the territories concerned. The magnificent contribution, in men and money, which all parts of the Empire have made to the British war effort has been entirely a voluntary contribution. It need not have been made unless each separate community had freely decided to make it.

With regard to the great self-governing Dominions— Canada, Australia, New Zealand, South Africa and Eire, or Southern Ireland—they would not even have been at war with Germany at all, if they had not decided upon that course through their own Governments and their own free parliamentary institutions—which most of them did, immediately on the declaration of war by Great Britain—for they were by no means automatically involved in the state of war between Great Britain and Germany. The South African parliament decided by only no more than a small majority to declare war, and Southern Ireland even chose to remain neutral, and remains neutral to this day. Since the Statute of Westminster was passed in 1931 by the Parliaments of Great Britain and of the Dominions, each one of them is what is described as an "autonomous community," and is specifically declared to be bound by no law passed by the British Parliament after that date. They are equally bound by no action which is taken by the British Government. Each of them has its own Government, which makes its own decisions, and its own Parliament, which passes its own laws, votes its own taxes and spends its own revenue. They are free to take whatever measures they think fit for their own defence or to make whatever contribution they think fit to the joint defence of the Commonwealth. They fix their own customs tariffs (sometimes, as in the case of Canada, severely hitting British trade) and their own immigration laws (sometimes excluding certain classes of British subjects). They appoint their own diplomatic representatives (Canada, Australia, South Africa and Eire have their own Ministers in several foreign capitals) and they receive diplomatic representatives from foreign countries. There is a German Minister in Dublin at this moment.

The position of the Dominions is that each one of them is an independent State, entirely on an equality with Great Britain, and that they are loosely attached together by an unwritten alliance, which has no stated obligations, but which is represented by the fact that the King of England is separately the King of each one of them, and also by the fact that they have all—except Eire—agreed to maintain, in London, a single Court of final appeal in matters of law. This Court, which is the Judicial Committee of the Privy Council, is one more example that the idea of justice lies behind all British political conceptions.

It may be argued, however, that there are British overseas possessions which are not self-governing Dominions, and great overseas territories administered by Great Britain which are also not self-governing; and that if the self-governing Dominions are in a position to defend themselves to some extent against British rapacity and exploitation, these other countries are not. There is India, for instance. There are the Colonies. There are the territories held under mandate. All of these, it may be urged, are valuable assets to Great Britain, both in the way of trade and in the way of providing lucrative posts in their administration for young Englishmen—the latter particularly in the case of India.

To these arguments there are conclusive replies. First, in regard to commercial benefits, it can be pointed out that if England—in the sense of the English commercial community, and not the British Government—carries on a prosperous trade with her Dominions and other possessions, she also carries on a prosperous trade with overseas countries which have no political associations with Great Britain, notably with the United States, with Brazil, the Argentine and other South American republics and with China. Moreover, the British Dominions and Colonies are free to trade with other countries than Great Britain, and do in fact do so; for less than half of their imports are British. Second, with regard to employment for Englishmen in India, it can be shown that although India contains a population of about 330 million people, there are now only 715 European Civil Servants and 450 officers of the Police Service; and that even some years ago, when there were fewer native and more British Civil Servants, the proportion to population was still very small. Moreover, young Englishmen, many of whom are of an adventurous temperament and like to go and seek their fortunes abroad, do so in other countries, besides those of the British Commonwealth. They can be found all over the world.

So indeed can Germans. This would suffice to knock on the head the argument that Germany needs colonies as living space for her surplus population, even if it were not already knocked on the head by the fact that even when Germany had colonies, very few of her surplus population went there.

That was very largely the fault of the way in which the German colonies were developed. It was also due to the climatic conditions of the German colonies, which were not attractive to European settlers as distinct from European managers of native labor; and it may be said that similar climatic conditions obtain in almost all the colonies—as distinct from the great Dominions—which European countries could hand over to Germany. Germany would therefore have had nothing to gain, from the point of view of "living space," by the acquisition of such colonies. In any case, it remains true that Germans who have wanted to emigrate could emigrate and have emigrated to independent foreign countries, where they thought they had a better chance of making a living than in any colony, and where the climate is more agreeable for European out-of-door workers.

Finally, there is the argument that in the countries of her "Empire" Great Britain was reserving to herself a sort of "corner" in the sources of supply of raw materials and that these sources of supply should be shared out afresh, in order that each European country should possess a reasonable proportion of them.

The main fallacy of this argument is that it is based upon an exclusively war-time conception of the control and distribution of raw materials. In time of war, it is certainly very valuable to Great Britain, that, as I have already pointed out in another chapter, large supplies of raw materials are available in countries which are under the political control of herself, her Dominions or her Allies, and that in the case of certain raw materials, this should be true of almost the entire world supply. For, under war conditions, Great Britain is not only assured of being able to obtain these raw materials herself, but of being able to refuse them to her enemies—although her control of the seas would in any case prevent her enemies from taking them home.

However, these conditions do not apply in time of peace.

Then, any one who can pay for and remove the raw materials can obtain them, whether the private individuals who sell them are British subjects or not, or are resident in countries belonging to the British Commonwealth or not, and whether the private individuals who buy them are Englishmen or Germans or men of any other nationality; and the terms on which they can be bought are the same, whatever the nationality of the buyer. Although the Free Trade policy which was previously the rule with regard to the imports and exports of all British possessions has been modified as far as imports are concerned, there is no restriction whatever upon exports —of course in peace time.

What is still more important is the fact that, according to the Report of the League of Nations Committee on Raw Materials in 1937 "the total present production of all commercially important raw materials in all colonial territories—again, as distinct from the independent Dominions—is no more than about 3 per cent of the world production." Consequently, a new deal in colonies which produce virtually no meat, wheat, wool, coal or iron, would not give any appreciable increase in the possession of sources of the really important raw materials to Germany, which at present has no colonies.

It is not without interest to remark that the spirit of liberty, independence and self-government, which is so characteristic of the Dominions of the British Commonwealth today, is also to be found in those possessions and colonies which are on the way to self-government, but have not yet completely achieved it. Indeed, it is to be traced in the history of all British Dominions and Colonies, except those isolated points of purely strategical significance, of which I shall speak later. It is to be discovered even in the circumstances of their acquisition.

The basis of the British Commonwealth is trade, and particularly trade by sea. This is what makes the British Commonwealth unique in the history of the world. There have been many other Empires, but all of them have been based upon conquest and upon the exploitation of the conquered peoples. Very little of the British Empire has been conquered; but when it has, the enemy has nearly always been a Power which was exploiting the native peoples, and the British purpose has always been to establish commercial relations with the inhabitants. Parties of adventurous travellers belonging to the "nation of shopkeepers" have begun by making journeys to distant lands, in order to sell British goods to the natives or to acquire the natural products of the country and sell them at home. To do either of these things, and especially to cultivate the products of the country, the British travellers became settlers, and a colony was founded, which sometimes also served as an outlet for surplus population at home. These are the beginnings of by far the largest part of the British Commonwealth of Nations.

In some other cases, the sovereignty over what were then called colonial territories has been acquired as the result of a treaty with another European Power. In others again, the inhabitants have placed themselves under British protection, and have eventually become British subjects.

The cases in which the acquisition has been by conquest are rare; but it may be remarked that when they have occurred, they have never been the result of a deliberate intention to subdue a foreign people and to maintain domination over them by armed force, as happened, for instance, throughout the history of the Roman Empire, but has not happened in the history of England since the fifteenth century, when Henry V invaded France and his successor was driven out by Joan of Arc. Expansion has nearly always been undertaken by the British Government rather reluctantly, and has been forced upon it by the necessity of protecting an already existing British settlement of traders from external aggression.

This was the case in South Africa, but most particularly in India, certain points on the coast of which were, in the seventeenth century, no more than trading stations of the East India Company. This company had neither the means nor the desire to conquer territory, and was considerably embarrassed when it gradually found itself involved, first in conflicts with French rivals and eventually in the control, administration and defence of land and population. This administration was only completely handed over to the British Government in 1858.

Nowhere better than in North America has it been possible to see the two most characteristic features of British colonization—foundation by peaceful settlement and development by local self-government. The Colonies which have now become the United States of America were founded and developed in this way in the seventeenth century; and it was because, in the eighteenth, England unwisely attempted to interfere with the local liberties, which she had hitherto left undisturbed, that she lost the Colonies, but learned a lesson which she has never since forgotten.

Canada is a good illustration in another way. French Canada was acquired in the middle of the eighteenth century as the result of successful war against France; but although there was at first some danger that an attempt would be made to anglicize the colony, the far-seeing decision was eventually taken to guarantee to the French Canadians the full protection of their religion—they were and are Catholics—their language, their laws and their customs.

Thus was inaugurated the practice of the safeguarding of the rights of minorities, which has ever since represented one of the guiding principles of British colonial administration, and is being faithfully observed today in dealing with the problem of India. The French Canadians, though they form nearly a third of the population of Canada, are nevertheless a minority; for they occupy only what is called Lower Canada, whereas the rest of the Dominion has progressively been settled by British immigrants, and first of all by those introduced through the activities of the Hudson's Bay Trading Company ever since the middle of the seventeenth century. However, although they are a minority, the French Canadians, having their minority rights guaranteed, have always been excellent British subjects.

Canada is the oldest of what are now the great overseas Dominions, although Eire, or Southern Ireland, which also holds Dominion status, is much older still, and had a highly developed cultural civilization as early as the ninth century—but Eire stands almost in a category by itself.

In Australia, the first colony was established, entirely by British settlers, in 1788, five years after the loss of the North American Colonies. This colony was called New South Wales. During the nineteenth century, the remaining Australian States were founded, and were united as the Australian Commonwealth in 1901. The population of no more than 6,600,000 is entirely British, except for 17,000 aborigines in the Northern Territory.

The colony of the Cape of Good Hope was acquired by treaty from Holland in 1814, and its population, as well as that of two of the three other States, which are today included with it in the Union of South Africa, is still largely Dutch in race and language. The Union of South Africa, however, now furnishes the most eloquent of all illustrations of the wisdom of the British policy of local autonomy. It was only four years after the end of the long and bitter war between the British forces and the Dutch Boers of the Transvaal that what was then considered by many to be the dangerous experiment of granting self-government to the Boers was put into effect. It was so successful that the Union of South Africa, including two mainly British and two mainly Boer States, was formed only three years later, in 1909. Moreover, in the Great War, two of the British Generals of the South

African forces fighting against Germany were men who had been Generals fighting against Great Britain in the Boer War, and one of them, General Smuts, is now Prime Minister of South Africa and Commander-in-chief of the South African forces fighting against Germany and Italy. The total population of the Union of South Africa is 9,600,000; but of these only 2,000,000 are of European stock, the remainder being of colored races.

The youngest of the Dominions is New Zealand, for its foundation as a British Colony dates back only to 1840. It is also the smallest of the Dominions in population. This is only 1,600,000, and rather more than half of it is of the native Maori race. New Zealand is nevertheless a very prosperous country, and one of the most advanced in the world in social legislation.

The population of India is far larger than that of any other dependency which owes allegiance to the British Crown. It amounts to nearly 339,000,000 for India alone and nearly 353,000,000 if Burma is included. The area of India and Burma together is 1,800,000 square miles, which is hardly two thirds of that of Australia and not half of that of Canada; but the population is 53 times that of Australia and 34 times that of Canada.

The political constitution of India is at present in an intermediate state. The supreme authority is still the Government of Great Britain, as it has been since 1858; and that authority is exercised through the India Office in London and through the Viceroy or Governor-General in India, in regard to whom the two Houses of the legislature—containing both nominated and elected members—act only in an advisory capacity. However, it is already an accepted principle that the views of the legislature shall be followed on matters of tariff policy, in which Indian interests shall definitely be placed above those of Great Britain. In fact, tariffs hostile to Great Britain have existed in India ever since 1919.

As for the ultimate intentions of the British Government, they go a great deal farther in the direction of autonomy, and definitely aim at complete Dominion status for India. In 1935, the British Parliament passed the Government of India Act, which authorizes the establishment of a federal system for the whole of India; and under this system the Governor-General will act on the advice of a Council of Ministers responsible to the two Houses of the legislature, matters of defence and external policy being alone reserved for his direct authority—that is to say the authority of the British Government. The Lower House of the legislature, which is called the Assembly, will be elected by universal suffrage, including votes for women.

However, it had not been possible, before the war, to arrive at agreement among the varied elements existing side by side in Indian politics, and to bring federation into existence, and the solution has had to be postponed until the return of peace.

These elements are unfortunately, some of them, in acute conflict with one another; and the problem, for which no solution has yet been found, is to create proper safeguards for the rights of minorities.

The main division, which cuts right across Indian life, is that between the Hindus and the Moslems, antagonistic both in race and in religion. Historically, the Moslems arrived in India as conquerors of the Hindus, and they possess military qualities which the Hindus generally lack; but they are less intelligent, less highly civilized, less politically conscious and, above all, far less numerous—they represent only 22 per cent of the total population, whereas the Hindus represent 68 per cent.

There is another division, which cuts across the Hindus themselves. It is between those of the higher castes and those who belong, from their birth, to what are called the depressed classes, the "untouchables," those who have no caste at all.

There are 50,000,000 of these, in the total of 239,000,000 Hindus.

Another division again is one which is not between individuals or classes, but between States. What is called British India, divided into provinces and administered by the Indian Government, contains three quarters of the population of India, but not much more than half of its area. The remainder consists of natives States, some Moslem and some Hindu, ruled by Indian Princes, under the suzerainty of Great Britain, but otherwise independent. Naturally enough, they also are anxious that their rights, which would be minority rights as far as the whole of India is concerned, shall be safeguarded.

When the new Constitution comes into force, the Federation will consist, not only of the Provinces now included in British India, but of the native Indian States, which would be under the control of the federal Government, legislature and judicature as far as matters of federal importance are concerned, and would be subject to federal taxation, but would otherwise be independent, and would even be independent in the administration of federal legislation within their States, where the form of internal Constitution to be adopted would be determined by their rulers.

The Hindus, who are, as I have said, both the most numerous and the most politically conscious of the Indian races and sects, form the great majority of what is called the Congress party—though the actual chairman of the party happens to be a Moslem. This title of "Congress" is apt to be misleading to any one not familiar with India; for it does not represent an Assembly of many parties, but a militant political organization, which is opposed by the almost unanimous body of the 90,000,000 Moslems, by the 50,000,000 of the "depressed classes," by the 7,000,000 Christians, the 3,000,000 Sikhs and the Indian native States, which govern a population of about 80,000,000.

The ingenious methods of passive resistance, to which the

Congress party, under the leadership of Mr. Gandhi, have resorted, make the efficient Government of the country difficult, especially as a certain proportion of the party have not been content to proclaim the right of conscientious objection to military service, a right which has been recognized in England for British subjects, but demand the liberty to agitate actively against recruiting—for there is no compulsory military service in India except for British-born subjects—and also against working in munition factories. Their attitude is all the more paradoxical, as they do not conceal their complete want of sympathy with Nazism.

This is the bare outline of the difficult situation in India, from which some issue will have to be found before representative self-government, which in its nature depends upon mutual toleration between majority and minority, can become a practical reality.

What is it, then, which has enabled Great Britain for so long to govern India? What has caused the British Government of India to be both accepted and respected? It is certainly not force; for in normal times, the number of British troops in India is not more than 57,000 men, who could be swept into the sea by India's 350,000,000. It has been suggested that it is the very existence of the antagonism between the Hindus and the Moslems, since the Moslems would at once butcher the Hindus if the British, who at present keep order, were to depart, and that this is why the Hindus therefore tolerate the British presence; but it would not suffice if there were a general antagonism to British administration.

Perhaps the real and profound reason is that British justice has been established in India, and that Indians of all races and religions have learned to have confidence in British justice. An American observer who admits frankly that he finds much to criticize in the British Government of India, declares that the great benefit which it has brought to the country is "the system of law courts, which recognizes all men as equal before the law."

I have already pointed out in an earlier chapter how closely interwoven the whole political and social system of England is with the sense of justice and of law. The very freedom which is the political ideal of the Englishman is freedom under the law. The Englishman knows that, at home, he gets a fair deal from the justice of his country. Every one who comes under the rule of England, be he white or brown or black or yellow, discovers that he gets a fair deal from British justice; and an illiterate Asiatic coolie can invoke the law of Habeas Corpus, if he thinks he is illegally detained, can carry the case on appeal to the Privy Council in London and can obtain satisfaction under a right which was won by Englishmen from a feudal King six centuries ago.

This right of appeal from the courts of the Dominions and Colonies to the British Privy Council is the only administrative link, apart from the persons of the King and his representative, the Governor-General, which remains, since the Statute of Westminster of 1931, to bind the Dominions to the mother country. It is not without symbolic significance that this last surviving bond—which, remember, does not exist in the case of Eire—should be one of law. For it is British justice which is chiefly responsible for the fact that, not only in India, but in many places all over the world, races which are not English consent to be ruled by the English.

For they do consent. That is the point. And they do get a fair deal. They are decently treated—or, in exceptional cases where they are not, they can get justice.

Moreover, their own customs, their own point of view, are respected.

This may be seen in the case of the many British possessions which are not great self-governing Dominions, but are Colonies, Protectorates or Mandated Territories, and are to be found, in addition to the Dominions, in Europe, Asia,

Africa, the two Americas and Australasia. Some of them are large, like Newfoundland, which was given the status of a Dominion, but abandoned it temporarily because of financial difficulties, like Burma, which is now administratively separated from India, like Ceylon and Jamaica, like Nigeria, with its native population of 20,000,000, like the Gold Coast and the Sudan and Northern and Southern Rhodesia and Bechuanaland and Tanganyika and Kenya and the Malay States. The same thing may be seen in the case of many smaller Colonies. There is not one of them which would willingly cease to be governed by Great Britain; and there is not one where local needs and the local point of view are not considered, not one where some step has not been taken in the direction of self-government. The advance, which generally begins by taking the form of a partly elected advisory council, is in many cases small, because the United Kingdom, in following the principle that control should be relaxed if the population shows signs of being able to manage its own affairs, regards itself as the custodian, not only of the rights of minorities but of the interests of the native peoples, which must not be sacrificed to those of European immigrants. In other cases, the advance has been great—Southern Rhodesia, for instance, is almost in the position of a Dominion.

The essential differences between the Colonies and the Dominions are that, in the Colonies, whatever the degree of local self-government which obtains, issues of foreign policy are in the hands of the British Government, which is consequently responsible for providing security against aggression, although the Colonies are expected to provide supplementary forces, according to their capacities. The British Government also appoints and controls the Governor, who is the head of the executive, and reserves the right to legislate or to disallow legislation. It controls financial and tariff policy, with the reserve that any tariff preference for British goods must be accompanied by a British preference for colonial exports and the still more definite reserve that Great Britain neither exacts nor receives any tribute, taxation or money payment, but that on the contrary she spends money on the Colonies.

Finally, there is a category of small colony, whose importance is directly linked with the defensive system of the whole British Commonwealth.

Just as most of the Colonies began in the form of coastal settlements for trade and specifically for maritime trade, with little thought of the inhabitants of the country beyond doing business with them and if necessary being protected from them, so a certain number of island harbors were acquired on the trade routes, in order that this merchant shipping should be able to put in for food, for water, for refuge from tempest and, later, for coal. These harbors gradually served as bases for the protection of the merchant shipping; but the far-reaching significance of sea power was for long but dimly understood; and it was first of all for commercial purposes that Great Britain acquired that chain of naval stations around the world, which have largely contributed to her present command of the seas, and are thus at the very foundation of her defensive, and still more of her offensive, strategy.

The main links of this chain, apart from Great Britain itself and the ports of the Channel, are Gibraltar, which closes one issue of the Mediterranean, Aden, at the end of the Red Sea, which closes the other issue, and Malta and Cyprus, in the Mediterranean itself; Jamaica and Bermuda in the West Indies; Ceylon, Singapore and Hong-Kong in Asiatic waters. In addition, Great Britain has agreements with Egypt and Iraq, under which British naval, military or air forces—sometimes all three, but air forces only in the case of Iraq—are maintained in those countries in time of peace.

It will be noticed that all of these bases—with the exception of Iraq—are on the sea; and this emphasizes the fact that the defence of the British Commonwealth is, first and last, maritime defence, and also, as I have just said, that even the offensive power of the British Empire is mainly maritime. It has always been sea power which has enabled the British Commonwealth to defend herself, and it has always been sea power which has enabled Great Britain to defeat her enemies. The battle of Waterloo was fought on land, but it was really won on the sea; and it was won, not so much by the spectacular naval victories of the Nile and Trafalgar, but by the constant pressure, which denied the use of the sea to Great Britain's enemies and prevented them from receiving supplies transported from overseas.

This is so true that, under normal conditions, the defence of the entire British Commonwealth is assured by the British Navy alone. There virtually is no British Army in peace time, except what is required for the maintenance of order in India and other territories. The Navy undertakes the whole responsibility.

Moreover, although certain Dominions do, in peace time, contribute important units to the British Navy—a contribution which is entirely voluntary—this contribution forms a relatively small part of the whole, and it may be said that Great Britain not only provides, but pays for the naval defensive system of the Empire.

As for any military defensive system, it can hardly be said to exist at all in peace time in the Dominions. As will be seen, there are certain liabilities of military service by the male population, but there are virtually no military forces.

These facts and their relative importance are hardly appreciated in time of war by the ordinary reader of the newspapers. He learns of the magnificent contributions in men, materials, energy, courage and labor, which are being made by the Dominions to the combined military effort; and he sees the news of the splendid and gallant achievements which have been placed to the credit of Dominion troops in the Army and the Air Force. But he does not realize three things

—first that this military and air contribution has had to be improvised since the beginning of the war, second, that the men could not have been transported safely to the scene of operations, if it had not been for the existence of the far from improvised British Navy, and, third, that in spite of the brilliant successes of the Army and the Air Force, it is the constant pressure of the British Navy—"the Silent Service," as it has long been called in England—which is really winning the war.

The means by which this pressure is exercised is the blockade.

The blockade of Germany is the real, the effective British offensive against Germany, the offensive which will eventually produce the conclusive results, as it did in the last war. It is by preventing Germany from obtaining the supplies of all sorts—not food alone—which she needs, that her strength will be worn down; and the blockade of Germany naturally implies also the blockade of the countries which are controlled by Germany; for everything which reaches those countries is immediately at the disposal of the Germans.

It is not that Germany can be forced by starvation to surrender. She is quite capable of feeding herself and the countries under her domination as well, on condition that she does not divert to war purposes and transform into armaments the foodstuffs themselves and the labor which might be used in production—on condition, in fact, that she does not prefer guns to butter, and does not actually turn the butter into guns, or rather, into munitions; for fats can be made into glycerine, which is an important element in explosives, and so can grain or sugar.

The point therefore is that if, not even Germany herself, but the countries which she has conquered, are fed from outside, this food—or other food, which the Germans would have been obliged to abstain from taking or to furnish themselves, if the outside food had not been forthcoming—can be taken by Germany and used, not only for food, but for armaments.

The fact that the Germans realize that the blockade is the really dangerous weapon directed against them is shown by their desperate efforts to break it. Their purpose in conquering Holland and Belgium and Norway and France was not so much that these countries could themselves be of much value to them—for their reserves have been rapidly exhausted—as that their possession might enable Germany to cripple British sea power and thus break the British blockade; and the Germans' sense of the primary importance of doing this was such that they were prepared to face— temporarily, as they thought—even an increase in the British blockade through the closing of a number of previously neutral ports, which had allowed a certain amount of leakage. They hoped, and hope, to turn the tables on Great Britain by a counter-blockade, which, if it were successful, would bring her to her knees much more rapidly than her own blockade of Germany.

That is the real struggle. Germany is fighting desperately to defeat the blockade by reversing it—that is to say, she is making a sortie against the British offensive, the British siege.

It will be the nation which will get the cargoes which will win the war. Britain holds the key points of Dover, Gibraltar and Aden, where she can, in the case of Dover, prevent cargoes from coming out of the English Channel, and, in the case of Gibraltar and Aden can close up both ends of the Mediterranean. The fall of France has opened the French Atlantic and Channel ports to Germany; but these can be blockaded by warships.

Strategically considered, the military operations all round the Mediterranean, and especially in North Africa, represent an attempt on the part of the axis powers to break the blockade by obtaining the control of the Suez Canal and of Aden; and the advance of the troops of General Wavell was part of the British reply to that attempt.

Such are the broad lines of the strategic situation, both in time of peace and in time of war. They do not diminish the great value of the share of the Dominions and Colonies in the British military effort; but they put it into its right perspective.

The double fact that the defence of the Empire is essentially maritime and that it is normally assured by the United Kingdom has determined the different ways in which each Dominion has interpreted the peace time requirements of defence in general and its own voluntary contribution in particular. The Australasian Dominions, Australia and New Zealand, placed important forces at the disposal of the Royal Navy, and thus secured the special protection which their isolation and other circumstances demanded. In 1938 Australia was furnishing four cruisers—which have since become six—five destroyers, one seaplane carrier and three smaller craft, and New Zealand two cruisers and four other craft. These ships were manned, partly by officers and men from Australia and New Zealand, but also by officers and men from the United Kingdom, and they operated under the command of the Royal Navy of the United Kingdom. The heroic part which the New Zealand cruiser *Achilles* took in the battle of the River Plate will not be forgotten. Nor will the sinking of Italy's swiftest warship by the Australian cruiser, *Sidney*.

Canada, before the war, had six destroyers, one flotilla leader and one mine-sweeper (four others were being built). She also had forty other vessels of less importance. She had a Naval personnel of seventeen hundred officers and men. South Africa had a Naval Defence Service, and had a number of men listed in the Royal Naval Volunteer Reserve, but no vessels of greater importance than mine-sweepers and patrol ships. In 1928 a small Royal Indian Navy was created; but in the ten years of its existence up to the war, it had not yet been able to provide any serious addition to the Naval defence system furnished by Great Britain.

In regard to military forces, what had been done by all the

Dominions before the war was to maintain what was virtually a militia, on a voluntary basis with regard to Australia and New Zealand, which had abandoned compulsory service, and on a nominally compulsory basis with regard to Canada and South Africa, but with compulsion rather as a liability than a severely applied system. In Canada, the militia numbered about 7000 officers and 80,000 men. In Australia, the total military forces came to less than 40,000, in New Zealand to no more than 9000, and in South Africa to 15,000.

Each of these four Dominions had done something before the war to create the nucleus of an Air Force. In Australia, it numbered about 300 officers and about 2500 men, and it possessed 40 front line aircraft and 20 others. In New Zealand the total was 600 officers and men, 28 first line aircraft and 70 others. In Canada, there were 300 officers, 2500 men, 200 first line aircraft and 200 others. In South Africa there were 38 first line aircraft and 28 others.

I have quoted these modest figures in order to bring out the magnitude of the military and aviation effort of the Dominions since the outbreak of war. Those who have read of the achievements of the Dominion troops in Africa and of the Dominion airmen everywhere, and those who remember their achievements in the other War, may be inclined to think that these are great military nations, with large armies always on a war footing. It is important to make clear that on each occasion virtually the whole organization had to be created after the outbreak of war.

I have said nothing of India in this connection, for India is in a special position. It has a regular, professional, long service, native army, raised by voluntary enlistment and officered by Englishmen, as well as by Indians. This army, which amounts to a total of 260,000, exists primarily for the purpose of keeping order in India and on the Indian frontiers, and its members are not liable for service overseas. They are sent only if they volunteer.

It is impossible to give the complete figures of the Dominions war effort; for even if they were available and could be published, they are increasing so enormously every day that any that could be stated would soon become valueless. I can, however, offer some general indications of what had been done at certain dates.

By the beginning of 1941, 60,000 Indian troops had volunteered for service out of India, and had been despatched to the front, and there had been 18,000 applications for 350 places in the Indian Air Force.

Canada, who sent 400,000 men overseas in the last war, had, in this war, by the end of 1940, sent four divisions, numbering at least 50,000 men, to Europe, and had, at the same date, 150,000 men on the active list and 300,000 in reserve. All men between twenty-one and thirty-five became liable, at the beginning of 1941, to four months military training, instead of the one month established on the outbreak of war, and 6000 were being called up every month. By April, 1941, Canada possessed an active Naval personnel of 23,000, and had increased her Naval craft to 155 vessels. At that time, her war industries were turning out a million shells a month and making steel at the rate of two million tons a year—double her output in the last war. One factory alone was producing aerial bombs at the rate of 100,000 a year and 3000 tanks of the latest type were being built.

Perhaps the greatest Canadian effort, however, is in connection with the air. She was arranging to organize, during 1941, twenty-five Canadian air squadrons for overseas service, all the pilots to be graduates of the British Commonwealth Air Training Plan, and to double the number of 36,-000 men already in air training.

The Commonwealth Air Training Plan itself is operating in 50 air schools in Canada, and will, before the end of 1941, be operating in 60, in addition to 7 schools for instructors, which, in the first instance, are staffed by officers from Great Britain. It is taking pupils from the British Isles, from Australia and from New Zealand, and is turning out pilots at the rate of 25,000 a year and air crews at the rate of 30,000.

When we look at Australia, a country almost as big as the United States, but with a population hardly that of New York City, we find her war contribution in men to be, proportionately, at least as remarkable. Compulsory military training was introduced a few months after the beginning of the war, and, at the end of 1940, Australia had sent more than 120,000 men overseas, while 200,000 had been called up for home defence. The prowess of the Australian and New Zealand elements in the British forces in North Africa is already legendary. The personnel of the Australian Air Force had already risen to more than 40,000 by the beginning of 1941, and the 25 Air Training schools in the country were already turning out pupils who were being sent to Canada for their finishing instruction. It was calculated that, by 1942, there would be some 30,000 Australian pilots, observers and gunners fully trained, half of this number being pilots.

New Zealand shows up no less brilliantly. Before the end of 1940, more than 20,000 New Zealand soldiers had been sent to the war area, and as many were either training in New Zealand or waiting to be called up. The native Maoris had a battalion of their own, which has since distinguished itself at the front. New Zealanders serving in the R.A.F. numbered 1000, and 50 of them had already won war decorations. New Zealand was planning to train 4000 pilots a year, and 5000 men (out of 14,000 who applied for enlistment) were already serving in the New Zealand Air Force.

As for South Africa, compulsory service was made effective as soon as the Dominion decided to enter the war, and although compulsion is only strictly applicable to Home Defence, practically the whole of the 100,000 men serving in the fighting forces at the end of 1940 had agreed to go anywhere in Africa. A strong body of them followed the two-thousand-mile route Northwards to Kenya colony, and their achievements on the Southern front of Abyssinia have since become well known.

The contribution of these Dominions in fighting men is, however, far from representing the whole of their share in the struggle. Their financial and industrial effort has been magnificent. As Mr. Menzies, the Prime Minister of Australia, said in England, when he referred to the fact that the Australian Income Tax had been trebled, "Australians are not counting the cost. If we come out of this shooting match broke, we shall be better off broke than conquered." Australia has been building destroyers, tanks and several types of aircraft, and has been making shells. In New Zealand, war expenditure, per head of the population, already stood at more than £5 by the end of 1940 and will have been at least doubled by the end of 1941. In South Africa, munition industries are mobilized on a war footing, with the hearty cooperation of the local Trades Unions, and the defence vote for the year 1941 amounted to £46,000,000.

The industrial effort of all the British and Allied Dominions, Colonies and other Dependencies East of Suez was organized and coordinated in an important conference held at Delhi, in India, towards the end of 1940. The countries and Colonies taking part in it were those whose shortest and most direct means of communication with the Eastern end of the Mediterranean was by means of the Suez Canal, and they included India, Australia, New Zealand, South Africa, Southern Rhodesia, Burma, Hong-Kong, Ceylon, Malaya, the East African Colonies and the mandated territory of Palestine, as well as the Dutch East Indian Colonies, whose population is 60,000,000.

This conference, which was called the Eastern Group Supply Conference, was based upon the principle that all the countries taking part in it should be self-supporting in a military sense, and that they should be able to arm, equip and supply the forces which they were contributing to the

North and East African campaigns. Such was already to a great extent the case. The Australian and New Zealand troops were equipped in the main by their own countries, and so were those from South Africa. South African aeroplanes were based on Rhodesia and the South African Union. The Indian units were to a great extent supplied from India.

The potential resources of what may be called the Eastern group of the British Empire, with its population of nearly 500,000,000, are almost inexhaustible, and the purpose of the Conference was to mobilize them. This has to a great extent been done. The industrial production of India has been turned over to war production on an immense scale. Steel, artillery, machine guns, rifles, rubber tires and blankets are among the many things which are being manufactured in great quantities. Burma is supplying valuable raw materials in the form of petrol, lead, zinc, tin and teak. The virtual monopoly of the world's rubber output by British Malaya and the Dutch East Indies between them is well known.

These supplies are being brought together and directed towards the African battle fronts, and not the least of the economies which are thus being effected is that of shipping.

It should be emphasized once more, however, that neither the supplies themselves nor even the troops for whom they are destined could be, or could have been, transported to Africa if it had not been that the British Navy holds the command of the seas. Nor could the supplies and the troops which Canada has sent and is sending to Europe have succeeded in safely crossing the Atlantic—the first 50,000 Canadians reached England without the loss of a single man.

British sea power is the key to the whole situation.

The threat to British sea power is by no means negligible. It has been and is severe. Its severity was largely increased by the collapse of France, which placed bases for aeroplanes, as well as for submarines, within easy striking distance of the whole Southern cost of Great Britain. The submarine menace is pointed, not so much directly against the British Navy as against the Merchant Service, and is an attempt, as I have already shown, to establish a counter blockade against Great Britain. It has largely been defeated by the convoy system, and the British losses have to a great extent been made good, not only by rebuilding, but by the Norwegian, Dutch, Belgian and French shipping, which came under British control when these countries were conquered on land by the Germans. It is being effectively combated with the supremely valuable assistance in ships and men which is now being given by the United States.

As for the threat from the air, as Admiral Lord Chatfield has pointed out, it would never have been believed, before September, 1939, that it would be so relatively ineffective against ships of war—for it should be remembered that this is the only part of the air menace which need seriously be considered, since the bombing of towns, which was to destroy British morale, has failed so signally in its object. During the first eighteen months of hostilities, Lord Chatfield continued, the single British cruiser lost in the Mediterranean was the only major casualty from air attack and although there have been other such casualties since then, in the battle of Crete, they do not reverse his conclusion that the outstanding lesson of this war is the proof, once again, that it is ships which command the sea, and that they will continue to do so for fundamental reasons.

Chapter XI

THE MEN AT THE HELM

It is clearly impossible to give, even in outline, the portraits of all the men who are guiding the British ship of State through the storm, and still less to attempt to give to the contribution of each man its just place in proportion to the whole. Much of the most important work is being done anonymously. Either those who are doing it have no desire for recognition, or they are satisfied with the purely professional approval of their immediate circle, or else they would perhaps be glad enough to be recognized, but are nevertheless ready to give their utmost in key positions without thanks.

What I can do is to present sketches of one or two of the personalities, who, for one reason or another, have come to represent, in the imagination of the British people, the tremendous effort which, in fact, the people as a whole are making.

First of all must come the King, and with him the Queen. In writing about other aspects of the life of England and the British Commonwealth, I have referred to the way in which the King, in spite of the very limited political power which he possesses, is not only an impressive figurehead and a symbolic expression of the unity of the national spirit, but a very important personal influence. This influence extends beyond his office, and has been to a great extent the creation of himself and the Queen. Their simplicity, their high sense of duty, their family life, their graciousness and their transparent good will have certainly touched the heart of England.

The great dynamic inspiration of the country, is, however, in this hour of crisis, the Prime Minister, Winston Churchill. It is difficult to add anything to what is now known about him all over the world, to put an extra touch to the portrait which every newspaper reader, every cinema spectator has vividly before him. His habits and his personal idiosyncrasies are now public property. Every one has been told how he goes to bed when he arrives at his official residence in Downing Street at about six in the morning—the King having insisted that he pass the night elsewhere, for reasons of security, just as he insisted that the King and Queen no longer sleep in Buckingham Palace. Every one has been told how, from his bed, he dictates until ten o'clock, as he finds literary composition come better if he is lying down, and he has written all his twenty and odd books in this way, including the life of his ancestor, the great Duke of Marlborough (it may be added that many authors have chosen the recumbent position for their work, as it sends the blood to the head, and that among them was the historian, Lecky, who always wrote lying face downwards). Every one has been told that he takes an hour's siesta after lunch, that he will sometimes undress and go to bed for half an hour before dinner in the evening —not to dictate, but to sleep—and that he can take cat naps whenever he likes during the day—a faculty which was also possessed by Gladstone.

We all know that he smokes fourteen of the largest and finest Havana cigars a day, can generally be seen with one in his mouth or clutched in his fingers, "and enjoys every one of them," as he says: that he likes good, plain food, and especially cold roast beef: that he takes coffee, but never drinks tea: that he has an iced whisky and soda with his lunch and an occasional sip of vermouth when he is working in the afternoon, and pauses to allow his ideas to resume their flow: that the great hour of his day, for conversation, as well as for the informal, but often vital, discussion of policy, is the dinner hour, when he and the beautiful Mrs. Churchill— whose grandfather was a duke, as was his own—receive a dozen guests, the men always including sailors and soldiers, and the women being of the handsome and witty kind who, he says, give sparkle to life: that he allows himself to be completely managed by Mrs. Churchill in all matters concerning the renewal of his wardrobe, but that he usually wears a short black coat and striped trousers and the square-shaped black hat which has already become legendary: that although he is sixty-six years old, short legged and rather heavily built, his remarkable physical alertness enables him to jump for the rope ladder and board a man-of-war in a choppy sea, when younger and lither men hesitate, and that it is only a few years ago that he stopped playing polo, which he had kept up ever since he was a young cavalry officer: that he has been a brilliant and successful journalist, and was a war correspondent during the South African war, in the course of which he was taken prisoner by the Boers and escaped: that he dislikes bores, ceremonies and routine, and holds Cabinet Meetings at short notice all over the place, and not exclusively in the historic Cabinet room at 10 Downing Street: that he has a habit, distressing to his secretaries, of holding documents in the palm of his hand, and making pencil notes which become illegible, as he stabs holes through the paper: that he is inquisitive, persistent and good-humor- edly aggressive; and that he hates to hear people whistle.

Now some of these things are personally picturesque; but some of them are trivial, and not many of them are signifi- cant. To understand the real nature of the man, one must look for indications of something more profound—something

which will help to explain the unique prestige which he commands today.

He has not always enjoyed that prestige. English political
leaders and the English public in general had always been a
little shy of him, a little afraid to trust him—not because they
doubted his honesty for a moment, but because they questioned his solid soundness of judgment. They thought back
to the distinguished but rather capricious politician, Lord
Randolph Churchill, who was his father. They remarked
with some uneasiness that he has never been tied by the traditions of party consistency, as most Englishmen are, and although he began as a Conservative, he immediately became
the "enfant terrible" of his party, and he did not hesitate to
join the Liberals when Free Trade, to which he had never
concealed his fidelity, became the main issue, and he did not
hesitate to become a Conservative again when problems of
national defence came into the foreground.

Although perhaps he saved Great Britain just before the
outbreak of the last war, when he was First Lord of the Admiralty, by issuing to the Fleet, on his own responsibility,
the order to keep to their stations in the maneuvers which
they had just terminated, and thus to be virtually mobilized, before either mobilization or war had been declared,
and although his action at the Admiralty and the Ministry
of Munitions during the war was constantly approved, both
by the experts and by the public, yet, when once the war was
over, people again began to say that of course he was a brilliant man, but that he was not of the stuff of which Prime
Ministers were made. He was not safe. He was unstable.

Above all, he was versatile; and I have already indicated
with what suspicion the average Englishman regards any one
who possesses that quality. He was so clever in so many ways
that in every one of the departments of which he had been
in charge—Board of Trade, Home Office, Colonial Office,
Ministry of Munitions, Treasury, Admiralty—the permanent

officials declared that he immediately understood the technicalities, not only better than any previous Minister with whom they had had to deal, but often as well as they themselves, who had given their lives to the subject. Besides, when he was out of office, did he not earn his living as a writer of books and even newspaper articles, and did he not amuse himself by painting pictures, and not at all bad pictures either? None of these things inspired confidence.

And then he had always seemed so sure of himself; and the English do not like that. His first book, written when he was a young army officer, had dealt with the Tirah campaign, and it had been scornfully described as "Hints to Generals, by a Subaltern." He has never had much patience with tedious people, and that made him enemies in a country where, unfortunately, many of the bigwigs are dull; and he has never restrained his tongue from biting epigram on his political associates. And yet he has no more striking characteristic than his personal loyalty; and it was he who stood up in the House of Commons after Narvik to defend Neville Chamberlain, the Neville Chamberlain whom he had once described as "the undertaker from Birmingham" and as "a good Lord Mayor of Birmingham in a lean year."

Nor does he ever bear any ill will. I can remember that when I last saw him, I said that I rather hesitated to speak to him, as my brother had been the candidate who had tried to turn him out of Parliament at the last election. "Oh, yes, I know your brother," he answered. "I like him very much."

So this is the man to whom the English people suddenly turned instinctively in the hour of their greatest danger. He had been quietly but firmly shouldered away from office, not only for some time before the present war, but even for some time after it began. Yet, when the moment came, the demand for him was unanimous, was irresistible.

What was at the basis of that demand? His ability, yes;

but not his ability first of all. What England needed at that moment was the inspiration of his courage, his determination and his fighting spirit; and England got that inspiration.

You will remember his first warning to the English people on taking office—that they must be prepared to face what would be no easy task, and that all he could promise them was "blood and toil, tears and sweat"; and I cannot forbear from quoting once more two passages which are now memorable. One is from the speech that he made after the retreat from Dunkerque, when every one expected the immediate attack upon England, which, thank God, did not come at that moment:

"We cannot flag or fail. We shall go on to the end. We shall fight on the seas and oceans. We shall fight with growing confidence and growing strength in the air. We shall defend this island whatever the cost may be. We shall fight on the beaches, we shall fight on the landing grounds, in the fields, in the streets, and in the hills. We shall never surrender."

The other comes at the end of his speech to the House of Commons after the collapse of France:

"Freedom shall be restored to all. We abate nothing of our just demands. Czechs, Poles, Norwegians, Dutch and Belgians, who have joined their causes with our own, all shall be restored. If we fail, the whole world, all that we have cared for, will sink into the abyss of a new Dark Age made more sinister by the lights of a perverted science.

"Let us therefore brace ourselves to our duty and so bear ourselves that if the British Commonwealth and Empire last for a thousand years, men will say: This was their finest hour."

There were also the concluding words of his tribute to the R. A. F. after the great German air attack upon England in September, 1940, had been beaten off:

"Never before in the field of human conflict has so much been owed by so many to so few."

Now these magnificent phrases were not flights of eloquence coming white hot from the passion of a great natural orator, as they might have been, for instance, in the case of Lloyd George. Churchill is not a great natural orator. He is a man who, with indomitable perseverance and power of will, has made himself into a great orator in the face of almost insuperable natural disabilities. He has a lisp and he has a stammer. The lisp he has never quite conquered; but he has fashioned a technique in public speaking which makes it almost imperceptible, though it breaks out in private conversation to a degree which sometimes makes him difficult to understand. As for the stammer, that also is not permanently suppressed in ordinary talk, especially when he gets excited; but he has quite conquered it when he addresses an audience, as also has the King, who suffers from the same nervous defect.

Just as Churchill's manner of utterance is something carefully schooled, so is his every effect something carefully prepared. He writes his speeches, critically balancing and choosing every word as if it were a jewel, and he learns them by heart. He studies every joke and every gesture before a mirror. The impression of spontaneity, and even of momentary hesitation in selecting a word or a phrase, are themselves rehearsed and acted.

Moreover, every speech that he makes is entirely a new speech. He hates the idea of repeating himself, and even of using a telling phrase which has ever served him before. He says it is unlucky.

Churchill, as an orator, has intelligence, he has wit, he has fire and he has the heroic note when he needs it; but, above all, he has limpid clarity and simplicity. The amateur or critic of language can find in his speeches marvels of literary composition; but they are never above the head of the ordinary man. Aristocrat though he is by birth and tradition, Churchill is always close to the soil. He is always in touch with the man of the people.

And yet he never descends to vulgarity. Even his jokes, even his banter of his enemies, are in good taste. They are never offensive. Nor are they vainglorious. Churchill does not prophesy triumph. He encourages effort.

Looking, as he does today, with his round, red, comfortably sensuous face, like something between a bulldog and Mr. Pickwick, Churchill, as he stands to deliver a speech, is very much a British Everyman. Well planted, with his feet slightly apart, and his hands grasping the lapels of his coat, his short, rather heavy and slightly swaying figure could almost be that of the traditional English John Bull.

So much for Churchill the orator. What of Churchill the statesman?

First of all, he has subordinated everything to the vigorous pursuit of the war. Well might he say, as Clemenceau used to say in 1918 to those who made one objection or another to his political action, "Je fais la guerre," and refuse to discuss the matter further, relying upon the virtually dictatorial powers which the French Parliament had granted him. Churchill could make this reply, not only because he has the same singleness of purpose, but because the British Parliament has granted him almost as wide a discretion.

However, that is not quite the way in which he sees his duty. What is remarkable in his use of the power which he has been given is his anxiety to carry the War Cabinet, the House of Commons and the people along with him at every step. He carries the Cabinet with him by holding almost daily meetings. Neither Cabinet Government nor collective Cabinet responsibility has been abolished in England. They have merely been concentrated in the small War Cabinet of eight. He carries the House of Commons with him by constantly supplying it with information, constantly consulting it and constantly giving it opportunities for advice and criticism, which he welcomes instead of deprecating. He has proved his desire to carry the British people with him by having included no less than three members of the Labor Party in the War Cabinet, and three more—all in key positions—among those Ministers who do not belong to the Cabinet.

There is another indication of his reluctance to exercise uncontrolled power, and particularly of his desire to have constantly at his ear some one to warn him of whatever danger there might be in his own daring, his own readiness to take risks; and that is his deliberate inclusion in the War Cabinet of two men who were associated with the more cautious and more temporizing policy which had preceded his. He had frequently expressed his absolute disagreement with this policy in the past. In the matter of relinquishing the right of the British Navy to control and use the ports of Ireland, for instance, he had strongly attacked Neville Chamberlain before the war for handing the ports over to the Government of Eire. Yet he has in his Cabinet two men who were closely associated with Neville Chamberlain in this and other expressions of the policy of "appeasement." They are Kingsley Wood, now in charge of the national finances as Chancellor of the Exchequer and formerly Neville Chamberlain's Minister of Health before being his Secretary of State for Air, and, most notably, Sir John Anderson, long considered to be Neville Chamberlain's most trusted personal adviser. Moreover, when he formed his Cabinet, he included, as his Foreign Minister, one other, Lord Halifax, who had indeed since been entirely converted to the need for vigorous resistance, but who shared the Cabinet responsibility for the Chamberlain attitude and was associated with that attitude by the British public.

However, this refusal to be entirely separated from the more cautious elements in British politics in no way indicated any lack of forward determination on Winston Churchill's part. He came into power to give effect to the dogged British combative spirit, and he expresses that spirit in himself and in his every action. His snatches of sleep at odd moments are only short breaks in long days and nights of constant work, always on active duty, always cheering up the thrusters, always hustling the laggards, always exulting in meeting difficulties and mastering them.

Some of his hustle he may have inherited from his American mother, whose father was Leonard Jerome, at one time owner of the *New York Times*. Certainly, he has always been able to speak to the people of the United States with sympathy and understanding; and he looks forward to what he describes as the inevitable "mixing up together" of the affairs of the two great English-speaking nations "for mutual and general advantage" without any sort of misgiving. "I could not stop it if I wished," he said. "No one can stop it. Like the Mississippi, it just keeps rolling along."

In this, as in everything else, Winston Churchill looks at things as they are, and deals with them as they are. In a country where many people either fail to see the facts at all or are inclined to ignore them in order to nourish some pleasant illusion, he is the courageous and wholesome realist. He has shaken up the complacency of his countrymen by frankly telling them how things stand. I think his countrymen are grateful to him, and that this is one of the reasons why they trust him.

I referred just now to certain elements in the composition of the War Cabinet. One of its most important features is that the three Defence Ministries—Admiralty, War Office and Air Ministry—are not separately represented in it, and can only make their views known through the Prime Minister himself, who is also Minister of Defence, and thus coordinated demands, which have sometimes been shown in the past to be in bitter and dangerous competition with one another.

A second feature is that, out of the seven members other than the Prime Minister, no less than three are without portfolio, or hold offices which have no departmental duties. This allows them to give their whole energies to Cabinet business. Of these three Ministers, one is Sir John Anderson, whom I have already mentioned. He is a Scotsman, of under sixty years of age, who has been a Member of Parliament only since the year 1938, but who previously had a long experience in various branches of the Civil Service in England, ending up with five years in India, as Governor of Bengal. The other two are members of the Labor Party, first, Mr. Arthur Greenwood and, second, Major Attlee, the chairman of the party, who has never been a workingman, but is one of several Labor members who have had a public school and university education, and were attracted towards Labor by being convinced Socialists and by having worked among the East London poor in the educational organization called Toynbee Hall. The remaining members of the War Cabinet are the Chancellor of the Exchequer, Mr. Kingsley Wood; the Secretary of State for Foreign Affairs, Mr. Anthony Eden; the Minister of Aircraft Production, Lord Beaverbrook; and the Minister of Labor, Mr. Ernest Bevin.

The three Labor members of the Government who are not in the Cabinet are Mr. Hugh Dalton, Mr. Herbert Morrison, and Mr. A. V. Alexander. Each of the last two began his working life before he was fourteen, Mr. Morrison as an errand boy in a shop in London and Mr. Alexander as an office boy in a business in Bristol. Mr. Morrison, whose father was a policeman and his mother a domestic servant, gradually worked his way up from errand boy to shop assistant and then to telephone operator until he became a Member of Parliament in 1923 at the age of thirty-five. He was Minister of Transport in the Labor Government of 1929. He was also a Member of the London County Council, and became leader of its Labor party, which commanded the majority, in 1934. Mr. Alexander also held office in the 1929 Labor Government. He was First Lord of the Admiralty, and it was his success with the Navy at that time which induced Mr. Churchill to offer him the same post now.

Of all the Labor members of the Government, however, the most picturesque and the most powerful personality is undoubtedly Mr. Ernest Bevin, the Minister of Labor, who may even be said to be the outstanding figure in the War Cabinet after the Prime Minister himself.

His beginnings were even harder than those of Mr. Morrison and Mr. Alexander. He was born in 1884, and he was not yet eleven years old when, both his parents being dead, he started work as a farm boy in Somersetshire at the princely wage of sixpence a week. He gradually made his way to Bristol, where he was at first a page boy in a restaurant, and then, as he grew up, a street-car conductor, a clerk and the driver of a milk cart. He was thrown out of work, and for five years could get nothing to do. "One had to eat," he says, referring to that time, "so I stole."

At the age of twenty-six, he found himself in the position —purely honorary, of course—of secretary of the unemployed movement in Bristol, and eventually he joined the Carters' Section of the Dockers' Union. This was the beginning of a Trades Union career which led him eventually to becoming, in 1922, at the age of thirty-eight, the General Secretary of the enormous Transport and General Workers' Union, into which he had organized the amalgamation of thirty-six smaller Unions. It was in this capacity that he was a leading figure in the unsuccessful general strike of 1926, the other two large Unions promoting it being those of the Miners and the Engineers.

As the representative of his Union, he afterwards did important work at the International Labor Office at Geneva, and helped to create the Scientific Advisory Committee, which would have brought scientists into touch with Trades Union leaders, and would have enabled the latter to obtain advance information of impending technical changes and prepared them for the consequent necessary action, if the Trades Unions had only shown the intelligence and foresight to make use of it.

The dramatic turning point in Ernest Bevin's career came in 1935, when the British Labor Conference at Brighton discussed the question as to whether Labor should give its support to the principle of sanctions against Italy over the invasion of Abyssinia. Some time before, Bevin had been tempted to join the extreme Socialist wing of the Labor movement, largely in consequence of his dissatisfaction at the secession of Ramsay MacDonald to form the coalition National Government; but the discussion over Abyssinia made him throw in his lot against the Pacifists and the Socialists, and his tremendous speech—"if you support the League, you must take the risks" was his argument—swept the Conference. From that moment British Labor was committed to a strong foreign policy and to the principle of collective security, and Ernest Bevin was committed to the line which was to carry him forward to the position, which he has now taken, of using all his great influence to induce every workingman in Great Britain to contribute his utmost to the winning of the war— "save the lives of our lads," he says.

Bevin is convinced that this war is the workers' war, because the victory of the dictators would mean the slavery of the workers; but he is also convinced that this war must mark the end of class privilege and a real equality of opportunity for every one. As it is, he has done more to improve the status of the workers since he has been Minister of Labor than he was ever able to do during the years when he was merely a Trades Union Leader. At the same time, he has persuaded the Trades Unionists to allow many of their rights to be suspended during the war, to accept women as workers and to admit beginners to be trained.

He dislikes and distrusts politicians. He despises them as "intellectuals," that is to say, as theorists. He had never been in Parliament before the war, though he tried to get in once, and he is rather disposed to regard discussion as waste of time. He wants to "get on with the job," and he is certainly domineering by temperament. He listens to objections with a smile, and then smashes them with terrific force.

As a speaker, the strength of his personality and his tremendous voice make him formidable; and he is one of the few Ministers who are successful on the radio. He speaks with great directness and sometimes even with a touch of brutality, and both are effective.

Of medium height, thick set and even heavy, holding himself well, Ernest Bevin has a round and rather fat, clean-shaven face, a firm mouth with almost pouting lips, but a pleasant smile. He has a direct look from his eyes through his thick-rimmed spectacles. He often speaks with one hand in his trouser pocket, and uses the other hand with the fist closed to make his gestures.

One of the characteristics of the present Government—and really an innovation in our time—is that it is almost exclusively English, at least in its leading members. The War Cabinet contains only one Scotsman and no Welshmen or Irishmen. Moreover, every one of the leaders is an Englishman of a different but very representative kind. Nothing more English than Winston Churchill, in one type, than the elegant Anthony Eden, in another, than the sturdy Ernest Bevin, in another again; and nothing more English, in a fourth, than Lord Halifax.

The English do not, in general, go to church as regularly as they did; but they remain a deeply religious people. It is only necessary to remember the tremendous stir which was created, a few years ago, by certain proposed alterations in the Book of Common Prayer to recognize how far down the religious sentiment goes. I am not sure that it can be described as Protestant sentiment. Nor can it be described as Catholic. It is Anglican.

One side of this Anglican religious sentiment could hardly be better represented than by Lord Halifax. He is the very figure of the Christian English gentleman, and every Englishman knows what that means. He would no doubt find himself at variance on doctrinal matters with many other English Christian gentlemen; for the Anglican Church is wide enough to include an Extreme Right and an Extreme Left, and he belongs to the Extreme Right, to the section called in England High Church. His father even distinguished himself by agitating for many years in favor of a reunion of the Church of England with the Church of Rome —but upon a basis of Anglican autonomy which did not reveal a great sense of practical possibilities.

Viscount Halifax is a devout churchman. He has also inherited a family tradition of the duty of public service; for his grandfather, the first holder of the title, did much to place the Government of India upon a firm basis after it had been taken over from the East India Company. He is a great Yorkshire landowner and a great territorial and almost feudal magnate in those remote moors, where feudal traditions still stubbornly survive. Finally, he is a very keen foxhunter, and he has been heard to say that if he guided his life entirely by his personal preferences, he would rather be a Master of Fox Hounds than Prime Minister of England. He became Joint Master of the Middleton Hunt when he returned to his home in 1931, after having been Viceroy of India for five years.

To any one who is not English, it may seem to be a little difficult to reconcile these apparently contradictory attributes; but, to an Englishman, they go quite naturally together. They are all part of the English aristocratic tradition.

For Lord Halifax is, above all, an aristocrat of the most serious English kind, which has nothing to do with the smart set. The black clothes and the hard, round hat, which he always wears when he is not in the full dress of a tall hat, are some indication of this seriousness. His manners are those of meticulous, old-fashioned politeness; but he is incapable of familiarity, has nothing of the common touch and possesses neither the power nor the desire to impress his personality upon the multitude. He is willing neither to overrate nor to underrate himself. When he arrived in the United States to take up his present post of ambassador, one of his first public acts was to apologize to the representatives of the Press for having kept them waiting, and then to read them a statement in what one of them called "a deep hollow voice, as from an empty cathedral."

And yet he is, in his personal relations, far from being what would be called dull. The Prime Minister has publicly described him as "a man of light and learning, whose company is a treat"; and he can maintain the level of conversation, which is set by his wife, considered by the same high authority to be one of the wittiest women in England.

His watchword in thought is religion. In action, it is duty, as he sees it through his religion—"what is right must be done"—and he has never allowed difficulty to interfere with the performance of his duty, any more than he has allowed it to interfere with whatever he has made up his mind to do. When he was born in 1881, he was a magnificent child, but he had a withered left arm. At Eton and Oxford he played games in spite of it, and excelled at lawn tennis. He rode in spite of it, and became a splendid horseman. He commanded a Yeomanry regiment in the other war in spite of it; and today it is hardly to be noticed in his gaunt, lean and angular six foot five of solemn impressiveness.

Lord Halifax was married at the age of twenty-eight to a daughter of the Earl of Onslow, and he was already in Parliament as a young Conservative member, when war broke out in 1914. After the signing of peace, the Hon. Edward Wood, as he then still was, held various offices continuously during the various periods when the National Government or his own party was in power—Parliamentary Under Secretary for the Colonies from 1921 to 1922, President of the Board of Education from 1922 to 1924, Minister of Agriculture from 1924 to 1925. In 1926 the then Prime Minister, Mr. Stanley Baldwin, offered him the post of Viceroy of India. He hesitated much as to whether he ought to accept; and it is said that he only did so after he and his father had gone into church together to pray, and had agreed, on coming out, that it was his duty to go.

As the Viceroy of India must, by tradition, be a Peer of the Realm, and as he had not yet succeeded to the family title, he was made Lord Irwin; and it was as Lord Irwin that he spent the memorable five years, which have perhaps done more than anything else in our time to prevent the Hindu population, which is the great majority of the people of India, from becoming irreconcilably bitter in their struggle for political autonomy. First of all, Lord Irwin became convinced that Mr. Gandhi, the Indian nationalist leader, was a religious man, like himself, and a sincere man, like himself; and, which was perhaps more important, he convinced Mr. Gandhi of his own sincerity and honorable reliability. Secondly, he also became convinced that Dominion status was the proper solution of the Indian problem; and it was largely owing to his having acquired this conviction that the Government of India Bill was eventually passed through the British Parliament, four years after his return home. The aspects of his relations with Gandhi which strike the imagination—his walk alone through the Indian village to the Mahatma's house to see him, the prayers which they said together, their long talks upon religious and moral issues, the decision which Halifax nevertheless once had regretfully to make of having Gandhi imprisoned, and Gandhi's description of him, even at that moment, as "the noblest of Englishmen"—are the picturesque background to the central fact that the two men agreed to keep Anglo-Hindu relations as sweet as the circumstances could allow them to be.

After his return to England and the death of his father—who had managed to keep alive until the age of ninety-four in order to see him again—Lord Halifax, as he had now become, resumed his parliamentary and ministerial career, and was successively President of the Board of Education, Secretary of State for War, Lord Privy Seal, Lord President of the Council and, eventually, Secretary of State for Foreign Affairs, which he was made in 1938, after the resignation of Mr. Eden over the failure to apply sanctions against Italy. He remained Foreign Secretary and a member of the War Cabinet until his departure for Washington at the beginning of 1941.

This was the period of his association with the Chamberlain policy of what has been called the Appeasement of Germany—an association which had indeed already begun before he reached the Foreign Office, when Chamberlain sent him to Germany in 1937 upon what even then proved a fruitless attempt to establish really friendly relations. History will perhaps be able to determine—though it is by no means certain—in what proportions that policy was pursued, firstly, in the genuine hope and expectation that it would be possible to come to terms with Germany; secondly, in the desire to be able to show that Great Britain had left no reasonable stone unturned in her efforts to reach a settlement by agreement, and thus to build up a great moral case for the Government before its own people, the peoples of Europe and the people of the United States, and thirdly, with the simple practical purpose of gaining time for a rearmament which had been neglected.

It is doubtful whether Halifax, or even Chamberlain, ever really felt any confidence that Hitler would keep the promise which he made at Munich; but they had to act as though they did; and there is no question that when Hitler marched into Czechoslovakia in March, 1939, in flat defiance of his pledged word, he sacrificed any moral standing which he had previously held. There is also little question—and Doctor Beneš has since declared it to be so—that the acquisition and digestion of Czechoslovakia gave Great Britain a few more months to prepare her defence.

As far as Lord Halifax was concerned, his mind was made up from the moment of the German entry into Prague; and there seems to be no doubt that it was only the insistence of the British naval and military experts for a little more time which prevailed upon him not then to resign in protest against the British acceptance of the German action. In any case, it is certain that, from this time onward, Halifax was behind the progressive stiffening of the British attitude and particularly behind the guarantee to Poland, which was eventually the occasion for the British declaration of war.

It was therefore a fully determined man who rose from his seat in the War Cabinet to be the first British Foreign Secretary to pass directly from that high office to the occupation of the post of ambassador to a foreign country, the first ambassador to whom the Prime Minister has ever personally given Godspeed on the great British warship which was to take him to his post, the first British ambassador who has been welcomed on board his ship by the President of the United States. His determination was publicly expressed more than once before his departure from England. In December, 1939, he spoke of "the rank growth of the doctrine of brute force in the world" and added that "there can be no temporary truce or patched-up armistice, which would bring no real relief."

The American people no longer needed to be convinced of the justice of the British cause. They had reached that conviction before Lord Halifax landed in America, and that was not the purpose of his mission. Its object was to persuade

America to send arms and munitions and ships to Britain, and, above all, to send them at once—to make America understand that urgency was the essence of the whole problem.

I have said that the leading members of the Cabinet are English; but there is a notable exception in addition to Sir John Anderson, who is Scottish. This is Lord Beaverbrook, who is Canadian, although also of Scottish origin. It is appropriate enough that the North American continent should be represented in the ranks of the Government at this time; and the United States is indeed represented in another way. I have already recalled that the mother of the Prime Minister was an American citizen before she married Lord Randolph Churchill, and it may be added that both Admiral Sir Dudley Pound, the First Sea Lord of the Admiralty, and Sir Archibald Sinclair, the Air Minister, are the sons of American women.

As for Lord Beaverbrook, he is perhaps really more Scottish than Canadian; for although his mother was Canadian born, his father went to Canada from Scotland, and he himself has lived most of his life in Great Britain and in the United States.

Although he is now Minister of Supply, after being Minister of Aircraft Production, he is more generally known to the British public as the much-advertised proprietor of the *Daily Express*, the London daily paper with the largest circulation, and also of the *Evening Standard* and the *Sunday Express*; and he did his best to remain no more than a newspaper proprietor—perhaps because he had had enough of ministerial life when he became the first British Minister of Information towards the end of the other war. However, there was no more chance of his resisting the Churchill hustle than there usually is of other people resisting his own hustle. The Prime Minister telephoned to him every day to urge that it was his duty to accept; and finally he gave in.

I have said that he is a much-advertised person, and it

need hardly be added that he did the advertising himself. He encouraged the cartoonists of his papers to represent him as a symbolic little imp, rather like the conventional figure of Puck, with a huge head on a tiny and wizened body, and the principal feature in that head an enormous mouth, perpetually expanded into a grin from ear to ear. He also had himself written up as a rough-and-ready Far Westerner, breaking into the soporific calm of the London journalistic world with a number of newspaper "stunts."

The description was perhaps not far from the truth, as far as the "stunts" are concerned; but the portrait is largely fanciful. Lord Beaverbrook is neither tiny nor wizened, but is of medium height and has recently become rather broad; and although his mouth is large, and he can produce the wide grin for the photographer, he in fact smiles rarely. He is really rather simian in appearance, with long arms, and legs on the short side, and with a round clean-shaven face and flat nose.

The two outstanding elements in his personality are his unerring sense of publicity and his immense dynamic faculty for getting things done, and done quickly.

He may think that his publicity sense is in abeyance, now that he has temporarily forsaken the newspaper world for that of public administration; but it breaks out at every turn. There was the aluminum shortage, and his appeal to housewives to give their saucepans in thousands. Not only did he soon have so much aluminum—including at least one artificial leg—that he was obliged to announce that he had enough for the present; but every kitchen and every family in the land had been awakened to the need for the quicker production of airplanes. There was the gift of £100,000 from Jamaica to help build Spitfires and the way in which, properly advertised, it set the ball rolling so that money poured in.

As regards his capacity for getting things done, no one who

has worked with him, either at the Ministry or on one of his newspapers, will forget the way in which he can bark, in that harsh, staccato voice—which he is able, however, sometimes to make tender and friendly—"I'll tell you what I want you to do, and I want you to do it today."

He does succeed in getting things done, and he succeeds by the use of his own special mixture of friendly confidence, noisy bullying and sly humor. He also gets them done by adopting the method which he found so successful in his newspaper offices, which was to break up the watertight compartments—rabbit hutches, he used to call them—and throw every one together in general collaboration. In Fleet Street it meant putting the editor and every one else into one vast room, which was uncomfortable and tended to be noisy, but at least excluded open idleness and made for speed. In the Ministry of Aircraft Production, it has meant virtually pooling all the manufacturing firms, snatching raw materials from one and giving them to another. In both Fleet Street and the Ministry it was accompanied by a drastic simplification of methods and staffs.

And yet Beaverbrook was not a dictator in his newspapers in the sense of interfering with the work. He was a principal contributor and an adviser—"I read those papers, but I don't write everything in them," he used to say. His plan was to back up his editor and every one on his staff as long as he was satisfied with them, and to dismiss them as soon as he was not; and this is, as far as possible, his plan at the Ministry. There he sits at his large writing table, with its unexploded German clock bomb upon it, in his large office with its tall windows, looking out upon a splendid view of London and the sky. Sometimes he broods. Sometimes he gets excited and makes his familiar gesture of raising both of his arms and shaking the open palms of his hands. He does not indulge in easy optimism; but he does not interfere with those who are working for him as long as he feels confident that they are producing or will produce results. Results are all that he wants.

The Government cannot perhaps be called a Ministry of young men, but it certainly cannot be called a Ministry of old ones. Its oldest member among the holders of important offices is Lord Simon, the Lord Chancellor, and he is only sixty-seven, a year older than the Prime Minister and Mr. Amery, the Secretary of State for India, who are both sixty-six. Lord Beaverbrook is sixty-two. Lord Halifax and Mr. Kingsley Wood are both sixty, and Sir John Anderson and Major Attlee a couple of years younger. The juniors are a group who are just over or just under fifty. They include Mr. Duff-Cooper, the Minister of Information, Sir Archibald Sinclair, the Air Minister, Captain Margesson, the Secretary of State for War, Captain Oliver Lyttelton, President of the Board of Trade until July, 1941, and since then, roving Minister for Near Eastern affairs, and Mr. Anthony Eden, the Secretary of State for Foreign Affairs, who is the Benjamin of the War Cabinet, for he is only forty-four.

The position and the outward personality of Mr. Eden are in curious contrast. Young, very good-looking and very well-dressed, he might well seem to be one of the many polished, agreeable but hardly very responsible or energetic junior secretaries in that Foreign Office or that diplomatic service, of which he has twice been the chief at an age when most politicians are still at the beginning of their career. Yet he has shown courage, initiative, activity and character, which entirely belie this superficial impression. When he ended his first tenure of the office of Secretary of State for Foreign Affairs, it was because he preferred to resign rather than sacrifice his convictions upon a matter of high policy; and today he does not hesitate to jump into an airplane and speed across a war-torn Europe in order to place the British case, in the most forcible and persuasive manner, before Allied Governments.

Politicians are always more in the public eye than the leaders of the fighting forces; and among the latter the generals are always better known than the admirals, although the Navy is still, not only the "Senior Service" in Great Britain, but the main bulwark of British defence as well as the spearhead of British attack. However, the Navy has always been content to remain, not only the Senior, but the Silent Service; and it is neither surprised nor indignant that for ten people who have heard of Lord Gort or General Wavell, there is hardly one who knows the name of Admiral of the Fleet Sir Dudley Pound.

And yet the First Sea Lord and Chief of the Naval Staff carries from day to day and all the time a responsibility which is far greater than that of any military chief. The whole of the seas of the world are his province; and although he does not direct any tactical battle action, it is on his orders that units of the Fleet are sent from place to place, it is he who, with the political First Lord of the Admiralty and the Naval Staff, determine strategy, and it is therefore he who will largely make or mar the result of a battle. He obtains no particular credit if things go right, but he gets all the blame if they go wrong. After the last war, Joffre said one day, "I understand that some people cannot make up their minds as to which French general really won the Battle of the Marne. I know quite well who would have lost it."

As a junior officer, Sir Dudley Pound, who is now a man of sixty-three, specialized in torpedo work, and when he held the rank of lieutenant, he was sent to the Admiralty as expert assistant to the Director of Naval Ordnance. He obtained his first command of a ship in 1915, and did well at the Battle of Jutland. After the war, he was Chief of Staff to Sir Roger Keyes in the Mediterranean. He was Second Sea Lord at the Admiralty from 1932 to 1935, and then once more became Chief of Staff to the Commander-in-Chief of the Mediterranean Fleet, who was now Sir William

Fisher, and he succeeded him in 1936 as Mediterranean Commander-in-Chief himself. It was only a couple of months before the present war began that he became First Sea Lord on the death of Sir Roger Backhouse.

As a commanding officer, Sir Dudley Pound has the reputation of being a keen disciplinarian, whose bark is, however, worse than his bite, and of being the typical "breezy fellow," which a naval officer is expected to be. What is perhaps a clearer indication of his character is that he has always devoted himself to the welfare of the Lower Deck, in the sense not only of making the men comfortable on board, but also of ensuring that their families at home receive reasonable and proper allowances.

The name of Sir Andrew Cunningham has crept into the newspapers because the cooperation of the Navy contributed very largely to the British military successes in North Africa, and he was and is Commander-in-Chief of the Mediterranean Fleet. He is a man of fifty-eight, and has seen most of his service in torpedo craft—either torpedo-boats or destroyers. He distinguished himself particularly at the Dardanelles, and, after the last war, he became a captain at the early age of thirty-six, after having won the Distinguished Service Order three times—that is to say, he now wears the D.S.O. with two bars. Later he commanded the whole flotilla of destroyers in the Mediterranean, and in 1939 succeeded Sir Dudley Pound in the complete command of that sea.

Cunningham is a short, tight-mouthed man, with a very loud voice. He is a glutton for work, is extremely efficient, and is said to be a grim disciplinarian. He is also an expert navigator, and could "cut an egg in half with a battleship," as the sailors say. His Hampshire home is the house which once belonged to Nelson's Admiral Collingwood.

Sir James Somerville, who commands a flying force in the Western Mediterranean, is one of the Navy's most brilliant and dashing officers. He combines a boundless physical energy, which has made him adopt the habit of rowing four times round his ship before breakfast, with the rather surprisingly sedentary hobby of making ship models. A few of the public may happen to have heard of him because, at the beginning of the war, when he was at home in England invalided, he gave a few broadcasts on naval matters for the B.B.C.

Sir Charles Forbes, the Commander-in-Chief of the Home Fleet, is nearly three years younger than Sir Dudley Pound: for he is a man of sixty-one. He is one of many successful officers who began by specializing in gunnery. During the first winter of the last war, he was in charge of what was then the largest and newest British battleship, the *Queen Elizabeth*, at the Dardanelles. Later, he was Jellicoe's Flag-Commander at the Battle of Jutland; and he saw active service at sea throughout almost the whole of the war. After it, he was Deputy-Director of the Naval Staff College for two years, and afterwards became Director of Naval Ordnance. He then commanded the Destroyer Flotillas in the Mediterranean; and his last post before commanding the Home Fleet was to be second in command of the Fleet in the Mediterranean. Thus the man who now holds the most arduous and responsible fighting command in the British Navy has had an experience of the most wide and varied kind.

The names of the leading R.A.F. commanders are hardly better known than those of the leading admirals; for what strikes the imagination of the ordinary man is the prowess of the individual airman rather than the skill of the dispositions of his officers. Most people are aware, however, that Sir Charles Portal, after having been Air Member for Personnel on the Air Council, recently succeeded Sir Cyril Newall as Chief of the Air Staff.

Sir Charles Portal is of Huguenot descent, and his hobby is falconry. After a more or less spectacular university career at Oxford, where he was best known as a furious motorcyclist, he joined the Army and proceeded to France. In November, 1915, he was able to transfer to what was then known as the Royal Flying Corps, where he became, first, an observer, and four months later, a pilot, and where he had many heroic fights, in one case accounting, by himself, for three German machines, out of the five which attacked him. For these and other exploits he received the Military Cross and the D.S.O.

Before his recent promotion to the highest post at the age of forty-seven, he held the Bomber Command, which had previously been in the hands of Sir Edgar Ludlow-Hewitt.

There have been other changes in the Air Force commands; and, since the French collapse, there have been changes in the Army commands also. The Commander-in-Chief of the British Military Forces in France was Lord Gort, known to his friends as "fat boy Gort" ever since the time when he joined the Grenadier Guards. His dashing Irish gallantry in the last war not only won him the Military Cross and the D.S.O. with two bars, but that rare and coveted distinction, the Victoria Cross. After the British Military Forces in France ceased to exist as a Command, Lord Gort became Inspector General of Training in England. Curiously enough, after the last war, he was given the important task of supervising the revision of the higher Army Training manuals in the light of war experience. More recently Lord Gort became governor general of Gibraltar.

Sir John Ironside, "Tiny" Ironside, as he was nicknamed in consequence of his great height and breadth, was succeeded as Chief of the Imperial General Staff a year ago by Sir John Dill, who commanded the First Army in the British Expeditionary Force in France, but who would no doubt have arrived earlier at the position which he now holds if Mr. Hore-Belisha, when he was Minister for War, had not insisted upon reducing the age limit, which just ruled him out and just let Sir John Ironside in.

Sir John Dill eventually took over the crushing responsibility of this post when British fortunes were pretty low—that is to say, at the end of May, 1940, when the Norwegian adventure had failed, and the British troops in Flanders were struggling back to Dunkerque. It is a striking illustration of the long-distance planning which is necessary in military operations, as it is characteristic of the confidence, courage and foresight of Sir John Dill, that it was at this black moment that he immediately made the plans for the British offensive in North Africa, and, as early as July, despatched, via the Cape of Good Hope, the tanks and guns which eventually enabled Sir Arthur Wavell to carry out this very successful campaign.

Sir John Dill had long known what was coming in France; for the military correspondent of the *Sunday Times* has recently revealed that as far back as September, 1939, when he arrived in France in command of the Second Corps, he had said, "The only question about Hitler's attack on France is whether he will make it now with the 100 divisions that he can spare from Poland, or wait until the spring, and make it with 200."

He has held the most important technical posts in the Army in peace time—Commandant of the Staff College and Director of Military Operations and Intelligence at the War Office—and the most important command at home—that of Aldershot.

Of all the generals, however, the man whose personality has fired the popular imagination is Sir Arthur Wavell, whom, by what was a great piece of good fortune for Great Britain, the opening of the war found in the wide and important Command of the Middle East, said to be territorially the most extensive Command in military history, for it covers an area of more than two million square miles.

I say that it was by a great piece of good fortune that he was in that position at that moment; for although, before the war, he was universally regarded by soldiers as far and away the cleverest man in the Army, that very fact tended to make him suspect. Like Winston Churchill, he was considered by the authorities to be neither sound nor safe. He hated routine. He was, in fact, just the sort of man whom the authorities in England tend to shoulder out of power until the last moment of crisis, and then sometimes call in when it is nearly too late. The very appointment, which he has recently held with such brilliance, was given to him almost as a snub and to side-track him from the succession to that of Chief of the Imperial General Staff, to which he seemed to be on his way when he obtained the Aldershot Command in 1938. For when he was at Aldershot, he did a thing which, to the routine mind, was unpardonable. He wished to demonstrate that the amount of equipment prescribed by regulations for troops on active service was enormously excessive and cumbersome. So he put into maneuvers one Division which carried absolutely everything that was laid down. Its transport extended for fifteen miles. The regulation equipment was reduced; but Wavell was withdrawn from Aldershot and placed in the Military Operations Branch of the War Office. This in fact gave him a useful insight into the workings of the central machine and also enabled him to visit the Army Department and the War College at Washington; but it was not promotion, any more than in reality was his appointment to the Middle East, for he was then under the orders of General Weygand.

His going there was, however, fortunate in several ways. One of them was that he already knew the country by personal experience and family tradition. His father and grandfather were both generals, and both were connected with service in the Middle East and North Africa; and he himself, before 1914, had made the pilgrimage to Mecca and Medina in disguise. He also had direct military knowledge of Middle Eastern conditions, and had acquired it under the best of teachers, Field Marshal Allenby. He went to Egypt

with that great general in 1917, and rose to be his Chief of
Staff. Allenby, who was himself far from having the routine
mind, liked the wide and original intelligence of Wavell,
who responded with an admiration which is expressed in his
two books, *The Palestine Campaign* and *Allenby, a Study in
Greatness*. He learned much from Allenby; and the tactics of
his own attack on Sidi Barrani were almost a replica of those
of Allenby's attack on Ghiza—the same brilliant use of de-
ception, the same swift exploitation of the enemy retreat. It
was during the Allenby campaign that Wavell happened to
be associated, in the capture of the Kufra Oasis, with the
Italian officer who has since become Marshal Graziani. They
exchanged gifts of daggers, each inscribed "United we are
the masters."

Wavell's service under Allenby was not his only experience of soldiering in the Middle East before his present
Command. In 1937, he was sent to Palestine to break Arab
terrorism there, which he did by a method of flying columns
and with a severity which earned him the nickname of "the
great bloodhound" among the Arabs, but also won their respect; for he never acted with cruelty or brutality.

Wavell is fifty-eight years old. He had a distinguished
public school career at Winchester, where he held a scholarship, and where my own brother, who was his immediate
rival all the way up the school, remembers him as a very
silent boy. He is still a placid, silent and close-mouthed man
—"guinea-a-word Wavell" he is called in the Army, for when
he does speak, it is always to say something which is worth
listening to. From Winchester he passed to the Military College at Sandhurst—passed in first and passed out first, just
as, later, he passed first both in and out of the Staff College.
He became an officer in the famous Scottish kilted infantry
regiment, the Black Watch, and saw active service in the
South African war, on the Indian Frontier and during the
last war in France. It was in that war that he lost his left eye

at Ypres, and today a reserve stock of glass eyes is included in his personal luggage; but he maneuvers his eyeglass so skilfully from one eye to the other that it is difficult to know which is the false one, and in any case he sees everything with the one good eye that is left to him.

After his recovery from the loss of his eye, he was sent for a year as Military Attaché with the Russians in the Caucasus, and spent his spare time learning to speak the language fluently. He went back to Russia a few years ago to attend the military maneuvers, and was much impressed by the use of parachute troops, which, in North Africa, he has been the first British general to adopt. Another innovation with which he was closely associated was that of the creation of the first completely mechanized force in the British Army. This was when he was serving as Operations Staff Officer with the Third Division in 1928.

The ingenuity of his many tactical innovations in the North African campaign has already passed into legend. There was the dummy British camp on the road to Sidi Barrani, with its wooden replicas of tanks and ammunition dumps and constant movement of lorries to and fro—arranged so that the Italian airmen should obtain the impression that this was the British base camp, whereas the real one was much smaller and in the desert to the South. The day before the attack on Sidi Barrani, there was the open marching up of troops, as if for a frontal assault, and their secret removal in lorries by night, with the result that General Maletti's Armored Division, surprised before dawn by an attack from another angle, was caught before the men could man the tanks. There was General Wavell himself, seen calmly sipping a cocktail on the verandah of the fashionable restaurant, the Mena House, at the foot of the Pyramids—and no doubt seen by Italian spies —on the very afternoon which actually preceded the opening of the Sidi Barrani attack. There were the instructions to the artillery and the Air Force to be ready to destroy the Italian drinking water distilling plant at Bardia, but on no account to do so until instructions at the last moment, so that the Italians should then not have time to lay a pipe-line from a more distant source of supply. There was the dropping of tons of Epsom Salts into wells which the Italians would be likely to use. There was the taking of Sidi Barrani, Bardia and Tobruk, each by surprise and each in a different way. There was the sweeping past the still unconquered Tobruk immediately after the taking of Bardia, when the normal thing would have been to spend weeks on consolidating the position.

All of these tactical audacities are based upon Wavell's conviction that plodding war is quite unsuited to the British temperament, whose real genius is lightning attack, rapid blows and the knock-out.

It must not be supposed, however, that Wavell is an excitable or nervous person. One of his strongest characteristics is his composure. When he heard of the Italian capture of Berbera, in British Somaliland, at an earlier stage of the war, he refused to allow the news to interrupt his morning swim, and, not only does he ride regularly, but he frequently plays golf and is always "fit." His office was a small, bare room, and everything in it arranged in an orderly way. On Sundays, he and his wife and three daughters, two of whom are secretaries and the third a nurse, gave the most placid cocktail parties in their Cairo home. He was constantly on the move, by air, to and from various points in his wide Command. However, when he is flying, although he occasionally takes the controls for a time up aloft—but never to take off or to land—he usually sleeps in the air, leaving instructions to wake him up if anything interesting is to be seen, or else he reads poetry.

For Wavell is very fond of reading poetry. He has Shakespeare almost by heart, and he has recently been re-reading the whole of Browning, for whom he has a great admiration. His tastes are catholic, however, for they also include the

Jeeves stories of P. G. Wodehouse. He is, typically, the intellectual soldier and is the author of twelve articles in the *Encyclopedia Britannica*.

Such is the trim, rather "chunky" and strongly built, medium tall, good-looking and personally very charming man, who has been in command of a composite force of Englishmen, Scotsmen, Australians, New Zealanders, Free French, Poles, Czechs, Indians, Arabs, Ethiopians, Maoris, Punjabis and Mauritians, could understand all of them and sympathize with all of them in their different ways, and had to supply all of them with their different kinds of food and drink. This is the man who had encouraged these various troops to sing on the march—the Australians bellowing the absurd "Wizard of Oz" and the Free French rolling out their fine, traditional "Sambre-et-Meuse." This is the man, of whom the German general Keitel is reported to have said, "The British have only one good military leader; but he is very good indeed."

INDEX

Achilles, 302

Aden, 298, 301

Admirable Crichton, The, by J. M. Barrie, 128

Advertising, journalism and, 157–161

Agriculture, second among main productive industries of Great Britain, 193, 200; production before the war and today, 201–203

Ainsworth, Harrison, 231

Air attack, relatively ineffective against ships of war, 308

Air Force, 300

Aldermen, 212, 219

Alexander, A. V., 319, 320

Alice in Wonderland, by Lewis Carroll, 238

Alice Through the Looking Glass, by Lewis Carroll, 238

Allenby, 337, 338

Ambassadors, the appointment of, 46

America, and the British cause, 327; sons of American women at the British helm, 328

Amery, 331

Anderson, Sir John, 317, 319, 331

Answers, 163

Appeasement of Germany, 326

Applause, in the House of Commons, 50

Archbishop of Canterbury, 41

Archery, 267

Argentine, Great Britain's investment in, 283

Aristocracy, character of English, 21, 24

Aristocratic class, 62, 63; still holds the influence in England, 21, 66; and voluntary taxation, 65

Army, 299, 300; women in, 109, 110

Arnold, Doctor (of Rugby), 132

Art, influence abroad, 224, 225; characteristics of, 225; realism, 251, 252; impressionism, 252; pictorial, 253

Arts, women in the, 108

Ashley Dukes' Mercury Theatre, 254

Astor, J. J., newspaper proprietor, 170

Astor, Lady, 50

Athletics, prominence given to, 127, 128, 132, 133, 140–142; as distinguished from games, 266–268

Attlee, C., M.P., 319, 331

Attorney General, the, 25

Austen, Jane, 234

Australia, and the second World War, 284; first colony established in, 291; united as Australian Commonwealth in 1901, 291; population 291; peace time requirements of defense, 302, 303; war contribution, 305–307

Baden-Powell, Lord, 64

Bagehot, quoted, 36

Baldwin, Stanley, 325

Balfour, Lord, 3

Bank notes, 213

Bank of England, 213, 214

Bar Council, the, 29

Barrie, J. M., 240, 241, 243; quoted, 128, 181

Barrister, the, 28–31

Baseball, 271

Basketball, 271

Beagling, 261

Beanfeast, the, 88

Beaverbrook, Lord, 167, 319, 331; heritage, 328; as newspaper proprietor, 328, 330; British Minister of Information in World War I, 328; a much-advertised person, 328, 329; physical appearance, 329; character, 329, 330; his sense of publicity, 329, 330; capacity for getting things done, 329, 330; as Minister of Aircraft Production, 330

Beerbohm, Max, 228, 235

Beer drinking, 80–82, 113, 259

Belloc, Hilaire, 237; quoted, 180, 238

Beneš, Doctor E., 327

Bennett, Arnold, 234

Bentley, E. C., 231

Bermuda, 298

Betting, 259

Bevin, Ernest, character, 322; dislikes politicians, 322; as a speaker, 322; physical appearance, 322; as Min-

ister of Labor, 319, 321; his beginnings, 320; as Trades Union Leader, 320, 321
Big-game shooting, 265
Billiards, 269
Bills, 52–54
Binyon, Laurence, 229
Black-coated workers, 86
Blackpool, 89
Board of Education, 41; powers of, 122–124; the President of, 122, 123
Boarding schools, 131, 132; Prefect system in, 132; compulsory games, 135
Boat race, eight-oared, 143, 269
Boat racing, college, 143, 149
Boers, 291
Book of Common Prayer, 322
Book public, in England, 230, 231
Bowls, 268, 270
Boy Scout movement, 64, 65
Bradbury, Lord, 221
Breakfast, English, 112
British blockade of Germany, 300, 301, 391
British Broadcasting Corp., 255
British colonization, characteristic features of, 288–298
British Commonwealth of Nations, 21; merchant navy of, 190; area and population, 282, 283; trade basis of, 288, 289; acquisition of colonial territories by conquest rare, 289, 290
British Empire, resources of, 189, 196, 199; gold and dollar assets in the United States, 199; control of raw materials in war time, 199, 200; naval defensive system of, 298–302; military defensive system of, 299–301; strategic situation of, in peace time and in war time, 299–302; defense of, essentially maritime, 302; potential resources of the eastern group of, 307. *See also under* British Commonwealth of Nations
British Isles, inhabited by four peoples, 1
British justice, 295, 296. *See also* Justice
British Malaya, rubber, war contribution of, 307
British navy, 184, 308
Brontë, Emily, 239
Brooke, Rupert, 229
Browning, 227, 228

Buchan, John (Lord Tweedsmuir), 231
Building trades, 193
Burma, 297; raw materials, war contribution of, 307
Burne-Jones, 240, 251, 252
Business people, 61
Byron, 226

Cabinet, has no existence as far as the law of England is concerned, 35; members of, must be members of Parliament, 37; executive acts of state decided upon by, 37–40; and the principle of collective responsibility, 38; number of ministers in, 44. *See also* Cabinet Ministers and War Cabinet of Eight
Cabinet Government, system of, 36–56
Cabinet Ministers, as representatives of the King, 37, 38; term of office, 38; chosen by the Prime Minister, 40–44
Cambridge, women students in, 103, 104; open scholarships in, 121; divided into number of separate colleges, 127–129; boat race between Oxford and, 143; no grouping by faculties at, 147
Campbell-Bannerman, Sir Henry, 3
Camrose, Lord, newspaper proprietor, 167
Canada, war contribution, 284, 304; French Canadians in, 290, 291; peace-time requirements of defense, 302, 303
Canned foods, *see under* Tinned foods
Cap and gown, 139, 148
Cape of Good Hope, British acquisition of, 291; population, 291
Carroll, Lewis (C. L. Dodgson), 238
"Cash and carry," 198, 199
Casson, Lewis, 255
Cathedral schools, 130, 131
Catholic Church, and education, 124
Celtic dialect, 2
Central Criminal Court, 30
Ceremonial, Englishman's passion for, 49
Ceylon, 298
Chamberlain, Neville, 313, 317; his policy of "Appeasement of Germany," 326

Chancellor of the Duchy of Lancaster, 43
Chancellor of the Exchequer, 41
Chaperon, the, 103–105
Charing Cross, 214, 216
Charitableness, characteristic of the English, 14
Charterhouse School, 217
Chatfield, Admiral Lord, quoted, 308
Chesterton, G. K., 236, 237; quoted, 180, 181
Children, parents' preoccupation about happiness of, 115–117; new freedom of association between parents and, 117; and manners, 118; team instinct, early development of, in boys, 119
Children's books, 239–241
Choral singing, 250
Christmas pantomime, 246–248
Christ's Hospital, 217
Church of England, and education, 124
Church schools, 124
Churches, in London, the bombing of, 217
Churchill, Lord Randolph, 312
Churchill, Winston, 42, 208; quoted, 7, 33, 314, 315; habits and personal idiosyncrasies of, 310, 311; as an author, 310, 313; successful journalist, 311; war correspondent, 311; taken prisoner by the Boers, 311; character, 311–314; polo player, 311; the English public and, 312–314; lack of party consistency, 312; as First Lord of the Admiralty, 312; painting, hobby of, 313; defends Neville Chamberlain, 313; and his vigorous pursuit of the war, 314–319; as an orator, 315; as a statesman, 316–318; reluctance of, to exercise uncontrolled power, 316, 317; physical appearance, 316; in touch with the man of the people, 316; attitude toward the United States, 318; mother of, was an American citizen, 318, 328
Churchill, Mrs. Winston, 311
Citizen, civil liberties of the, 36
Civil liberties, 36
Civil proceedings, 30, 31
Civil Service, 46; women in the, 107
Class consciousness, in education, 125–129, 134. *See also* Class distinction
Class distinction, 59, 60, 62–75, 82, 83,

et passim; tendency is towards abolishing, 84, 93
Clemenceau, quoted, 316
Clergy, the, 46, 47
Clinics, school, 125
Clothes, *see under* Dress
Club habit, the, 75
Club neckties, 130
Coal, important national asset, 184–186; the export of, 186; output of, as compared to that of the United States, 186; workers in mining of, 193
Coal Act of 1938, 186
Cock fighting, 258
Colleges, 146, 147. *See also* Universities
Colonies, *see under* Dominions
Comic paper, 249, 250
Commerce, women in, 106; foreign, 184–189, 194, 195; number of people employed in, 193; the romance of, 210, 211
Commission of the Peace, *see under* Justice of the Peace
Common law, 22, 26
Commons, *see under* House of Commons
Complete Angler, by Izaak Walton, 239
Compulsory games, for schools, 140, 280
Compulsory gymnastics, 140
Conservatives, the, 33
Constitution, *see under* English Constitution
Constitutional laws, 34, 35
"Contempt of Court," 178
Contents bill, 181, 182
Cooking, 74, 110–112
Cornish tin mines, 187
Cory, W. J., 229
Cotton, 193, 194
Council for Encouragement of Music and the Arts, 255
"Council Schools," 124
Country gentry, and the townspeople, 46, 47
Country House, 233
Country-house hospitality, 77, 78
Country life, 57–83
County Court, 30
Courage, of the Englishman, 6, 18, 253, 255
Court of Criminal Appeal, 30
Court of the Justices of the Peace, 29
Court of Quarter Sessions, 30

Coward, Noel, 244
Credit, 197, 198
Cricket, 268; the village match, 64; the annual school match, 142, 269; professional, 272, 273; test matches, 273; 274; described, 276–279
Criminal law, legal proceedings must take place in public, 28
Cromwell, Oliver, 155
Cross-examination, 28, 29
Crown, delegation of the authority of the, to the Cabinet, 38, 39; symbol of unity, 39
Cunningham, Sir Andrew, as Commander-in-Chief of the Mediterranean Fleet, 333; at the Dardanelles, 333; war decorations, 333; physical appearance, 333; character, 333; expert navigator, 333
Cunninghame-Graham, 242
Curling, 270
Cyprus, 298
Czechoslovakia, German entry into, 327; British acceptance of the German action, 327

Daily Chronicle, 159
Daily Express, 163, 166, 167
Daily Herald, 158, 166, 168, 172
Daily Mail, 163, 164, 166–168, 172
Daily Telegraph, 164, 166, 167, 172
Daily Sketch, 167
Daily Worker, 155
Dalton, Hugh, 319
Dancing, village, 82
Darts, 271
Daudet, Léon, quoted, 11
Day schools, 130, 131, 135
Dear Brutus, by J. M. Barrie, 240
de Blowitz, 182
Defendant, in criminal proceedings, 30, 31
Defensive strategy, 298, 299
Delacroix, quoted, 224
Delane, John, 173
de Madariaga, Salvador, quoted, 13
Democracy (in England), essentially aristocratic, 21, 24
Democratic spirit, in England, 63, 152
Derby, 260
Dickens, 225
Dill, Sir John, as Chief of the Imperial General Staff, 335, 336; in command in France, 335, 336; character, 336; technical posts in the army in peace time, held by, 336

Dinner parties, 73, 74
Dinner table, observances of the, 73, 74
"Division Lobby," 51
Domestics, *see under* Servants
Dominions, self-governing, completely autonomous, 38, 284; furnish Great Britain with raw materials, 187, 189, 196, 199; Great Britain's assets in, 198, 199; right of appeal from the courts of the, to the British Privy Council, 296; essential differences between the colonies and, 297, 298; status of, 283, 284; trade, 286–288; liberty, independence, and self-government characteristic of, 288; contribute units to the British Navy, 299; war contribution, 299, 302–306; peace time requirements of defense, 302, 303; industrial efforts of, 306, 307
Dover, 301
Doyle, Conan, 231, 241
Drama, 243, 244
Dramatic societies, amateur, 246
Drawing room, in the country house, 72; in the town house, 97
Dress, 113, 114
Duff-Cooper, Sir Alfred, 331
Dukes, Ashley, 244
Durham University, 144
Dutch Boers, 291
Dutch East Indies, rubber in, 307
Duty, the Englishman's sense of, 18
Dynasts, The, by Thomas Hardy, 239

Eastern Group Supply Conference, 306
East India Company, 290
Economist, 171, 175
Eden, Anthony, 319, 322, 325; physical appearance, 331; character, 331;
Education, of women, 103–105; state system of, 120–127, 134; and democracy, 120, 126; compulsory, 120, 122, 125, 162; open scholarships in the universities of Oxford and Cambridge, 121; reform in, 122–125; the church and, 121–124; class consciousness in, 125–129, 134; athletic versus scholastic honors, 127, 128; "public-school" education, in England, defined, 128–132; old public schools and universities the basis of the schoolboy code of honor in England, 130,

134; the university, 133; steps in, for middle-class boy, 135–151; effects of the war on, 153, 154

Efficiency, in totalitarian states, and in democratic states, 36

Egypt, 298

Eire, 1, 284, 291

Elementary schools, 120, 123; creation of a new category of, 124

Eliot, George, 234

Eliot, T. S., 230

Elizabeth, Queen, personal influence of, 310

Emotions, Englishman distrusts, 7

Employment, 193, 200–202, 206; of women, 105

Engineering, 193

England (including references to Great Britain), lyric poetry produced in, 5, 223–226; flower gardens in, 6, 61, 62, 79, 80; justice in, 20–32; parliamentary law, 20–26; 32–56; socially and politically aristocratic, 21, 57, 62, 63; common law in, 22; rule of primogeniture, 24, 66; liberties enjoyed by the private citizen, 36, *et passim;* local administration, 45; political system, essential features of, 55, 56; country life, 57–82; town life, 86–92; survival of old feudal tradition in, 63, 68; aristocratic class continues to occupy key posts in the Government, 66; social observances in, 73, 74; social barriers are breaking down, 75; under war conditions, 98, 99, 197–199, 253–256; education in, 120–154; coal fields, 184–186; iron industry, 186, 187; industrial, financial, and commercial greatness of, 184–221; raw materials, 186, 200, 287, 288; seaports in, 189; shipping as life line of, 189; merchant navy of, compared to that of other countries, 190; foreign trade, 185–189, 194, 195; Dominions, trade with, 189, 196, 197, 199, 286–288; the purchase of war material, 197–199; investment in Argentine Republic, 283; investments in the United States, 199; literature, the arts and the sciences, 222–256; book public in, 230, 231; sports, 257–281; colonies, 282–288, 304–307; dominions, self-governing, 284; and colonial administration, 290, 291; naval stations, 298; blockades Germany, 300, 301; colonies give aid to, in present war, 302–307; submarine menace directed against merchant marine of, 308; convoy system, 308; air attack, 308; attempts to establish friendly relations with Germany, 326; acceptance of the German action in Czecho-Slovakia, 327; declaration of war on Germany, 327; men at the helm, 309–341. *See also* British Commonwealth of Nations and British Empire

English Constitution, unwritten, 20, 21, 34, 35; Bagehot quoted on, 36

English Court of Law, 23

English language, 224

Englishman, the, distinct from the Welshman, Scotsman, and Irishman, 1–3; imagination of, 2, 5, 6, 9, 12, 17, *et passim;* wastefulness of, 2, 16; a dreamer, 3; instinctive judgment, characteristic of, 3, 18; distrusts intelligence, 4; sense of orderliness and decency, 4, 22, 23, 37; lack of artistic taste, 5; his poetic sense, 5, 222; as reader, 5, 230, 231; as nature lover, 6, 222; humor and wit of, 6, 7, 226, 236–239; habit of understatement, 6, 7; courage of, 6, 18, 253, 255; self-control, 7; distrusts emotions, 7; shyness, dominant instinct of, 8–10; lack of ease in conversation, 8, 10; reverence for womanhood, 9; impression made on other countries, 9, 10; snobbishness, characteristic of, 10, 75; pride and modesty of, 11, 18, 223; indecision of, 12; tolerance, 14; business relations, 15; learns by mistakes, 16, 17; respect for tradition, 17; moral principles, 17, 18; sporting spirit of, 19; passion for liberty and justice, 20–22; respect for the law, 21, 23, 37; social grace of, 49; passion for form and ceremonial, 49, 244, 246; preference for country, 60; gardening, a passion with, 62; the club habit, 75; preference for a house to a flat, 95; interest in practical, 222, 230; literary taste, 226, 230–232; theatre, regard for, 245; love for animals, 258; riding to the hounds, 262; cricket, character of, as revealed in game of, 276–279; deeply religious, 322

English village, the, physical aspects

of, 58, 79, 80; the squire, 59; social strata in, 60, 82, 83; flower gardens, 61, 62, 79, 80; class comradeship in, 63–65; cricket matches, 64; calling on new arrivals, 67; charitable and social services in, 67–69; the Village Institute, 69; the afternoon tea, 71–73; the garden party, 78, 79; shops, 80; post office, 80; public house, 80, 81; Flower Show, 82; dancing, 82

Equality, before the law, 20, 21, 26; social, 20, 21

Ervine, St. John, 244

Established Church, the, 69

Eton, 128, 131, 142

Eton jacket, 136

Evening meal, 86

Evening News, 167

Evening Standard, 167, 172

Examination and cross-examination, 28, 29

Executive and legislative powers, the close union of, 36. *See also* House of Commons, House of Lords, and Prime Minister

Exports, 185–188, 194–196, 200; during World War II, 197

Factory, the, 88

"Fags," 132

Fantasy, 238, 240

Farm buildings, 58

Farmer, 201, 203; usually tenant of landowner, 58, 59

Farms, 59

Fellowships, 146; qualities demanded of candidates for, 151

Feudal tradition, survival of, 63, 68, 69

Finance, foundations of, and conditions essential to financial greatness of England, 184; trade balance, 195–198; credit, 197; war expenditures, 197–199; investments, 198, 199, 283; inflation of currency, 204, 205; taxation, 204–206

Financial Times, 167

Fire insurance companies, 192

First Lord of the Admiralty, 45

First Lord of the Treasury, 41

Fishermen, 202

Fishing, 264

Fishing industry, 202

Fitzgerald, Edward, 228, 229

Flower gardens, liking of British for, 6, 61, 62, 79, 80

Flower Show, 82, 83

Fly-fishing, 264, 265

Fodder, 202

Folk songs, 250

Food, national supply of, 200–202; rationing in war time, 203, 204

Football, 268–270, 273; professional, 272, 274, 275; Rugby, 275, 276

Forbes, Archibald, 162

Forbes, Sir Charles, Commander-in-Chief of the Home Fleet, 334; specializes in gunnery, 334; in World War I, 334; experiences of, varied, 334

Foreign exchange, 195, 196

Form, Englishman's passion for, 49

Fox hunting, 261–263

France, conception of the law in, 22; freedom of the press in, 156; the fall of, 301, 307

Free Trade policy, 288

Freedom of the seas, 184

French Canadians, 290, 291

French Republic, 39

Frenchman, and the mental processes of the, 3, 4; his conception of the law, 22

Galsworthy, John, 233

Gambling, 259, 260

Games, as distinguished from athletics, 266–268

"Games master," 133

Gandhi (Mahatma), 295; relations with Lord Halifax, 325, 326

Garden party, 78, 79

Gardens, *see under* Flower gardens

Garvin, J. L., 172, 173

Gaskell, Mrs, 234

Generosity, characteristic of the English, 14

Gentleman, the, 60; defined, 85, 86

George VI, personal influence of, 310

George, Lloyd, 207

German colonies, 287

Germany, conception of the law in, 22; attitude of, toward colonies, 282, 286, 287; uses propaganda against Great Britain, 283, 284, 287; British blockade of, 300, 301; counter blockade against Great Britain, 308; England's attempt to establish friendly relations with, 326

Gibraltar, 298, 301

Gilbert and Sullivan operas, 237

Gilbert, W. S., 237, 238; quoted, 42

Girls, freedom allowed to, 103–105; and higher education, 104, 105
Gladstone, 42, 310
Glasgow Herald, 174
Golf, 268–271
Gort, Lord, nickname, 335; World War I decorations, 335; Commander-in-Chief of British Military Forces in France, 335; as Inspector General of Training in England, 335; made Governor General of Gibraltar, 335
Government, changing the, 33, 34; England's unwritten Constitution, 34, 35; the "separation of powers," 36; Cabinet government created, 36–56; King, limitations upon his direct power, 35, 37–39; co-operation between the executive and the legislature, 37; in the Dominions, 38; offices of the, 40–44; anachronisms in the, 41, 42; local administration, 45; changes in, when government goes out, 45, 46; lack of political influence in the lower appointments and promotions, 46; Act abolishing sex disqualification for post in, 109; present, almost exclusively English, 322, 328. *See also* Judicial System and Parliament
Government of India Bill, 325
Governor, 297
Grace, W. G., 273
Grammar schools, 131
Graves, Robert, 242
Graziani, 339, 340
Great Britain, *see under* England
Green Mansions, by W. H. Hudson, 242
Greenwood, Arthur, M.P., 43, 319
Greenwood, Frederick, 173
Grenfell, Julian, 229
Gwynne, H. A., 172

Habeas Corpus, 28, 296
Halifax, Lady, 324
Halifax, Viscount, 317, 322, 331; a devout churchman, 323, 324; character, 323, 324; Joint Master of the Middleton Hunt, 323; as Viceroy of India, 323, 325; Ambassador to the United States, 324; strong sense of duty, 324; physical appearance, 324; beginnings, 324; marriage, 324; various offices held by, 325, 326; relations with Gandhi,

325; purpose of mission to America, 327, 328; mission to Germany in 1937, 326; attitude toward Germany, 327; first British Foreign Secretary to occupy post of ambassador to a foreign country, 327; first ambassador to whom the Prime Minister has ever personally given Godspeed on a British warship, 327; first British ambassador who has been welcomed on board his ship by President of United States, 327
Hamlet, by William Shakespeare, 13
Hardy, Thomas, 230, 239
Harmsworth, Sir Harold, 167
Harmsworths, newspaper proprietors, 162, 166, 167. *See also* Lord Northcliffe
Harrow, 128, 131, 142
"Head of the river," 149
Headmaster, 135, 136
Hebrew conception of the law, 22
Henley, W. E., 229
High Court Judge, 28
High Court of Justice, 26, 30
High Court Trial, 28, 30
Hiking, 265
Hitler, and the Munich policy, 326, 327
Hockey, 271
Holland, freedom of the press in, 155
Home, the English, of today, 94–102
Home life, of the town dweller, 86–92, 100; in the suburbs, or the country, 57–82, 101
Hong-Kong, 298
Hore-Belisha, 335
Hospitality, in the Englishman's home, 77, 78, 94
Hospitals, supported by voluntary contributions, 67
House of Commons, historical facts concerning, 24; controls financial business, 33; selected by the nation, 33; and the system of Cabinet government, 36, 37; name defined, 46; salary-paid members of, 47; organization of, 47–49; system of election to, 47; number of members, 47; physical features of, 47–49, 51; parliamentary procedure, 49–54; seating in, 48, 51; Leader of, appointed by Prime Minister, 51; women members, 108, 109
House of Lords, judicial capacity, 30; chairman, 32; Government bench

in, 51; powers of, 53, 54; members of, 54, 55; women not eligible, 54
Housewives, English, and cooking, 111, 112
Hudson, W. H., 241, 242
Hudson's Bay Trading Company, 291
Humor and wit, 6, 7, 226, 236–239
Hunting, 59
Huxley, Aldous, 232, 234
Hyde Park, 92

Imagination of the Englishman, 2, 5, 6, 9, 12, 17
Imports, 185–189, 195, 196; during World War II, 197
Income tax, 205
India, Government of India Act, 1935, 293, 325; antagonism between the Hindus and the Moslems in, 293–295; area and population, 286, 292; employment for Englishmen in, 286; British acquisition of, 290; British administration in, 292–295; varied elements in the politics of, 293–295; the Congress party under leadership of Mr. Gandhi, 295; Royal Indian Navy, 302; peacetime requirements of defence, 303; native army, 303; war contribution, 304, 307; under the Viceroyalty of Lord Irwin (now Lord Halifax), 325
Individualism, English, 213
Industrial areas, 193, 194
Industries, productive, number of workers employed in, 193
Industry, women in, 106, 193; England as great industrial nation, 184–187; the romance of, 210–221
Infant mortality, 105
Infant schools, 135
Inflation, 204, 205
Inns of Court, 29
Instinct, Englishman relies upon, 3
Institute, the Village, 69
Insurance, maritime, 190–192
Inter-University Athletic meeting, 269
Intuition, of the Englishman, 3
Investments, British, 198, 199
Iraq, 298
Ireland, the national language of, 2; the mind of, 227; fly-fishing in, 264
Ireland, Southern, and the second World War, 284
Irish literary movement, the, 229
Irish theatre, the, 229

Irishman, distinct from the Englishman, 1, 2; temperament, 2; wit, 2; important part played by, in building up British nation, 2
Iron industry, 186, 187
Ironside, Sir John, nicknamed "Tiny" Ironside, 335; as Chief of the Imperial General Staff, 335
Italians, attitude toward colonies, 282

Jacobs, W. W., 238
Jamaica, 298
James, Henry, 233
Jerome, Leonard, 318
Joffre, Césaire Joseph Jacques, quoted, 332
Journalism, new form of, 162, 163
Journalist, the, 179, 180
Joyce, James, 234, 235
Judges, 25, 36; appointed for life, 24, 27; relationship with the Bench and the Bar, 26; their habiliment, 31, 32; forms used when addressing, 32; summoned to the House of Lords by "writs of assistance," 32; salary of, 67
Judges, High Court, 28
Judges of fact, 28
Judicial system, in England, 26–32; ceremonial side of the administration of justice, 31, 32; historical link between justice and Parliament, 32
Jury, the, 28, 29
Justice in England, 20–56, 295, 296; Parliament and, 32
Justice of the Peace, 23–25, 29, 68
Juveniles, 238, 240

Keitel, General, quoted, 341
Kemsley, Lord, newspaper proprietor, 167
Keynes, J. M., 205
King, the, limitations upon the direct power of, 35, 37–39; moral influence of, 39, 309, 310; the Prime Minister and, 38–40; subjects high regard for, 65; as symbol of unity, 309
King's Privy Council, 43
Kipling, Rudyard, 230, 232, 240

Labor, conflicts, 65, 66, 207; and present armaments drive, 206, 207; relations between employer and employee, 207; unions, 207; represented in War Cabinet, 208, 317, 319

Labor Party, 33, 34; represented in War Cabinet, 208, 317, 319; committed to a strong foreign policy, and to the principle of collective security, 321
Lacrosse, 271
Landowner, the, 58, 59
Latin America, British investments in, 199, 283
Latinists, the, 131
Law, women in, 108, 109
Lawn tennis, 269–272
Lawns, 78, 79
Lawrence, D. H., 234
Lawrence, T. E., 232, 241
Laws, enactment of, by both Houses of Parliament, 52–54
"Leader of the House," 51, 52
Leader of the Opposition, 52
League of Nations, 1937 Report of Committee on Raw Materials, 288
Lecky, 310
Legislative and executive powers, the, close union of, 36. *See also* House of Commons, House of Lords, and Prime Minister
Libel, 178, 179
Liberty, 20
Listener, 183
Literature, English, sixteenth-century Elizabethan poets, 224; character of, 224–227; influence abroad, 224, 225; not easily translated, 226, 227; new vogue for poetry, 229, 230; the novel, 231–236, 239; humor and wit, 236–239; fantasy, 238, 240; the juvenile, 238, 240; travel books, 241, 242; the drama, 243, 244
Liverpool, 189, 190
Livery Companies, the, 218–220
Lloyd-George, David, 3; quoted, 84
Lloyd's, 190–193, 213
Lloyd's Register, 192
Local Education Authorities, 123
Locke, philosophy of, 224
Lodging houses, 89, 90
London Bridge, 216, 217
London, city of, workers in, 60, 61, 211, 213; as financial center of the world, 184; historic tradition, 211–221; important as a seaport, 211; picturesque names for streets, 214, 216; the churches, 217; bombing in, 217; office of Lord Mayor, 218–220; the Livery Companies, 218–220; literary and artistic life goes on under war conditions, 253–256;
air-raid shelters and rest centers, 256
London Philharmonic Orchestra, 255
London University, 144
Lord Chancellor, the, 27, 32
Lord Mayor, 212, 218–220
Lord Privy Seal, 42
Lords, *see under* House of Lords
Lords Justice of Appeal, 27
Lower class, 91
Luncheon, 112
Lynd, Robert, quoted, 280
Lyttelton, Captain Oliver, 331

Macaulay, quoted, 258
MacDonald, Ramsay, 3, 42, 321
Magna Charta, 34
Maletti, General, 339
Manchester Guardian, policy and management of, 171; prestige enjoyed by, 173; as champion of freedom and enemy of injustice, 174
Manners, 49, 63
Manufacturing, 185, 186
Maoris, 305
Margesson, Captain, 331
Maritime insurance, 190–192
Maritime transport, *see under* shipping
Marius the Epicurean, by Walter Pater, 235
Marriage, 101, 102
Masefield, John, 230
Mason, A. E. W., 231, 241
Massingham, 159
Master of Fox-Hounds, 262
Masters, in the public schools, 133; in the preparatory schools, 133
Maugham, Somerset, 236, 243, 244
May, Phil, 252, 253
Medicine, women in, 107, 108
Menzies, quoted, 306
Mercers' Company, 220
Merchant Marine, 298; and the convoy system, 308
Merchant Taylors' School, 217
Meredith, George, 233
Metal trades, 193, 194
Middle class, 63, 70, 89, 110
Milk supply, 202
Milne, A. A., 243
Milton, John, 155, 156; quoted, 257
Minister of Finance, 41
Ministers (of the Government), 40–44. *See also* Cabinet Ministers
Ministers of State, 40
Ministry of Food, 202

Modesty, the English ideal of, 18
Moore, George, 233
Morgan, Charles, 233, 243, 244
Morgenthau, 198, 199
Morley, Lord, quoted, 38
Morrison, Herbert, 319
Mothers' meeting, 68
Munich, policy of, 326, 327
Music, 224, 250
Music hall, the, 244, 246
Musical activities, under war conditions, 254, 255

Napoleon, 15
National character, *see under* Englishman
National Health Insurance, 209
Naval stations, 298
Navy, and the defence of the British Commonwealth, 298, 299, 307; called the "Silent Service," 300, 332
New College scholarships, 145
New Zealand, war contribution, 284, 302, 305–307; population, 292; advanced in social legislation, 292; peace-time requirements of defence, 302, 303
Newfoundland, 297
Newnes, George, starts *Tit-Bits*, 162
News Chronicle, 166, 172
News-letter, the, 156, 177, 178
News of the World, 166
Newspapers, the first weekly, 156; the first daily, 156; originally addressed to upper and middle classes, 157; advertising, 157, 160, 161; circulation, 157, 159, 166, 168, 169; the Government and, 157, 158, 164, 178; freedom granted editors, 157–159; financial pressure, 158, 164; relative independence of, 158, 160; opinions and news messages anonymous, 159, 163; in the nineteenth century, 159, 161, 162; layout of, 161, 162; signatures introduced into, 162, 163, news "stories," 162; proprietors of, 162–164, 167–169; revolution in, 162–182; the editor is replaced by the proprietor, 163; the daily, 164–168; the Sunday paper, 165–167; concentration of ownerships, and control over public opinion, 167–169; and propaganda, 169; and political influence, 170; when policy of, is reversed, 170, 171; newspapers of opinion, 172; editors make reputation of papers, 172, 173; foreign correspondents, 174; prices of, 175, 176; disappearance of the comic papers, 176, 177; penalty for "contempt of court," 178; libel suits, 178, 179; changes in day-to-day conduct of, 179, 180; the office of a morning paper, 179, 180; the office of an evening paper, 181, 182; contents bill, 181, 182; no open-air newspaper stalls in London, 181; and the wireless, 183
Nicoll, Robertson, 173
Nigeria, 297
Nonconformists, the, 69
Norman Marshall's Gate Theatre, 254
North American Colonies, 290, 291
Northcliffe, Lord (Alfred Harmsworth), newspaper proprietor, 162, 166–168, 170
Novel, 230–236

Observer, 164, 172–174
Offensive strategy, 298, 299
Offices of the Government, 40–44
Old Age Pension Act, 209
"On the Foundation," 138
Oppenheim, Phillips, 232
Owen, Wilfred, 229
Oxford, women students, 103, 104, 153; scholarships, 121; divided into number of separate colleges, 127–129; boat race between Cambridge and, 143; no grouping by faculties at, 147; undergraduate privileges, 150, 151; democracy and, 152; in war time, 152, 153; special War Degree, 153

Pageantry, liking of British for, 244, 246
Pageants, historical, 246
Painting, in the nineteenth century, 224, 225; the Pre-Raphaelite painters, 225, 250, 251; contemporary, 251–253
Palestine Campaign and Allenby, a Study in Greatness, by Sir Arthur Wavell, 338
Pall Mall Gazette, 159
Pamphlets, 156
Parents, and children, 115–117
Parliament, historical link between Justice and, 32; authorizes taxation and makes laws, 32; Cabinet represents dominant political party

in, 37, 38; organization of, 46–52; supreme authority of, in the United Kingdom, 51; life of each, fixed, 55. *See also* House of Commons

Parliament Act, 55

Parliamentary discussion, 49

Parliamentary system, 20–56

Parson, the village, 68, 69

Partridge, Bernard, 241

Past, Englishman's reverence for, 49

Pater, Walter, 235, quoted, 236

Peers, to be created, 54; Irish and Scottish, 54

Peerages, hereditary, 54

Periodicals, 156, 157

Peter Pan, by James M. Barrie, 240

Pinero, A. W., 243

Playwright, the, 243, 244

Playwriting, revival of, 243, 244

Poetry, lyric, 5, 223–226; English have natural instinct for, 5, 222; revival of, 229, 230; new movement in, 230

Poland, British alliance with, 327

Police, 91, 92; right of, to call upon private citizen to assist in maintaining order, 23

Police magistrate, 30

Political liberty, 36

Politician, English, 48

Politics, regarded by aristocracy as occupation of a gentleman, 66; women in, 108

Polo, 269, 271

Poor Law, 68

"Poor Relief," 208

Portal, Sir Charles, Chief of the Air Staff, 334; heritage, 334; falconry, hobby of, 334; at Oxford, 334, 335; World War I decorations, 335; posts held by, 335

Post office, eggs can be purchased at, 80

Pound, Sir Dudley, 328; duties as Admiral of the Fleet, 332; specializes in torpedo work, 332; at the Battle of Jutland, 332; posts held by, 332; as a commanding officer, 333; character, 333

Prague, German entry into, 327

Preparatory schools, 123, 135, 136

Press, freedom of, 36, 155, 156, 168, 178; alterations in the, 162–182

Pride, of the English, 11, 34

Prime Minister, the, and the authority of the Cabinet, 38; his duty to the King, 38, 39; chooses Cabinet

Ministers, 40–44; a Minister without portfolio, 42; in time of war, 42; before the House of Commons, 49–52; may request dissolution of the House of Commons, 55; salary, 67

Prize Fellowships, 151. *See also* Fellowships

Prizefighting, 258

Proctor, the, 147, 148

Professions, the, women in, 106, 107

Propaganda, newspapers and, 169; Germany uses, against Great Britain, 283, 284, 287

Public house, the, 80

Public life, high standard of, 66, 67

Public schools, in England, 125–132; traditions, ideals, and standard of conduct at, 130, 141; Prefect system, 132; compulsory games, 132, 133; and class consciousness, 134; type of citizen produced by, 134, 135; Church of England schools, 141; the study of Latin and Greek classics, 141; educational aims, 141

"Punch and Judy," 248

Purchasing power, the maintenance of, 184, 197, 203; reserves of, 197

Purple Land, The, by W. H. Hudson, 241

Queen, the, 39, 65

Queen Elizabeth, 334

R. A. F., Winston Churchill's tribute to, 314, 315

Racing, 259, 260

Rackets, 269, 271

Raw materials, 186, 200

Religion, 322, 323

Religious education, 124

Religious liberty, 36

Reuter's News Agency, 159, 171

Richardson, Dorothy, 242

"Ridgway's Late Joys," 254

Robinson, John, 173

Royal and Ancient Golf Club, 268

Royal Exchange, the, 190, 191

Royal Indian Navy, 302

Royal National Lifeboat Institution, 191

Rubaiyat of Omar Khayyam, the, 228

Rugby football, 275, 276

Russell, George (A. E.), quoted, 235

Sabatini, Rafael, 232

Sabbath, the, sabbatarian conventions, 64; in an English town, 87,

88, 92; theatrical entertainment forbidden by law on, 88
St. Paul's, 130
Saint Paul's Cathedral, 216
Salisbury, Lord, 42
Sargent, John, 251, 252
Sassoon, Siegfried, 229
Savings Campaign, the National, 205, 206
Savings movement, voluntary, 205
Scholarship examination, at Winchester, 138
Scholarships, 121, 144, 145
Schoolboy code of honor, 130
Schoolmaster, 60
Schools, State, 120, 124–126, 134; upper and middle class boarding schools, 123; private preparatory, 123; milk and food provided for needy children in State schools, 124, 125; secular, 124; aristocratic air of patronage toward State schools, 124; medical care in State schools, 125; standard of conduct, 130; day schools, 130, 131; in war time, 153, 154. *See also* Public Schools
Science, 223
Scotland, Celtic dialect spoken in highlands of the north of, 2; thrifty habits of the Scotch, 2, 16; education in, 121; the mind of, 227; grouse shooting in, 264; fishing in, 264; golf in, 268, 270; game of curling, 270, 271
Scotsman, distinct from the Englishman, 1, 2; important part played by, in building up British nation, 2
Scott, C. P., newspaper proprietor, 171, 173
Scott, Walter, 231
Scottish folk songs, 250
Sea power, of Great Britain, 298–301, 307, 308
Seaman, Owen, 241
Seaports, 189
Seaside holiday, 89
Seaside resorts, 89
Second Mrs. Tanqueray, The, 243
Secular schools, *see under* Church schools
Self-control, English, 7
Servants, domestic, 98–100; consideration shown to, 70
Seven Pillars of Wisdom, by T. E. Lawrence, 232
Sexes, the separation of, for relaxation, 74, 75, 81

Shakespeare, William, 224, 225, 243
Shaw, Bernard, 232, 236, 237, 243; quoted, 2, 3, 13, 86
Shipbuilding, 194
Shipping, 184; life line of Great Britain, 189, 193; and foundation of her commercial and financial greatness, 189; England as world's leader in, 190
Shooting, 59, 77, 264, 269; big game, 265
Shopkeeper, the, 60
Shops, the village, 80
Shyness, characteristic of the English, 8–10
Sidi Barrani, 339
Sidney, 302
Simon, Lord, 331
Sinclair, Sir Archibald, 328, 331
Singapore, 298
Smuts, General, 292
Snobbishness, 68; in the reserve of the English, 10; defined, 62; and club candidatures, 75
Social ease, lacking in Englishmen, 8
Social equality, 20, 21
Social instincts, as shown in village life, 58–85
Social legislation, 208
Social observances, 73, 74
Solicitor, 30, 31
Solicitor General, the, 25
Somerville, Sir James, commands a flying force in the western Mediterranean, 333; character, 333, 334; making ship models, hobby of, 334
South Africa, and the second World War, 284; British acquisition of, 290; Union of South Africa formed in 1909, 291; population, 292; peacetime requirements of defense, 302, 303; war contribution, 305–307
Southern Rhodesia, 297
Speaker of the House of Commons, 48–51
"Speech days," 134, 142
Speech, freedom of, 36
Spender, J. A., 172
Sport, defined, 257–261; maintained in war time, 281
Sporting spirit, of the English, 19
Sportsman, defined, 261
Squire, the, 59
Stag hunting, 262
Standard of living, under conditions of war, 98, 99
Star, 172

51-22 09

State Secondary Schools, 120, 126; imitate the old "public school," 134; prepare pupils to pass into the universities, 134
Statue of Westminster, passed by British Parliament, 1931, 284, 285
Steed, Wickham, 161, 172
Stern, G., 242
Stevenson, Robert Louis, 231
"Stiles," 58
Stock Exchange, the, 213
Strikes, labor, 207
Suez Canal, 301
Sunday Chronicle, 166
Sunday Dispatch, 167
Sunday Express, 167
Sunday Times, 166, 167, 172, 175
Swinburne, Algernon Charles, 227, 228

Taxation, 204, 205
Tea, the Englishman's, 112, 113
Tea parties, 71–73
Technical schools, 120, 123, 124
Tenacity, the English ideal of, 18
Tennis, 79, 268–270
Tennyson, Lord Alfred, 228
Tess of the d'Urbervilles, by Thomas Hardy, 239
Textile industries, 193, 194
Theatre, 244; the English audience, 245; under war conditions, 254, 255
Thirkell, Angela, 242
Thorndike, Sybil, 255
Times Literary Supplement, 175
Times, The, erroneously referred to as the organ of London, 158; advertising in, 160, 164; layout, 161; editorial policy, 163, 170, 172; circulation, 166; ownership, 170; policy and management protected, 170; its prestige, 173, 174; special foreign correspondents, 174; letters written to, 174
Tinned foods, 111
Tit-Bits, 162
Tobruk, 340
Tolerance, a characteristic of the English, 14, 34
Tom Brown's Schooldays, 130, 132
Tower of London, the, 217
Town houses, description of, 95–97
Town life, 86–92
Towns, private houses in, 95–97; flats replacing private houses in, 95, 99
Townspeople, and the country gentry, 46–47

Toynbee Hall, 319
Trade, foreign, 185–189, 194, 195; with the Dominions, 189, 196; balance of, 195–198
Trades Union Congress, 208
Trades Unions, 207, 320, 321
Tradition, 40
Transport, workers in, 193
Travel books, 241, 242
Treasure Island, by Robert Louis Stevenson, 231
Trollope, Anthony, 234
Turnstiles, 58

Under Secretaries, political, 40, 44, 45
Understatement, the Englishman's habit of, 6, 7
Unemployment insurance, 209, 210
United States, coal output of, as compared to that of Great Britain, 186; British imports from, 188, 189; merchant navy of, compared to that of Great Britain, 190; British investments in, 198–199; aid to Britain, 197, 198, 308; "cash and carry" attitude of, 198, 199; Winston Churchill's attitude toward, 318
Universities, 127–129, 134; fees, 145; terms, 145
University, the, life at, 147–153; traditions, ideals and standard of conduct at, 130; in war time, 152, 153
University police (bulldogs), 147
Upper class, 59, 60, 70; and education, 125
Upper middle class, and education, 125, 126

Village cricket, 64, 272
Village, English, *see under* English village
Voting, 47

Wages, under war conditions, 204; increase in, for working classes, 206
Wales, Celtic dialect spoken in, 2
Walpole, Hugh, 234
Walter, John, 170
Walter, John, II, 170
Walton, Izaak, 239
War, standard of living, under conditions of, 98, 99; voluntary service, 99; expenditures, 197–199; production, 203, 204, *et passim*; support

of labor, 206, 207; life, literary and artistic, during, 253–256

War material, the purchase of, 197–199

War Agricultural Committees, 201

War Cabinet of Eight, Labor represented in, 208, 317, 319; Cabinet Government and collective Cabinet responsibility concentrated in, 316; certain elements in composition of, 317–319; members of, 317, 319–331

War Savings Certificates, 205

Water polo, 271

Waterloo, Battle of, 299

Watts-Dunton, 228

Wavell, Sir Arthur, 301; experiences in the Middle East, 336, 338–340; highly regarded by soldiers, 337; his brilliance and dislike of routine make him suspect of authorities, 337; service under Allenby, 337, 338; heritage, 337; nicknames, 338; tactical audacities of, 338–340; character, 338, 340, 341; a good student, 338; in the South African War, 338; in France, 338, 339; loses left eye, 338, 339; as an author, 338, 341; military attaché with the Russians in the Caucasus, 339; and the North African campaign, 339; his fondness for poetry, 340; physical appearance, 341

Wealth, the distribution of, 99; national, 197–200

Wedding, English, the, 101, 102

Week-end, defined, 77

Wells, H. G., 232

Welshman, distinct from the Englishman, 1, 2; intelligence of, 2; love of choral music, 2; important part played by, in building up British Nation, 2

Westminster, 130; centralization of the judiciary at, 25, 26

Westminster Abbey, 214

Westminster Gazette, 159, 172

Whips (Junior Lords), 41

Whistler, James Abbott McNeill, 252

White, 239

Wicket gates, 58

Wilde, Oscar, 236, 243

Williams, Emelyn, 244

Wimbledon, 270

Winchester, 128, 131; life of the student at, 138–143; masters at, 139; annual cricket match against Eton, 142

Wine clubs, 149, 152

Wine drinking, 74

Wireless *vs.* newspapers, 183

Wit, and humor, 6, 7, 226, 236–239

Witness, the, 28, 29

Wodehouse, P. G., 238, 239

Women, Englishman's attitude toward, 8, 9, 74–76; in the Government, 47; in the middle-class English home, 101–102; revolution in the social economic and political status of, 102–110; higher education and, 104, 105; business and professional activities of, 105–110; salaries, 106, 107; their clubs, 110; and clothes, 113, 114; in the textile industry, 193

Women's Institutes, 69, 110

Women's Land Army, 110, 201

Wood, Kingsley, 317, 319, 331

Woolen industry, the, 187, 188, 193, 194

Woolf, Virginia, 242

Worker, town, 86–90

Working class, 60, 80–82; betting and beer means of escape for, 113, 259; savings of, 206; wages increase for, 206; better conditions of, 208–210

Workman's Compensation, 208, 209

Workshop, the, 88

Wren, Christopher, 217

"Writs of assistance," 32

Wuthering Heights, by Emily Brontë, 239

Wykeham, William of (Bishop of Winchester), 131

Yeats, W. B., 177, 229

Yorkshire Post, 174